GOLDEN FOOTPRINTS

Memoirs of an African Development Worker

SAMUEL DUBINYALE BRAIMAH

STEP BOOKS

STEP PUBLISHERS
ACCRA, GHANA

GOLDEN FOOTPRINTS:
Memoirs of an African Development Worker

ISBN: 978-9988-3-2824-5

Published by
STEP PUBLISHERS
P. O. Box AN 11150, Accra-North, Ghana
stepwriters@gmail.com. www.stepbooksghana.org
Tel. +233 (0)302 513487

Cover design by John Kuzah

Printed and bound in Ghana by
Yamens Press Ltd.

Dedication

This book is dedicated to my parents Yobi Bariki and Forkampa Braimah (pronounced *Bourema* by the local community). Their combined vision to send me to school and give me better opportunities in life as well as their individual commitments to a high level of integrity laid the foundation on which the values that defined my career were built. I will forever be grateful to them for being the unseen architects of this book.

Foreword

Sam Braimah entitled this biography '***GOLDEN FOOTPRINTS: Memoirs of an African Development Worke***r'. This is extremely moving. In the last chapter we learn of the chronic health problems that have left him bedridden. He does not complain or blame, but simply records this situation as it is. I hope his readers and friends will take a moment to recognise what a remarkable man he is, and how much he has achieved. We also learn through the pages of this book of the consistent and critical support of his family.

I can neither summarise the content, nor would I attempt it. This is a sweeping account of a life dedicated to development, making the world a better place. In this brief foreword I will talk of my interactions with Sam. Reader please note, these were just a tiny part of his full and productive life.

In 2002 Sam attended the Health Economics and HIV/AIDS Research Division (HEARD) workshop on "Planning for HIV/AIDS in Sub-Saharan Africa". At that time HIV was spreading rapidly, particularly in Southern Africa. Sam had joined the fight against HIV/AIDS as a development worker with ActionAid. He understood AIDS was more than a medical problem, it was a major development issue.

HEARD, a new organisation, established in 1999, was desperately understaffed and was seeking a Senior Researcher. We both headhunted and wooed Sam. Apart from his obvious qualifications, his active problem-solving mind, evident appetite for work and extensive African experience, he brought a critical mentoring element to HEARD. At that point South Africa had been free for fewer than 10 years. Sam was a role model for the younger staff, especially those who had been victims of Apartheid. His stay was all too brief. At the end of 2004 Sam returned to Burundi as the head of ActionAid. This was a loss for HEARD and South Africa.

This is a long book, forty-three chapters divided into three parts. As Sam notes in his preface, it is not necessary read it from the first to last page, rather the reader can dip into it. The account of his MA is amusing and inspiring. In 1991 he was awarded a British Council scholarship to the University of Swansea for a master's degree in Economic and Social Development. Unfortunately, his first degree was in chemistry, so he underwent a crash course in economics and sociology. The economics clearly had an influence that went beyond books. Sam describes a wide range of income earning and money saving activities he undertook during his year in the UK.

The book is about the life and career of a multifaceted man. There are aspects that stand out, beyond service and commitment. Sam was open to new experiences and challenges – living in four African countries during his career. He was backed by a loving family, and in turn gave his children all the opportunities he could. He was also able to make friends from all levels of society. Running through the story is his deep faith in Christ. Sam is a practising Christian, who believes God has a plan for him. As the reader learns, Sam may be disabled, but he is far from finished.

Sam has touched many lives. Ghanaians have the reputation for entrepreneurship and valuing education. Sam epitomised this. More than this he lived his beliefs, and as such has had a deep impact on many. I feel blessed that I got to know him, and he came to Durban at a critical time in the development of HEARD. This book deserves to be widely read, it is a remarkable, honest, and inspirational account of an influential African development worker. It was an honour to write these words by way of introduction.

Professor Alan Whiteside OBE, D Econ.

Alan established HEARD in 1999. He is a Professor Emeritus at the University of KwaZulu-Natal and from 2014 to 2021 held a chair at Wilfrid Laurier University in Waterloo, Ontario, where he was based at the Balsillie School of International Affairs.

Acknowledgements

The number of people I have consulted, spoken to, communicated with and received support from in the writing of this book is such that it would be practically impossible to list all of them by name. I am very grateful to the following categories of people who have contributed tremendously to the writing of this autobiography:

My extended family members, particularly elder cousins who know more about my childhood than anybody else.

Colleagues who have been in school with me in Manga Primary and Middle Schools, Ghana College, Tamale, (now Ghana Senior High School, Tamale), Navrongo Secondary School, (now Navrongo Senior High School) and the University of Cape Coast.

Students and teachers who were in Bawku secondary school in the 1980/81 academic year.

Former staff members, partners and beneficiaries of World Vision International, African Centre for Human Development, US Peace Corps, ActionAid, University of KwaZulu-Natal, Oxfam and African Evaluation Association.

Scientists and researchers of the Savannah Agriculture Research Institute main station in Nyankpala and substation in Manga.

Natives of the Kusaasi and Bissa areas in the Bawku East, Bawku municipal, Binduri, Pusiga, Garu and Tempane districts.

The Christian Community particularly those who have been involved in the propagation of the Christian gospel and ministry among young people.

The whole of this book was written using the voice recognition features of telephone devices because of my loss of nerve coordination and sight. I am very grateful to my two children, Stephen and Salma Braimah, who painstakingly sat by my bed to edit the original texts that sometimes did not make sense and produced the first drafts of the first 30 chapters and then went on to put the whole manuscript together. My sincere thanks to Dr Charles Ibrahim Mahama, my classmate from Ghana College, Tamale, and currently a retired veterinary surgeon, who encouraged me to write this book, provided technical advice from the beginning and did the first proofreading and editing of the text. Mr. John Turl, a retired British teacher who taught at Mfantspim, Navrongo and Denu secondary schools in Ghana from 1969 to 1981 did a herculean job of proofreading and editing the whole book, supported by language advice from his wife, Emma. In the process they helped me to understand many English grammatical constructions to which I have never paid attention in the past. I am sincerely thankful to them for their enormous support.

My wife, Rachel Roda Braimah (né Rachel Roda Sogene), worked hard to provide the suppot I needed in my difficult physical situation to be comfortable enough to write the book. I will forever be grateful for her support.

The greatest gratitude is to the Almighty God who enabled all these people to provide the support needed in the writing of this book.

Contents

LIST OF FIGURES

Preface

My name is Samuel Dubinyale Braimah although my middle name has been wrongly spelt as Dunyale in my official documents throughout my education and professional career.

'*Golden Footprints*' is the story of my life and it chronicles my childhood experiences and indigenous knowledge that has always been left in the past to oral history. It also presents my experiences in management, leadership, organisational development and facilitation of integrated development projects and programmes, particularly in the Non-Governmental Organisation (NGO) world. In writing my story, I have communicated with over one hundred individuals to ensure the accuracy of my narrative and eliminate ambiguities.

Part 1 of the book is about my rural background and education. My rural northern Ghanaian childhood experiences were typical for my generation in that part of Ghana. Unfortunately, such experiences are never documented but narrated orally to future generations, the result being that the narratives gradually get distorted and finally disappear into oblivion among future generations. Indeed, many people in my generation could easily replace my name with theirs and the stories would be the same.

The portion of the book on indigenous knowledge articulates concepts and knowledge that have remained in the domain of oral history. For example, Chapter One deals with the concept of seasons in northern Ghana, which is quite representative of the savannah ecological zone that includes the northern part of la Côte d'Ivoire, southern Burkina Faso, northern Togo, northern Benin, northern Nigeria and parts of Chad and Cameroon. It is quite worrying that many people who do not come from that part of Ghana think that there are only two seasons there while all the ethnic groups in the area have specific names for the four or five seasons in a year. This silence about indigenous knowledge that is undocumented may not be unique to Ghana and readers from around the world may find analogies in other parts of Africa and beyond.

Part 2 documents my experiences as a development worker, having lived and worked in four African countries and made presentations and facilitated workshops in twenty others. I have also documented changes in traditional agricultural practices and grain production habits that could adversely affect climate change and the nutritional value of foods in the savannah ecological zone. I have worked for seven different organisations, namely, World Vision International, the African Centre for Human Development (now-defunct), the US Peace Corps, ActionAid, the University of KwaZulu-Natal, Oxfam and the African Evaluation Association. This part of the book describes my experiences in all these organisations. Several chapters have been dedicated to my experiences with World Vision International in Ghana and have been written to contribute to any full documentation of the history of the organisation in Ghana in the future. The most important component of Part 2 of the book is the elaboration of learning points derived from organisational strengths and weaknesses as well as my own failures and successes while working to facilitate development across Africa. I believe that these experiences will be significant lessons for development workers in present and future generations.

As a Christian, I believe in the sovereignty of God. Part 3 narrates the many occasions of divine interventions in my life although some of these instances of God's protection have been recorded throughout the whole book. It is my hope that these testimonies will contribute to conviction and faith in God. I believe that the writing of this book without holding any pen or pencil because of my loss of nerve coordination is a miracle of God. The details of my battle for survival and several interventions in my life are documented in this part.

The narration of some personal experiences has been written in a manner that relives the emotions and feelings that accompanied them. This has been done deliberately to ensure that readers enjoy both the facts and the narrative of my life story.

The book has 43 chapters and each chapter is written as a complete story. Indeed, one does not really need to read the chapters in sequence. The first 30 chapters were published in my blog entitled 'Memoirs of a Development Worker in Africa'. Several of these chapters have been extensively revised with the inclusion of new information and rearrangement of sections to avoid repetition and ensure consistency.

I invite readers to come along and follow my life story in the hope that it will provide lifelong lessons for future generations to come.

Employment Timeline

The table below provides my employment history as detailed in Part 2 for quick access and reference.

Figure 1: Employment timeline

Date	Organisation	Last Position	Chapter
1980 - 1981	Ghana Education Service	Chemistry Teacher	15
1981 - 1994	World Vision International Ghana	Head of Operations	16 - 26
1994 - 1995	African Centre for Human Development	Deputy Director	27
1995 - 1996	US Peace Corps Ghana	Associate Peace Corps Director	31
1996 - 1998	World Vision International Niger	Area Development Programme Manager	29 - 30
1998 - 1999	US Peace Corps	US Peace Corps Training Manager	31
1999 - 2003	ActionAid Burundi/ Burundi National Council for the Fight against AIDS	Programme Support Manager/Technical Advisor	32 - 33
2003 - 2004	University of Kwazulu-Natal, South Africa	Senior Researcher	34
2004 - 2011	ActionAid Burundi	ActionAid Country Director	35 - 37
2011 - 2013	Oxfam Niger	Oxfam Country Director	38
2013 - 2015	African Evaluation Association	Executive Director	41

PART 1: BACKGROUND

CHAPTER 1

THE CONCEPT OF SEASONS IN NORTHERN GHANA

In documenting my childhood experiences there is much that could be said about the survival strategies and money-making ventures that a schoolchild in the north of Ghana has to learn in order to obtain the personal needs that parents often cannot afford.

One of the exercises that has been part of my development experience, is that of producing work plans. The biggest failure of my first work plan in the NGO world was the lack of consideration of seasons in which activities should be carried out during the year. My mentors quickly drew my attention to this as it was necessary for determining when community members will be available to participate in project activities such as communal labour.

My childhood survival activities and NGO development plans were executed all year round so there is a need to understand the concept of seasons in northern Ghana. Although what I am writing here refers specifically to the Bawku area, the concept is similar in most of northern Ghana.

Many people who do not come from northern Ghana assume that the region has only two seasons – namely the dry season and the rainy season. Out of the desire to be courteous and not offend the visitor, the indigenous people of the north simply agree with this concept. I have even heard people say that Europe has four seasons, namely winter, spring, summer and autumn while we have only two seasons. However, when one goes into details it will be observed that northern Ghana has four or five seasons depending on the language of the people. In this chapter, I will be referring to the Bissa and Kusaasi people.

In the Bissa and Kusaal languages, the rainy season is divided into three parts. The first part of the rainy season is when the farmers come out to prepare the land and plant crops. This is called *Siirey* or *Sigiley* in the Bissa language and *Sigirr* in Kusaal. The season is characterised by very heavy rains that can soak through the ground which has become very hard as a result of several months of dryness. The season used to start in the third week of April every year but due to changes in climatic conditions it now starts at the end of May and sometimes June. In the absence of calendars, the local farmers looked at the leaves of trees and their flowering and fruiting times to be able to recognise the season. Most agricultural projects that require the learning of new farming methods and techniques by famers must necessarily be done during this season. Development workers implementing reforestation projects that involve the transplanting of seedlings should start during this season to allow the young trees to be watered by the rains for at least 3 months.

It is during the first part of the rainy season that vegetables spring up, particularly in low-lying areas. This brings relief and ends recurrent annual food shortages. Women quickly get hold of the early quick-growing vegetables to prepare sauces to relieve the hunger. It is common for households to eat only the vegetable sauce as a full meal. Two of the most common vegetables that spring up are *Gintareh* and *Gancor* in Bissa. For the development worker, the best time to provide food assistance to people facing food shortages in northern Ghana is the period from the beginning of March to the end of June. Such assistance will provide farmers with enough food to prepare their lands and have enough to eat until the next harvest.

The second part of the rainy season starts in July and ends in September and is called *Biyo* in Bissa and *Sieog* in Kusaal. It is during the second part of the rainy season that early millet is harvested. It is also during this season that the most dreaded children's disease that attacks the feet becomes prevalent. The disease is called *Buyaa* in Bissa and *Tinginsigli* in Agole Kusaal and is probably an infection caused by the persistent use of the feet in wet ground on the farms sometimes for whole days. The feet become very itchy and white patches appear between the toes. This painful condition troubled my life every year until I was in secondary school at the age of thirteen.

This part of the rainy season is characterised by long periods of rain lasting several hours and sometimes days. It is the period when farmers work hard to remove weeds from their farms to allow the crops to mature without interference. It is also the period when children make extra money from weeding in the farms of other people. Shepherding domestic animals such as sheep and goats can be very difficult at this time of the season because the shepherds may have to endure the rain several times a day. As long vacations for school children coincide with this season, school children in the village are free to work on family farms and also privately to earn income before the beginning of the next academic year. Malaria is very common during this season because of the abundance of stagnant water where mosquitoes breed. Any development worker implementing projects in northern Ghana may want to avoid communal labour and community meetings during this season.

The third part of the rainy season is called *Mosa* in Bissa and *Sapalig* in Kusaal. It is characterised by short rains and the raindrops are rather big and heavy. The rains in this season last only 15 to 30 minutes. It is the season when major crops such as millet, rice, groundnuts, sorghum, etc. are harvested. Any development work that seeks to teach farmers to cultivate new crops and tree planting projects should never be done in this season because the rains are coming to an end and the next season would be 6 months away.

The dry season is generally called *Kuyeh* in Bissa and *Oun* in Kusaal. The Bissa and Kusaasi make a distinction between the cold dry season and the warm dry season. The cold dry season starts in December and ends in the middle of February the following year. It is called *Nyeim* in Bissa and *Waad* in Agole Kusaal. This season is characterised by very cold weather and dry harmattan winds from the northeast. It is the season when most families go to the bush to cut grass for the roofing of their houses and as fodder for the animals. Getting up early to bath and run to school is very difficult during this season. It is the season when the water from the rainy season recedes very fast. Because of the persistent dry north-easterly winds this season is also characterised by bushfires. Farmers who are not fast enough to take their crops from the field can easily lose them through such fires. NGOs engaged in environmental education need to educate farmers before this season starts. Many young people migrate from the north to the south in search of manual jobs in cocoa farms at the beginning of the cold dry season.

The warm or hot part of the dry season is called *Lemaar* in Bissa and *Dawalig* in Kusaal and is probably the worst season in northern Ghana. It lasts from about mid-February to late April. Perennial food shortages occur during this season, particularly towards the end, as the rainy season approaches. The ground is usually hot, and children who go to school without shoes on their feet have to bear the discomfort until the season ends. The most common disease during this season is cerebrospinal meningitis and this has claimed many lives of both adults and children. Young people who migrated from the north to the south at the beginning of the cold dry season return to their native villages at the end of the hot dry season to engage in farming activities.

An understanding of these seasons, their peculiarities and effect on specific population dynamics is important for the execution of projects and programmes in northern Ghana. This understanding has helped me tremendously in my development career. I have been told by an agriculturalist who worked in the north of Ghana in the 1970s that if he had understood these concepts when he was in the field, he would have done many things differently. It may be very appropriate to teach these concepts of seasons from a local perspective in high schools, agricultural institutions and in development courses. Unless we are able to do this, Ghanaian school children will continue to learn one thing at home from their traditional parents and another thing in school from their class teachers.

CHAPTER 2

MANGA - WHERE IT ALL STARTED…

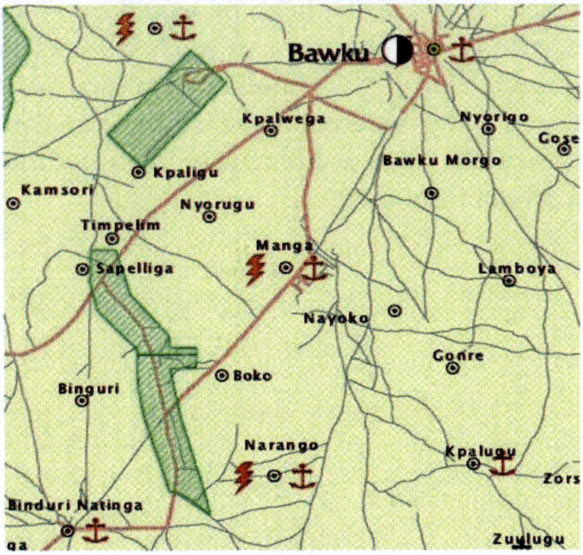

Figure 2: Map of Manga area

Memories of my childhood and my early school days cannot be documented without some account of Manga, the community in which I was born. My understanding and internalisation of poverty, as well as my development career, have all been influenced by my early life in this community.

In my travels, I have found four communities called Manga. There is a Manga village in the Bawku District of the Upper East Region where I was born. Travelling from Walewale to Nalerigu, in the current North-East Region, there is a community off the road called Manga. There is a third Manga off the road between Paga and Ouagadougou. I was really intrigued when I found a fourth Manga located between Kano in Northern Nigeria and Babban Mutum on the border between Nigeria and Niger. The community

I am writing about here is the Manga located about 6 km southwest of Bawku, on the road to Binduri.

The one major feature that has made Manga famous is what is commonly called the Manga Agricultural Station. In my childhood days, there were actually two research entities in the village, namely the Crops Research Institute and Soil Research Institute, both belonging to the Council for Scientific and Industrial Research (CSIR). Currently, the station is referred to as an outstation for the Savannah Agricultural Research Institute (SARI). I stumbled over some information in the year 2002 that showed rainfall records in the station that date as far back as 1933. It is, therefore, most likely that the station was established around 1930.

The agricultural station still features several trees such as Neem and Acacia that were planted when the station was started. A group of residential bungalows and houses accommodates the workers and officers assigned to the station. There is a garden with fruit trees such as mango, guava and citrus and also vegetables such as lettuces, cabbages, carrots, peppers and garden eggs. A borehole in the garden provides water which is pumped out by a windmill and directed into a reservoir for watering the crops. The third feature is a Teak (*Tectona grandis*) plantation that has flourished since the 1930s. This plantation taught me about climate change mitigation and adaptation long before the treaty known as the Kyoto Protocol was adopted in 1997. Finally, and most importantly, there is a series of farms for the cultivation of crops for experimental purposes and a number of scientific laboratories where the staff conduct their research. The station was manned by Europeans until 1958-9.

In spite of the early presence of Europeans in Manga, a school was not started until 1957 when Osagyefo Dr. Kwame Nkrumah, the first president of Ghana, embarked on an expansive education program. The introduction of the school resulted in a number of changes in the local communities. Before that, any family in the area who wanted to send a child to school had to send the child to either Bawku or Binduri. This meant that children had to be grown up enough to be able to go by foot to school over a distance between 5 and 6 km. Many children in the Manga and nearby communities now had access to school at a closer proximity. The new school population increased by 35 to 40 pupils each year until 1967, when the first batch of Form 4 leavers completed school and were replaced by Primary One pupils.

This meant that from the time that the school started, the number of children who had to walk these distances progressively reduced.

The last European to leave the Manga station was called Mr. Winiski, a Polish agricultural worker. After his departure, the station was run by Agricultural Technical Officers mainly graduates from Nyankpala and Kwadaso Agricultural Colleges.

Some of the principles, concepts and practices that Manga taught me and that have influenced my development career include practical farm loan system, reforestation, recognition and fighting land degradation and preservation of soil fertility and agricultural extension. These allowed scientists to interact and impart knowledge to rural community farmers. Pumping water out of a borehole using renewable energy, such as wind, and storing it in a reservoir for irrigation of crops in the garden was a practical method of teaching irrigation. The station had a programme that encouraged farmers in surrounding communities to take loans in the form of agricultural implements and tools and pay them back with farm produce. The farm produce was collected once a year during the cold dry season. I remember that my father paid his loan in the form of bags of groundnuts and completed the payment in 1963.

Apart from the teak grove in the Agricultural Station, there was also a small forest reserve at its northern side. One can see similar efforts at reforestation at the Binduri Forest Reserve near Bawku. There is also the forest reserve between Aboabo and Nyohini in Tamale. I have seen two forest belts, each about 50 metres wide and several kilometres long running east to west between the Nigeria – Niger border in Kano, in Northern Nigeria. On the road from Paga to Ouagadougou, there is a controlled forest near the town of Kombissiri where trained forestry workers selectively cut branches and bring them to the roadside for sale, thereby providing wood for fuel without depleting the forest. All these examples point to how early development thinkers in West Africa thought about reforestation.

In order to fight erosion, contours were constructed using graders 50 metres apart and perpendicular to the direction of flow of water across the villages around the Agricultural Station. The contours had a downhill ridge and an uphill trough. This meant that when the rain falls, water could be trapped in the uphill trough and prevented from moving down by the downhill ridge. The early Agricultural Officers brought the seeds of elephant grass and planted them on the ridges. The very strong roots of this kind of grass reinforced the strength of the ridges and also provided elephant grass for weaving designer mats and other types of household mats and baskets. Farmers were advised that if they had to plough their land to create small ridges for planting, the ploughing had to be done in the same direction parallel to the contours. This rule was well understood by the communities. I remember my father advising that if I ever had to plough land in a village where there are no contours, the ridges must always be perpendicular to the direction of water flow when it rains. It was the major strategy for fighting soil erosion.

In order to fight soil degradation, farmers were taught to produce compost manure. All households with cattle received instructions on how to establish a grass storage system near their house. The barn had a circular base, with a diameter of about 3 metres and a similar height with about six poles fixed to the ground at equal distances along the circumference of the circle. An aggressive effort was made by each farmer and their family members to collect grass during the cold dry season to fill the grass reservoir. Throughout the year, the grass was fetched in small quantities to cover the cow dung and wetness in the kraal and make it comfortable for the cows to lie down. The process of putting grass into the kraal normally starts in the month of April in the hot dry season and runs throughout the following 12 months. It is the farmer's duty to fence the kraal and keep the manure together. After 12 months, enough compost manure has developed to fertilise farms of the household. Officers from the Agricultural Station visited each household once a month to ensure that the compost manuring process was progressing as advised. They left notes on a card with the farmer for future reference by other visiting officers. Collecting the manure and spreading it on the farms at the beginning of the rainy season ensured soil conservation and increased fertility of the farms. I can never forget the smell of compost manure. The advent of chemical fertilisers and the decrease in the availability of grass due to population increase has gradually eroded this practice. The system of agricultural extension where technicians went out of the station to advise families and farmers on best farming practices was unique resulting in increased crop production by farmers around the station.

In recent times the station has been run by agricultural scientists, most of them with doctoral degrees and some of them have won national awards in agricultural research. According to Dr Alhassan Sugri (private communication), the officer in charge of the SARI outstation:

"The Upper East Region Farming Systems Research Group (UER-FSRG) was established in May 1993 and is based at the Manga Agricultural Research Station about 4 km South-East of the Bawku Municipality. The re-naming coincides with the decoupling of the Nyankala Agric. Station from the Crop Research Institute, Fumesua to the current status as CSIR-SARI. The UER-FSRG is tasked with analysing the farming systems of the region with the view to generating appropriate innovations that would improve the livelihood of the people. The focus is on characterizing and describing the farming systems, identifying and prioritizing constraints to increase agricultural production and generating suitable interventions to address the key problems of farmers through adaptive on-farm research. The Team has oversight responsibility of co-ordinating the Research, Extension and Farmer Linkage Committees (RELC) activities in collaboration with the Ministry of Food and Agriculture (MoFA) in the Upper East Region. The Team also provides backstopping in agronomy, crop protection, seed production, soil fertility management, postharvest storage and processing among others, of major crops cultivated in the UER. We provide technical services and collaborative works with MoFA and Non-Governmental Organizations (NGOs). The following few are crop varieties available to farmers: maize, cowpea, frafra potato or piesa, soybean and millet."

The Manga Agricultural Station drew its workers from the surrounding villages such as Boko, Nyorugo, Nayoko and Kpalwega and Manga itself. Because of the prolonged presence of Agricultural Officers in Manga, the community is perceived by people from other villages as being "very enlightened".

As a child, my understanding of what the world looked like was determined by this small village, and it influenced my thinking about what I wanted to be in the future. Agricultural Technical Officers were the biggest figures in the community. They were smartly dressed and rode big BMW motorbikes. They lived in bungalows made up of modern constructions, very different from the mud houses in which I lived. Walking barefooted behind these bungalows with the risk of being cut by a broken bottle or bitten by snakes, one could hear music coming from their gramophones and short wave radio sets. The officers' children who went to school with us looked different with sandals on their feet all the time. I went to the officers when I was looking for manual labour on their farms, as did many other children in the community. These technical officers had a huge impact on my life. As a primary school child, my dream was to become an Agricultural Technical

Officer and ride a big motorbike in the future. This background enabled me to identify with the poor and fit into any rural community across Africa.

In the year 2006, I sat in a shed outside a rural house near Djosson in Senegal. As donkey carts passed nearby and goats and sheep walked out of the yard to look for food elsewhere, I saw a replica of Manga. The smell of the animals' droppings, the sight of savannah trees and the dust rising between houses were very nostalgic. I had similar nostalgic feelings visiting villages near Yako and Tugan in Burkina Faso, San in Mali and Damagaram Takaya in Niger.

Figuring out which household was better than another was ingrained in me before I learned about "Community Wealth Ranking" in my development career. Some of the features that showed differences in household wealth included the use of corrugated iron sheets for roofing which was considered to be a mark of the highest-ranked household, ownership of a bicycle and a radio, ownership of bullocks and plough, etc. My family house was not roofed with corrugated roofing sheets; neither did we have a bicycle or a radio. However, we had two bullocks and a plough for the cultivation of family farms and renting to other farmers who did not have the same. My mother brewed *pito*, a local alcoholic drink brewed from sorghum. This turned our household into a social learning centre, where community members sat together to recount historical events and passed on oral traditions to the younger generation. During vacations and days I did not go to school I spent a significant amount of time sitting by these older people and learning from their accounts of history and traditional knowledge.

The concept of time that has been used for hundreds of years was the same when I was a child and is still the same today. Time was measured in days, market days and months. The concept of dates and weeks was introduced through Islam and Christianity. In the Bawku area, market days occur every three days. Community members are most likely to have a clearer image of three market days from today than of say nine days from today.

Community parenting, where every adult took it upon themselves to discipline children in the community, whether they knew the child or not, was the common practice in Manga. Most of what I have described about community life in Manga is likely to be the same across northern Ghana. It was out of this community that I emerged and I am still deeply rooted psychologically in Manga.

CHAPTER 3

FAMOUS PRACTICES OF MANGA TO REMEMBER

The history of Manga cannot be complete without mentioning the game of lawn tennis, the celebration of Christmas and the nurturing of bullocks for animal traction. These are famous practices in Manga to be remembered. One of the biggest weaknesses in Africa is the dependence on oral history and the absence of well-documented historical events. This has resulted in many historical facts being distorted, fading away or sometimes being forgotten completely. It is my hope that this narrative will be used for maintaining the history of Manga, and if possible, used as a foundation for launching future initiatives in the community.

There is a concrete platform standing in the north eastern corner of the Savannah Agricultural Research Institute substation in Manga that is currently being used for threshing millet and other cereals. The history of this platform is very intriguing. The officers who started the Manga Agricultural Station, who were mostly of European origin, tried to establish a sporting ground where they could spend their leisure times and keep fit. Some of them must have been tennis players and so they decided to construct a tennis court. My mother recounts how women in the communities around the station came together to collect Grade 1 gravel that was usually used by community members to compact the floors of their compounds. The women brought the gravel to the demarcated area in large quantities and beat it with their wooden implements until it was hard and compact. The officers then completed the court with a thick layer of concrete. This is where the officers used to go and play tennis starting around the 1940s. Young boys from the community came to the court as volunteer ball boys to pick up and return stray balls to the players. At some point the officers actually started to pay the boys some money to come as ball boys. All this activity must have stopped in the early 1960s as my memory of seeing the officers playing tennis remains very vague. I am told that there was an attempt to revive the game on this court in the 1980s but that has been discontinued. After nearly 70 years of existence the court is still so strong that a driver has told me that he drove a tractor on to it to thresh maize. Unbelievable! I wonder how much material was used in the construction of the foundation of this tennis court. There is a huge potential for reviving tennis in Manga particularly among younger school children by renovating this court and training the children to become professional tennis players. Indeed, the least that could be done would be to turn the court into a tourist site to tell the history of Europeans in the community. This is one piece of historical information that should be remembered.

The celebration of Christmas in Manga was introduced by the early workers of the Agricultural Station. I have very graphic memories of Christmas in 1965. I remember being sent by my father to buy gunpowder in an old beer bottle from the next community. I ran all the way to the house of the gunpowder seller and back home. It was the 23rd of December 1965, so Christmas was just two days away. Christmas Eve was coming up and my father did not want to miss his annual ceremony of firing a gun on the 24th and 25th of December. My cousins and I waited in anticipation as my father brought out his shotgun and cleaned and oiled it using a piece of cloth and a long feather. On the evening of 24 December, he came out proudly, gun in hand, put the required quantity of gunpowder into the gun, walked to the front of the house and 'BOOM'! - he fired it into the air. We all jumped up and down and shouted'*BURINYAA*!'. That is how we call Christmas in Ghana and I am still trying to find the origin of that word. He repeated the action once more and we shouted louder. Firing of the gun on Christmas Day surpassed what happened on Christmas Eve. He fired it three times in the morning and twice in the evening, by which time either the gun powder was finished or he had just enough left for the '*Nyewyay*'. That is how my father pronounced New Year and I had no idea what he was saying until I was ten years old. I remember this incident very well because it was the last time I ever saw the gun. The government of Kwame Nkrumah was overthrown in February 1966 and there was a rumour around the community that security personnel would be coming around to arrest anybody who had a gun at home. My father took the gun and buried it about 50 metres away from the house. When the rainy season arrived in April of that year, he tried to retrieve it, only to find out that its wooden components had been eaten by termites and the metal components had crumbled into a useless heap. My father never forgot to bemoan the loss of his gun during Christmas every year until he died in 1971.

There was also the feasting part of Christmas. For whatever reason, there was suddenly so much food at home. My father brought in some soft drinks and everybody got a little calabash of it to drink. I remember going back several times for more portions of the drink. One had to take advantage of this because the next time such a feast would happen could be a year away.

On Christmas Day each year, the officers in the Agricultural Station organised celebrations that have left deep impressions in the minds of all who lived in those days. Several households in communities such as Nayoko, Bokko, Nyorugo that surrounded the station brewed pito, the local alcohol, in anticipation of heavy patronage on Christmas Day. The officers organised an evening of celebrations that was patronised by all the staff members of the station as well as traders from nearby communities. By 4:30 p.m. one would find the station very busy with traders selling all types of food, Christmas paraphernalia, toys and sweets. My sisters and cousins joined the celebrations by retailing cola nuts and ginger beer. From the year 1965 until 1967 I joined the business part of Christmas celebrations by buying and retailing sweets and making a profit of up to 20%. Almost every child in Manga at the time got some form of new clothes to join in the celebrations and we normally just walked around showing off our new clothes. Those of us who lived near the agricultural station went from house to house and were offered gifts made up of mainly biscuits and sweets. Some officers gave us food, usually cooked rice served in a big bowl and shared by several children, and we never bothered to wash our hands before or after eating. I was one of many children who walked around barefoot in new clothes, a step higher than those who could not afford new clothes.

The nearby communities organised their own musical entertainment and converged at the Agricultural Station where they displayed their music and dancing skills. The entertainment sometimes lasted until the small hours of the following morning. Some of the dancing and music groups from the nearby communities were accompanied by two or three people firing muskets. The children went from one dancing group to another making comparisons to see which group danced best. The funniest part of the celebrations happened on the 26th of December when children ran back to the grounds where the entertainment had taken place the previous night and looked through the dust in search of coins that might have been lost by traders, entertainers or buyers.

The authorities in the agricultural station slaughtered one or two cows to contribute to the celebrations. I cannot remember how the meat was used but I am aware that there was normally food served for the officers and some of the important invited guests such as the village chiefs and medical doctors from Bawku Hospital as well as senior workers. All the entertainment normally stopped at some point for the senior officer in the station to make a short speech that was followed by prizes given to deserving workers of the station. This annual function became so popular that musicians from as far away as Bolgatanga and Garu came to participate in it and most of them still have fond memories of Christmas in Manga.

I have talked to several people in my generation who grew up in Manga, most of them Muslims and none of them knew that Christmas was a Christian celebration. We only found out about Christmas being the celebration of the birth of Jesus Christ in secondary school. The major talking point in the month of January every year was a description of the last Christmas celebration and how it compared to previous celebrations. I remember that in 1968 the biggest talking point was about the Bimoba drummers and dancers from Nakpanduri in what was then the Northern Region.

Currently, in 2021, the events described in the narrative above have been consigned to history. These celebrations diminished significantly in the 1970s and have completely disappeared since the middle of the 1990s.

The Manga agricultural station, started in the 1930s, is one of many that were established across northern Ghana. There were, for example, similar stations in Zuarungu, Yendi, Wa and Nyankpala. Farmers in the communities around these stations were taught modern techniques of farming to increase their crop yields and ensure food security. In Manga, one of the many modern farming techniques of those days taught to farmers was animal traction. The station had a herd of cattle numbering over 100. The cattle I saw in the late 1950s and early 1960s were said to have been imported into Ghana, most likely from Brazil or India. Farmers in nearby communities around the station were taught how to harness a castrated bull and turn it into a working animal that pulls a plough to till the land for farming. My father was one of the trainers who taught other local farmers how to use bullocks for ploughing. The implements that could be drawn by the bullocks included the plough, the harrow and the cart. These were linked to the bullocks by a chain and yokes that held two bullocks together.

There was a credit scheme that allowed local farmers to buy bullocks and the necessary set of implements on credit which they paid back using farm produce over 4 to 5 years. One could see a large number of farm implements in the station available for purchase by farmers. Buyers came from as far away as Garu, Tempane, Pusiga and Zebilla to buy the bullocks and the implements.

The idea that the use of tractors is better than animal traction has killed this program. In 1992, I worked in a tomato nursery in Yorkshire in the UK and witnessed the ploughing of the land in preparation for transplanting new tomato seedlings for the next crop season. The soil was so heavy as the tractor ploughed through it, and in a large commercial greenhouse, that it was impossible for the loosened soil to be eroded. The use of heavy agricultural implements such as tractors seems to have accelerated soil erosion in Manga and indeed, in northern Ghana, particularly in farmlands that are not flat but inclined towards a valley. It is interesting to note that up to this year (2021) many farmers in Burkina Faso still rely on animal traction and not heavy duty ploughing with tractors.

Although these old practices may never be revived, they should never be forgotten.

CHAPTER 4

THE FOUNDATION OF MY EDUCATION

It was one evening during the hot dry season – my mother's pito day (pito is an alcoholic drink brewed from a variety of sorghum called *Naga* in Bissa). This was the day my mother had pito for sale for the whole day. Small groups of people sat in various shaded places in the house drinking from small calabashes and talking about various events in history. Like all pito houses, this was a typical informal social education centre. The sound of a big motorbike approaching compelled the hum of conversation to halt. One of the Technical Officers from the Manga Agricultural Station arrived and stepped down with authority from his motorbike and cheerfully greeted everybody. I cannot remember exactly what happened but he picked me up and sat me on the fuel tank of the motorbike. He then went ahead and sparked the bike and we rode away towards the Agricultural Station but came back to the house after about 200 metres. He took me down from the motorbike and said something to my father in Mampruli which translates to "Your boy is very brave; send him to school". This incident has been remembered by my family members as one of the events leading to my going to school. I was the second person in my immediate and extended family to go to school after my cousin called Rebecca Talata.

The Agricultural Officer in this episode was called Mr. Mannyeba Dokurugu from Nabari in the current North East Region of Ghana. The incident only rekindled a burning desire in my father that he had nursed for decades. When the next opportunity to send me to school arrived my father took me by the hand and sent me to the Manga Primary School. In those days there was hardly an upper age limit for a child going to Primary One. The lower age limit was six years. With this situation, the class ended up with six and seven-year-old children sitting with ten to thirteen-year-old children and all the other ages in between the extremes. In the absence of birth certificates, the teachers devised a clever way of implementing the lower age limit. The child is told to hold his right hand over the head and touch the left ear with the middle finger. If the child could do so, he or she was considered to be six years or older. Otherwise, the child would be rejected. My heart was broken when I failed this assessment and had to go back home. I remember crying for so many days. When the second opportunity came, I passed the assessment. I was so full of joy that I was at long last going to school. I cannot remember whether it was the second term of the same year or the following academic year. This was in the 1959/60 academic year. My father went through the process of getting me school uniform. A khaki shirt and khaki shorts. The smell of the new uniform was just fantastic. Never mind if it was just one pair, I wore that pair five days in the week for one year before I got new uniforms for the following year and it was just great. This was normal and I cannot remember ever having more than one pair of uniform anytime in my elementary school life. I don't think any school-going child of my generation ever had more than one pair of uniforms.

In the school I began to get an understanding of the system. There was one boy, called the bellboy, in the senior classes who came out and rang a bell at specific times and shouted something. I just followed everybody and did as everybody did. Gradually I managed to decipher what the bellboy was saying.

The shouts included:

"Parade, please!" – the time for pupils to stand in parade, either to begin the day's school session or to end it.

"Change lessons, please!" – to signal for teachers to stop the lessons they were teaching and start the next lesson.

"Recreation, please!" – to signal the beginning of a 15 or 30 minute break period, where pupils had the opportunity to get out of class and interact informally.

"Classes over, please!" – the end of classes for the day.

That last shout was the best of them all.

For the first two weeks of going to school, I was amazed to see some children being dragged to school by their parents, kicking and screaming with their faces bathed in tears. I have never understood why they did not want to go to school.

Manga Primary School had a small market under a tree that has always been mistakenly called the blackberry tree. Indeed this tree is the West African Black Plum, botanical name *Vitex doniana*. Under this tree some women sold food to the pupils during recreation (the break time). This was where I practised my first sentences in Kusaal, the language of Kusaasis, because speaking ones local language – referred to as vernacular – was not allowed in class. My mother made sure she gave me one penny a day, equivalent to USD$0.20 today (2020), to take to school. This was the time we used pounds, shillings and pence in Ghana. The one penny coin had a hole in the centre. My one penny a day school allowance was upgraded to two pence a day when I got to Primary Four. And to three pence a day in Middle School. However, I must say that I was not at the bottom of the scale. I have heard of children who refused to go to school because their parents could not give them one penny a day.

In classes, we learned to count using pebbles and sticks broken from the nearby bushes. We learnt to write with chalk on wooden slates in Primary One. From Primary Two onwards we started to use pencils to write and crayons to draw. We were introduced to the use of pens in Primary Four. In those days we started with the use of stick pens. The pen was basically a well-modelled stick with a nib at the end. Children had bottles of ink in front of them and dipped the pen into the ink to write on paper. The biggest challenge was how to get the right amount of ink on the pen. This problem was partially solved with the supply of absorbent blotting paper. Writing with a pen was such a messy business. But then came the idea of a fountain pen. This pen could draw ink into an internal chamber to be used over some time and refilled when empty. The arrival of the ballpoint pen relieved us of the messy business of writing with fountain pens.

By 1966, my command of the English language increased tremendously because I took advantage of the libraries in the school. I read children's version of books such as The Merchant of Venice, Oliver Twist, Robinson Crusoe, Gulliver's Travels, Cinderella and many more I cannot remember. I communicated confidently in five languages – English, Hausa, Kusaal, Mooré and my native Bissa.

The teachers I encountered in my elementary school in Manga were simply amazing. The Head Teachers wore white shorts and white shirts and always made sure they displayed a number of pens in the front pocket of the white shirts. The other teachers wore black shorts and white shirts. All the other teachers were always in black shoes worn on socks that were pulled up until they were just below the knee. These were the days when teachers wore uniforms. The schoolgirls wore green dresses, while the boys wore their khaki shorts and shirts. This narrative would be incomplete without mentioning a few famous teachers of Manga Primary and Middle Schools. The first Head Teacher of Manga Primary School was called G. K Amadu. Other teachers who left permanent impressions on my memory include Mr. Felix Kofi Tease, who taught me in Primary Six and consistently gave us weekly exams for one year that forced us to learn hard the whole year. Mrs. Soale was the first female Head Teacher. Mr. Garaba Seidu was the first Head Teacher of the Manga Middle School. Finally, Mr. Francis Fusheine Seidu coached us in preparation for the Common Entrance Examination.

The motivation to go beyond Manga in my pursuit for education came in 1966 when the first batch of pupils from Manga Middle School qualified to go to the secondary school. This group of pupils actually set the pace for subsequent generations to follow and I document their names here for history and for posterity. They included George Abugnaba Abanga, Azinim Abukari, Awali Hayah, Daniel Asaana Aketa, Dauda Mahmudu, Mahama Hamidu, Musah Alhassan, Haruna Adamu, Haruna Wahabu, Bawre Fusheini and Alice Azumpua Atogsi. Before 1966 there were only two children from Manga, Edward Bukari Fusheini (1960) and Musah Sumani (1963), who went to Navrongo Secondary School and they went from the Bawku Middle Boarding School. Musah Sumani is the first child from the Bissa community in Manga to go to secondary school.

The excitement of promotion from Primary School to Middle School was beyond description. The boys graduated from khaki shorts and shirts to khaki shorts and white shirts. The girls graduated from green dresses to yellow skirts and white blouses. School provided a number of opportunities that children who did not go to school missed. When the Ministry of Health needed to do vaccinations against any of the six childhood killer diseases, such as polio and measles, schoolchildren were vaccinated first. Non-fat dry milk and wheat provided by missionaries and churches were distributed through the schools. If one fell sick and was taken to Bawku Hospital, schoolchildren were given priority. For me, there were two major accomplishments. In the first place, I was beginning to understand what the Agricultural Technical Officers in the Manga Agricultural Station were saying. Secondly, I was on track to accomplish my dream of joining their ranks one day in my life. My idea of the world expanded beyond Manga. I had discovered the world out of Manga and as far as Mognori, Kulungungu, Bitou in Burkina Faso, Pusiga and Garu.

By the end of 1967, I had developed the ability to perform multiple tasks. A simple village boy had become a Middle School pupil who worked hard to stay within the top bracket of students. I had seen the first two batches of students take and pass the Common Entrance Examination and proceed to Secondary Schools and I desperately wanted to be in the next batch.

The phenomenon of inadequate school infrastructure has always been a problem in sub-Saharan Africa since time immemorial. Manga was not an exception. The first batch of pupils to go beyond the primary school into middle school in the 1963/64 academic year attended middle school form one classes in the classroom that was meant for primary school class 6 pupils. In order to compensate for this arrangement, one class in the primary school was held under a tree. In the 1964/65 academic year, two classes were built from zana mats woven from elephant grass as classrooms for the form one and two pupils of the middle school. The actual school block for the middle school was ready in the 1965/66 academic year. I was in the batch that went to the middle school in the 1965/66 academic year. In those days, one wrote an external examination to get promoted to middle school. I remember that one of the questions in the external examination was 'which is heavier? 1 pound of paper or 1 pound of stones?' the answer to this looks obvious but was difficult for many pupils at the time.

My memories of these difficult school infrastructure challenges significantly influenced my drive to support the construction of schools in Ghana, the Republic of Niger and Burundi. Evolving development approaches have called this 'service delivery' with the understanding that engaging duty bearers (the government) and advocating for them to provide such infrastructure while sensitizing rights holders (community members) to claim their rights is a more sustainable approach to development. The reality is that advocacy can be a slow process and unless it is accompanied by tangible interventions such as the construction of schools, it will take a long time to accomplish its goals while poor children wait in vain for action and miss the opportunity to go to school.

I was a typical schoolboy who went home every day after school and made sure that he did the normal domestic chores such as ensuring that domestic animals were properly cared for. I did all the extra activities a boy would do to earn some more money including fishing, working on the family farm and on the farms of other people. These activities enabled me to afford a few extra necessities such as buying a few extra clothes. I used the bright lights from the Tilley lamps used by the Agricultural Technical Officers when they played cards in the night to do my extra studies. It looked as if I was on course to accomplish the dream I had nurtured for seven years.

Developing competencies in reading, writing and speaking English as well as acquiring knowledge in Maths and Social Studies in school were complemented by the strong values at home and in the community.

It must be said that life in primary and middle school was not as rosy as narrated above. Three challenges confronted every primary and middle school pupils of my age. The first was survival through the heat, cold and rain of the different seasons. Imagine trying to run home barefoot for lunch and back to school in the hot dry season, when the temperature was 40 degrees Celsius. The second was the wide age range in classes, where the minimum age in Primary One was 6 years and there was no upper age limit. This meant that some of the older boys bullied the younger ones in the same class. I know of a case where a pupil left school because of beatings from other pupils. My mother's memory of this case was the child crying and passing by our house with a mixture of tears, phlegm from the nose and blood from the mouth, dripping on his shirt. The third survival had to do with beatings from teachers. The cane spent more time in the hands of many teachers than the chalk and the duster. Beatings from the hands of teachers in primary and middle school could really be brutal. Several children have been known to leave school because of beatings from teachers. There were situations when the relatives of children confronted a teacher who had beaten a child.

The process of going to Secondary School was as exciting as any pupil could imagine. It started with the arrival of the Common Entrance Examination forms in the school. This was followed by a selection of pupils whom the teachers thought were capable of passing the exams. Thankfully I got selected with many other pupils to complete the forms. For the first time in my life, I was going to complete an official form. I now had the uphill task of going home and convincing my father to provide the necessary finances for paying for the form and taking the required passport-sized photograph. My father consulted one of the Technical Officers who convinced him that the best route to becoming like one of the officers was to go through secondary education.

The form was made up of hard paper and the fields were square boxes. I now discovered the difference between my first name and my surname. I completed the form as diligently as I could, but there were three difficulties I had to overcome: the question of the date of birth, the choice of a secondary school to go to and a photograph to be attached to the form. The date of birth issue was settled at home by my parents as my father had a sort of record in a small document box he kept in his room. After a lot of consultation with friends, my class teacher and Agricultural Technical Officers, I settled on Ghana College, Tamale as my first choice. The schools were listed on the back of the form and each school was given a code. The other big issue was the passport-size photograph. It was yet another first for me to have my photograph taken. I remember stopping several times on the way home to pull the photographs out of the envelope and stare at the image of my face. The completed forms were collected and sent to the West African Examination Council (WAEC) and the preparation for the Common Entrance Examination started in earnest.

Extra classes were held by teachers who had gone through secondary school for pupils who were preparing for the Common Entrance Examination. I attended these classes with a lot of enthusiasm as if my life depended on them. My contact with Bawku Secondary School elevated the anticipation of moving beyond Manga. I had gone to participate as a spectator in several Speech and Prize-Giving Days of the school. This was one of my biggest motivations to go to Secondary School one day. When other secondary schools came to play football matches against the Bawku Secondary School team, the Manga Middle School students, such as myself, were there to cheer those who had already succeeded in making what we believed would be the next step in our education.

The Common Entrance Examination finally arrived and my colleagues and I reported smartly to Bawku Secondary School. Unfortunately for me, I had surgery on my left thumb a few days before the exam, so I wrote the exam with my left thumb in a bandage and the whole of my left hand in a sling. This was definitely not the best way to write an examination that would represent a major milestone in my life.

One hot afternoon, I returned late from lunch to find everybody in the parade grounds preparing to march on into their classes. My passing the exams to go to Ghana College in Tamale was announced. A mixture of feelings ran through me – embarrassment, elation, confusion and other emotions that defied description. Somebody managed to send the message to my home before I arrived. My father was over the moon in excitement when I got home. The arrival of letters that indicated several other pupils had qualified to go to secondary school gave me a very comfortable feeling that I would be leaving in the company of others, even though the rest were going to different Secondary Schools such as Bawku Secondary School, Navrongo Secondary School and Notre Dame Secondary School. I was the only pupil who qualified to go to Ghana College.

This foundation of my education played a major role in my career as a development worker in Africa. Whether in northern Ghana, Niger or Burundi, anytime I found myself confronted with challenges in education, this is the background that motivated me to go out there and support children who could become major actors in the development of their countries.

CHAPTER 5

MY FIRST TURBULENT TRANSITION

I have made several transitions between jobs in my career of over 35 years as a Development Worker. These transitions were not only between language zones, geographical zones and African cultural zones but also between organisational cultures. There are usually three stages in every transition. In stage one, it is evident that one is no longer in culture A but has to live in that culture until one leaves it. Stage two is when one has left A but has not yet arrived in culture B. The third stage is when one has arrived in culture B and is going through the process of induction and integration into the new culture. Going through these stages in my first real transition was very emotionally draining. The preparation to leave the Manga Middle School environment and enter into Ghana College was stage one of my turbulent transition.

The excitement from the news that I had qualified to go to Ghana College in Tamale disappeared within 24 hours. My class teacher told me that I had an interview to attend and until I was told that I had passed the interview and received my admission letter I should not jubilate, although the school had not yet witnessed a situation where a pupil had failed an interview. I had to take note of the date for the interview as well as the location and time. My jubilation was replaced by apprehension. After all this hullabaloo, if I failed the interview, I would be back in Manga Middle School – exactly where I started. The wait for the interview seemed to last forever. It was difficult to concentrate in class. At home, I just went through the motions of doing domestic chores. Finally, the day arrived and I was supposed to go to Bawku Middle Boarding School and meet Mr. A.F. Clayton, the Headmaster of Ghana College. Just as I was about to step out of the house at 6:00 am I noticed a huge cloud of rain coming from the east. My father quickly improvised a raincoat from an old transparent polythene bag that used to contain fertilizer and I set off to defy the rain and have my interview. I arrived at the interview location about 20% wet; the improvised raincoat had done 80% of its job. The wait was long and tiring and it rained all day. By 3:30 pm, Mr. Clayton had not come, and the Bawku Middle Boarding School Head Teacher advised me to go back home and wait for further communication. This introduced another period of waiting. The following week, the school received a letter saying that the heavy rain of the day had also covered Tamale and that was the reason for the failure of the Headmaster to come to Bawku. I was given a new date for the next interview and this time I was requested to travel to Tamale and meet the Headmaster in his office. This introduced waiting number three. It also introduced a new set of challenges.

This was going to be my first time travelling outside the Bawku district. Secondly, this was going to require transport fares to Tamale and back to Bawku. Thirdly, I was going to an unknown town that was far bigger than Bawku. Transport money was obtained with the support of one of the teachers in the school who fulfilled his promise of giving me a cash reward if I passed the Common Entrance Exam. I made all the necessary inquiries about transport to Tamale. Two days before the interview I set off on a bus to Tamale. The advice was to give a full day between the day of travel and the day of the interview. The bus left Bawku at 9:00 am. Travelling to an unfamiliar place can be nerve-racking. I just had no clue how long the journey would take. I stayed wide awake every inch of the journey. I wondered whether travelling a total distance of 480 km for a 30-minute interview was really worth it. It was my first experience of travelling more than 30 km out of Manga and I was visiting the largest town in northern Ghana. This would be considered as a significant accomplishment even if I did not get admission into secondary school.

Finally, I arrived in Tamale at 5:00 pm holding a brown paper bag in which was my school uniform and a storybook to read. I got out of the bus in front of what was then the Rivoli Cinema, and was greeted with loud music blaring from the nearby shops. Confused and frightened, I did not know where to go. Then, out of nowhere, a bicycle pulled up and the rider said that it looked as if he knew me. Yes, this was somebody from Manga - a miracle! It was the beginning of many more miracles in my life. He asked where I was going and I said I had no clue but I knew I had an interview in two days' time. This man, Mr. Issah Musah, was the Head Teacher of Viting Middle School (now Viting Senior High School) at the time. He took me to his home and I had a place to sleep and prepare for the interview.

After one full day of getting acquainted with life in Tamale town, the date of the interview arrived and I went to the Headmaster's office at Ghana College with the assistance of my host. Mr. Clayton was a British national sent to head the school from the British Council. The major question I can remember is whether I had read a full storybook before and whether I could recount it. I recounted the story of Oliver Twist with every detail including the names of all the characters – The Artful Dodger, Charlie Bates and the famous quote "Please sir, can I have some more". The interview lasted for less than 30 minutes. I received some assurance from Mr. Clayton that I would get a letter from him within the next few days. The first part of stage one of my transition was over and I was on my way back to Manga.

The second part of stage one started when I received a letter two weeks after the interview to say I had gained admission into Ghana College, and the letter was accompanied by a prospectus which detailed all the items I would need to buy before reporting. That was the first time I had seen the word 'prospectus' and its meaning was told to me by my class teacher. The list was a long one but it contained words I had never seen in my life. Words such as 'cutlery' and 'pyjamas' were completely new to me.

I now had to complete stage one of the transition, by staying in class, concentrating on lessons and writing all the relevant examinations to complete the year. The arrival of letters for other pupils in the school who had qualified to go to other secondary schools gave me the comfortable feeling that I was not alone in this transition process. One began to have a false sense of not being a part of the class anymore. The end of the year and the beginning of the long vacation heralded the end of stage one and ushered in the beginning of stage two of the transition process.

During the long vacation that started in the middle of June, I was right in stage two of my transition. At this point, I was no longer a pupil of Manga Middle School but I was not yet a student of Ghana College. The major activity during this period was the battle to buy as many items on the prospectus as I could. I remember the struggle to explain the need to buy different types of footwear such as bathroom slippers, sandals, sports shoes and leather shoes for special occasions. All this footwear is called *kusor* in Bissa and my father could not understand how I was upgrading from no shoes on my feet to owning four different pairs. This was the biggest investment in my education by my father. Meanwhile, I had to continue working on family farms, working on the farms of other people for money, going fishing for food and income and performing all my household chores. The three-month wait dragged on and on but stage two finally ended when I felt I had got almost all the items on the prospectus and was ready to go to secondary school.

Stage three of my transition started on 19th September, 1968. That was the day before I was supposed to report to Ghana College in Tamale. By 6:00 pm I had packed all that I needed into the brand new wooden box that had been bought for me. All my belongings including bedsheets, sandals, pillowcases, underwear, towels, the famous pyjamas, toilet and washing soap, blanket etc. did not even fill half of the box. By putting my pillow into the box, I managed to occupy the extra space. I had no clue that students used a trunk for their clothes and a 'chopbox' for provisions such as gari, sugar, milk and other food items. Although I learnt this later in school, I never managed to have a separate box for such provisions throughout my seven-year education in secondary school. The night of 19th September was so long I thought there was something wrong.

In the absence of a watch or a clock, one had two options to determine the time in the village. The first was to wait patiently until the cock crowed. The second was to walk out of the room and look at the position of the stars in the sky. After the third attempt to look into the skies my father called from his room and told me to be patient and sleep. For some reason, the cocks were not crowing that night. It seemed like somebody had put sleeping pills in their water or they had simply gone on strike. Finally, the first cock crowed. That was a signal that it was 3:00 am. By 6:00 am I was well dressed and ready for Tamale. My father accompanied me to Bawku and gave me a piece of rather lengthy advice. The major points I can remember are "Never do things because other people are doing them", "Never take what does not belong to you", "Always be prepared to help somebody in need even if you do not have enough; you can always share what you have" and "Life is like a grindstone, if you make yourself like millet it will grind you into powder. If you make yourself like a stone, it will grind you but with difficulty. If you make yourself like ball bearings, it will grind but you will never be crushed". I recognised that these are universal principles that make sense in real life. I am forever grateful to my father for his high level of integrity, ensuring that his actions did not contradict his words, giving him the moral authority to impart such advice. My prayer in life has always been that God will enable me to attain such moral authority to advise my children and the youth in a similar fashion.

By 3:30 pm on 20th September, 1968, I made my big arrival in Tamale and then took a taxi to Ghana College. My new life had just begun. I was helped by other Form One boys to carry my box to my room and shown the bed I would sleep on. This was an upgrade from the mat back at home in Manga. I noticed that all of us who had come to Form One had lost our real identity. Everybody just called us "Form One". I was the first pupil from Manga Middle School to come to Ghana College. One encouragement was that there was another pupil from my school, George Abugnaba Abanga, in the third year of Ghana Government Secondary School (now Tamale Senior High School). George was the first bellboy I knew in Manga primary and middle schools.

The first function in the school was the parade and roll call at 5:00 pm on that day. The House Master, Mr. R. R. Lalaji arrived on his motorbike. He was an Indian so neatly dressed that I became conscious of my own shabby dressing. He addressed all of us in front of the dormitory. I understood less than 5% of what he said. I was busy trying to concentrate on staying in my footwear that kept slipping. I screamed at myself in my head "Dubinyale! Calm down. Don't panic. You have survived Primary and Middle School as well as the shepherd grounds. You will survive this one too".

Unlike Manga, in Ghana College, beatings by teachers had become history but bullying by other students was upgraded to a different level. I remember a Form One boy being instructed by a senior student to kneel down by his bed and fan him until he fell asleep. This punishment continued until almost midnight. A senior student once gave me three vicious slaps. I cried for more than two hours, not because of the pain from the slaps but because my own father had never given me a slap in the face. I later discovered that he was just one class ahead of me. Sixteen years after this incident, I met the same guy on the road begging for a lift in the car I was driving. I stopped and gave him the lift but made sure he recognised me and I reminded him of the incident. He said "Yes sir" and stepped out of the car, holding both hands in front of him and said "Thank you sir". I acknowledge east appreciation moved on. In my opinion, bullying is the bigger boy's way of making up for what might be a deficient intellectual capacity.

On Monday, 23rd September I moved along with everybody else and found myself on parade in the assembly hall. Mr Clayton, the Headmaster, made us sing a hymn accompanied by a musical instrument that looked like a giant accordion standing on the ground, played by Mr Thompson. It was my first encounter with a piano beyond the accordion I knew in Manga. The hymn was :

"He who would valiant be 'gainst all disaster,
let him in constancy follow the Master.
There's no discouragement shall make him once relent
his first avowed intent to be a pilgrim."

I quickly observed that many students knew only the first line of the chorus of the song that started with "there's no discouragement ...." so that line was loudly amplified. I waited for and joined in that amplification. I did not understand a word when the headmaster addressed the assembly. I clapped and laughed when everybody else clapped and laughed without knowing exactly what I was clapping and laughing about.

The idea of going to eat in the dining hall was new to me. My best experience of eating on the table was in the traditional restaurants called 'chop bars' in Bawku market but the tables were at the same level with the bench on which the customer sat. This time in Ghana College, the tables were real dining tables and seated four students on a bench on each of its long sides and one student each seated on metal chairs and the short sides. These two students were called the 'table heads' and were usually Form 4 or 5 students. I was immediately confronted with the challenge of how to use cutlery. In which hand was I supposed to hold which piece of cutlery? At home I had never used a fork and a knife. All I knew was the use of a spoon to drink local porridge or to eat rice. As I fiddled with the cutlery, wondering what to do, a lady sitting by me who was obviously senior to me saw my predicament and came to my rescue. What she was trying to show me was to hold a fork in my left hand and the knife in my right hand and guide the food into the fork and take it to my mouth. What about the spoon? Porridge was served during breakfast and so there was a place for the spoon. A tough experience but I ended up learning how to eat with cutlery. My most memorable dining hall experience is about the loss of the cutlery of one of the seniors on my table. In those days the four and five students had their cutlery kept by form one students and brought to them in the dining hall during meals. I kept the cutlery for a form 4 student with the nickname 'Wicked Fu Manchu'. Anybody who has watched the horror films featuring several actors including Christopher Lee as Dr Fu Manchu will understand the fear this nickname could strike in the hearts of fellow students. One day I lost the cutlery of this senior of mine. I cried all afternoon and any of my mates who try to find out why I was crying and learnt about my loss of the cutlery made cases worse for me by telling me that I would be 'skinned alive'. Interestingly 'Wicked Fu Manchu' received the news of the loss of his cutlery with a funny smile on his face and all I was told was to bring his food to the dormitory. The following day he gave me a new set of cutlery to keep for him. Amazing! He never laid a hand on me. The impression the nickname gave was not really right. The gentleman is now a senior minister in the Presbyterian Church of Ghana.'

Day One in Ghana College was crazy. It was basically about going into the office of the storekeeper, Mr Babatunde, for this and for that and for the other thing until we had all the exercise and textbooks we needed. My class was full of young excited children in the same age bracket as myself. The difference was that most of them seemed to know exactly what they were doing and I just tagged along. I later discovered that most of them were in exactly the same situation as myself.

I had to get used to all the new terminology. The teachers here were called Masters. The Head Teacher was called the Headmaster. There was an assembly hall and a dining hall; these did not exist back in Manga. You did not go back home after classes, you went to your dormitory to face seniors and manage to get some sleep before daybreak. We did not have one teacher teaching every subject; each subject had a separate teacher. Getting their names and their corresponding subjects was a new challenge. This adjustment took a few weeks but by the end of the first term in December 1968, I could call myself a secondary school student (a 'secondarian' - a word we cleverly coined from nowhere) and looked forward to going back home to meet my colleagues who had gone to other schools, and comparing notes.

CHAPTER 6

MY TRADITIONAL WEAR AND THE BISSA CLOTH WEAVING PROCESS

In preparing to go to secondary school in 1968, there was some difficulty in explaining the various items on the prospectus to my father, but there was one item that I could explain in five seconds. This was the item called traditional wear. After witnessing several Speech and Prize Giving days in Bawku Secondary School, I became aware that many students of northern descent wore smocks during these occasions, so I simply translated "Traditional Wear" to the word for "smock" in Bissa.

The term smock refers to a tunic made from locally woven strips of cloth. This used to be worn mostly by men from the northern part of Ghana but it is now worn by many people across the country as a part of fashion. By the following morning, my father had worked out the process of getting me a smock to go to Secondary School. It would involve the use of cotton planted on the family farm processed by my mother, woven by my father and made into the smock by himself. The issue of traditional wear is very dear to my heart.

Originally, the production of the material used for making northern Ghanaian cloths begins with the planting of cotton (botanical genus: Gossypium). The cotton used for making clothes is produced on a shrub called *lanni* in Bissa. This is distinctly different from the cotton obtained from the kapok tree (botanical name: *Ceiba pentandra*) which is mainly used as a filling for pillows and mattresses. Kapok is called *gyissi* in Bissa. Throughout my school days, many Bissa households would have a 10 to 15 square metre farm in front of the houses for easy access called *lanni sira* dedicated for the planting of cotton and vegetables. I am told that this traditional practice has all but vanished in Manga. Many Bissa children born in the 21st century hardly know what the cotton plant looks like. It was from this traditional cotton farm that my mother got her cotton that would be used for making my traditional wear.

Farmers used to cultivate cotton on larger farms away from the house as a cash crop. This was very profitable and common during the days of the Cotton Development Board in Ghana. However, the practice has significantly declined in northern Ghana. The market price of cotton in the international commodity market in June 2020 was $1.3 per kilogram. Some West African countries such as Senegal, Mali, Côte d'Ivoire, Burkina Faso and Benin are serious exporters of cotton cultivated by Farmer Cooperatives. Many people in the cloth-making industry have informed me that cotton produced in northern Ghana was among the best in the world. The authorities in Ghana may want to consider the revitalising of the cotton industry to compete with neighbouring countries and in the world market. It could also feed into the local garment manufacturing industry.

After harvesting the cotton from the farm, the Bissa women used two local tools to remove the seeds. The tools are a stone that has been polished to be extremely smooth on the top called *lanni gya* and a piece of metal produced by local blacksmiths about 15 to 20 centimetres long and up to 3 millimetres thick in the middle, also extremely smooth, called *kanni.* The women pressed the cotton between the metal piece and the stone and massaged out the cotton seeds. My father would normally divide the cotton seeds into two. One part was kept as seed for the next season while the other was given to my mother who crushed it and sieved out the powder to use for soup. At the commercial level, cotton seed can be crushed and the powder processed into cotton oil.

The next stage in the processing of the cotton was to spin the wool into thread, once again using locally produced tools. This tool is called *gendri* in Bissa and is the equivalent of a spindle. It is made up of a clay ball about two centimetres in diameter with a hole through it and a slender piece of stick passing through the hole. The ball fits tightly at the lower end of the stick and the spinner spins it from the top with the right hand (if right-handed) while holding the cotton wool about 40 centimetres away in the other hand with the cotton linked to the top of the stick.

Women can sit for hours spinning the cotton into thread. Sadly, with the advent of imported thread, this laborious process of spinning cotton into thread has been largely abandoned and can be found only in very rural communities in northern Ghana. A much better response to the influx of foreign trade would have been to introduce modern techniques of spinning cotton into thread as was done in the textile industries in the 1970s and

'80s. It is not clear the extent to which this has continued with the decline of cotton production in Ghana.

My mother went through the traditional process of spinning thread and it was from this thread and imported black thread that my smock material was woven.

Setting up the thread to weave the strips of material that were used to sew the smock was another painstaking process. The cloth is woven in very long strips. The process began by putting together all the thread that was needed for the setup. The local thread was presented wrapped around a 40 cm piece of stick and the final shape looked like a rugby ball with about 5 cm of the stick left free at both ends for handling by the user. With the disappearance of cotton in the rural communities, the local thread can hardly be seen again. Imported thread comes in bundles that can be opened and fitted onto a square holder that could measure between 30 and 35 cm on each side. The first stage of setting up the thread for weaving the smock involved unrolling it from its holder and putting it around wooden sticks, pegged on the ground at the corners of a square with each side equivalent to one quarter of the total length of the material to be woven. Boys would then go through the process of unrolling the thread from its holder and placing it around the sticks pegged at the corners of the square. The sticks were made smooth to prevent them from damaging the thread and pegged into the ground leaning away from the inner part of the square to assure that the thread around them does not slip over. The sticks are pegged up to 30 cm above the ground. One corner of the square was arranged to be the beginning and end of the set up. Walking around the square to put the thread around the sticks was done over and over again until the required quantity of thread was attained. For a strip of about 60 to 100 m long, one had to walk several times back and forth around the square to obtain the required quantity of thread in order to complete the setup. With two or three people doing this and at times jogging, it would take up to one hour to complete the setting-up process. I took part in this procedure several times from the age of 10 until 1970 just before my father died. This is the first part of setting up the warp, called *gyisiga* in Bissa, for weaving.

This laborious process has now been improved upon by modern weavers who wrap the thread around a revolving metal frame as shown in Figure 7.

After this, someone has to sit down and pass each thread at the beginning of the setup one at a time through the two main components of the loom, namely the heald frames, called the *dabsi* or *sassi* in Bissa, and the reed, called the *kwereh*, as shown in the photograph below. The shuttle looks like a miniature canoe and the thread on it moves from left to right and vice versa to weave the cloth. The Heald frames are responsible for the up and down movements of alternate threads of the warp to create space for the weft on the shuttle to move from one side of the warp to the other and weave the cloth. The reed determines the thickness and width of the cloth and beats back the thread from the shuttle to complete the weaving. Please see photos at the end of the chapter.

From about 20 metres away from the weaver to the end of the setup, the warp is rolled into a bundle that looks very much like a rugby ball. These pieces of equipment make up the traditional version of the loom. I remember on several occasions, sitting as early as 6:30 am and working through the day up to 4:00 pm to set up for my father to weave the smock material, which is usually about 10 to 14 cm wide. About 8 to 12 strips are stitched together side by side to make a cloth. With modern technology, I have seen the same material woven using improved methods so that one strip is about four to six times the width of the traditional strips, therefore, requiring less work to stitch them together into cloth.

In making the smock, my father sometimes gave me some pieces of material to stitch together by hand using a needle. In taking measurements for making the smock in the absence of a measuring tape, my father used a measure from the elbow to the tip of the middle finger. This measure, the old English 'cubit', is called *kanteega* in Bissa. He improvised a smooth stick, equal to the length of the *kanteega*, for measuring. I have personally spent time during my childhood days stitching materials together for women's wrapping cloth and maxi skirts.

My father went through the lengthy process of weaving the material and then sat down to stitch the pieces together to produce my smock. Thus everything was done by hand from beginning to end. This was the single prospectus item that was homemade and I wore it from 1968 till 1978 when I grew out of it.

The practice and activities required to prepare thread for weaving the smock material gave me basic lessons in systematic scientific work. This definitely impacted my future study of science. The nationwide embrace of the northern smock is a huge opportunity for promoting the industry, starting from the growing and processing of the cotton, through the use of modern techniques of spinning, to the use of more advanced technology for weaving the smock material.

My participation in my father's smock making was an activity for weekends and vacations and never interfered with my school attendance. His death marked the end of my involvement in that industry.

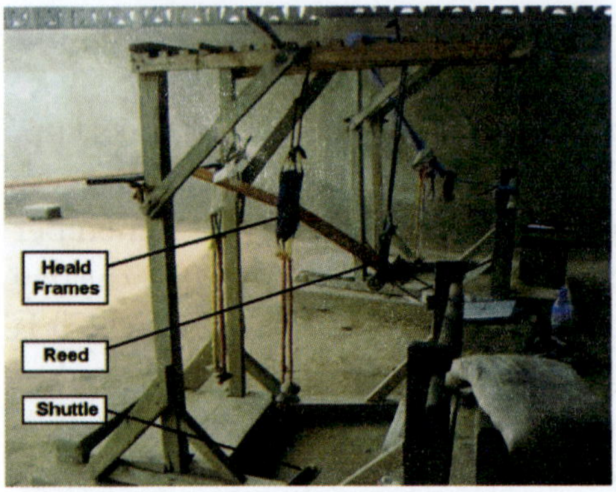

Figure 3: A traditional loom (side view)

Figure 4: A traditional loom (weaver's view)

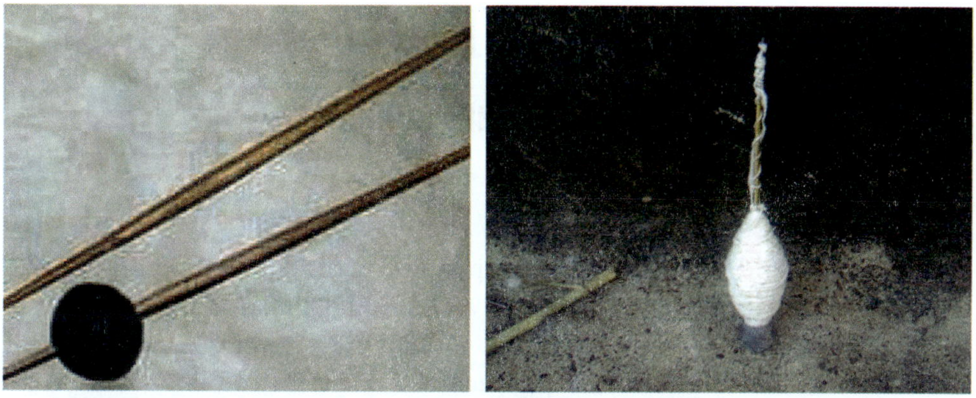

Figure 5: Gendri, with & without clay ball (left) and with spun thread (right)

Figure 6: The shuttle *(Kukorigor)* sitting on the stone used for extracting cotton seeds

Figure 7: The heald *(Dabsi)* on the left and the reed (Gombor) **on the right lying on the stone used for extracting cotton seeds**

Figure 8: Modern setup for the warp

CHAPTER 7

BUILDING ON THE FOUNDATION

I am told that the most important part of any building is the foundation. If my primary and middle school days formed the foundation of my education then my life in the secondary school from 1968 to 1975 built on that foundation. I spent five years of this time up to 1973 in Ghana College, Tamale and the other two years in Navrongo Secondary School. I will recount some major events that influenced my life during these seven years.

The first event is the accumulation of knowledge in English Language, Mathematics, Science and Social Sciences during these years. The second is my becoming a Christian in the year 1970. The third is the passing away of my father in January 1971. The fourth event is what I will call the drama of the 1973 year group in Form Five.

The accumulation of knowledge over a seven-year time frame is a very slow process. It includes going to classes every day during school days, listening to the teachers of all the subjects being taught, doing the exercises, the tests and everything else given by the teachers. Also, it includes reading widely on every subject under the sun. The secondary school is actually the environment in which one builds on the foundations of education and builds a character upon which the rest of life will be based.

One of the biggest historical events that Ghana College has come to be known for is the launching of a miniature rocket in the 1969/70 academic year. Three science teachers, namely Mr. R. R. Lalaji, Mr. A. A. Acharya and Mr. A. A. Dramani came together to design and launch this rocket, the first-of-its-kind in any secondary school in Ghana and most likely in West Africa. I was proud to be part of the students who witnessed this firsthand.

I have been asked whether we had nicknames for masters in secondary school. I can remember a nickname for the master who taught Typing and Shorthand, Accounts and Commerce. He had a problem pronouncing "commodities". He pronounced the word as "acommodities". As a result of this habit, we called him, "Mr. Acommo". I have consulted a few former students of Ghana College and nobody seems to remember his real name.

From Form One in Ghana College, I joined the Science Club, the Historical Society and the Scripture Union. A group of Christian teachers and workers came together to form the Chaplaincy Board in Tamale, which organised weekend conferences for young Christians in the Secondary Schools and Technical School. They were held at a location called the Presbyterian Youth Training Centre in Vitin on the Tamale-Yendi road. It was during one of these conferences that I gained a very clear understanding of the Christian gospel and I gave my life to Christ. My acceptance of Christ seemed to be received as a bad example back in my home community, which was predominantly Muslim. Some of my relatives had the perception that if a child was sent to school, that child could become a Christian. This fear has gradually been replaced by an understanding that formal education provides a certain guarantee for becoming competitive in the job market. I believe this decision was the greatest step in my life that transformed me into a Bible-believing Christian living on biblical principles. It has been the biggest influence on my career as a development worker in Africa.

Several members of the Chaplaincy Board who metaphorically held my hand and walked me through basic Bible study and prayer and helped me to understand practical Biblical Christian living are still alive and will most likely read this book. I hesitate to mention names to avoid leaving very significant people out of the list. In Navrongo Secondary School, my faith as a Christian was strengthened when the masters who taught me sophisticated principles in Physics, Chemistry and Mathematics sat with me in Scripture Union meetings and studied the Bible diligently with us – sharing their experiences. I am still in touch with two of these masters after over 40 years of separation.

The third major event that influenced my life in secondary school was the passing away of my father in January 1971. This was the most traumatic shock of my life at that time. The man I trusted to respond to all my needs and who committed himself to seeing me through education was gone. I did not even have the opportunity to explain my new faith to him. The very pillar of support on which I depended to accomplish my dream was gone. I mourned the loss of my father for one year, literally crying every day at some point or other. On the first anniversary of the death of my father, I took the decision that despite my loss I was going to work hard and realise big dreams in my life.

This is one of the motivations that kept me going through difficult situations in my career as a development worker in Africa.

The fourth big event that influenced my life while I was in secondary school is what I will call the 1973 Form Five year group drama. I must mention that in the second term of my Form One in Ghana College, in January 1969, there was a strike that led to the removal of A. F. Clayton as headmaster of the school. That was the first time I heard the word 'strike'. So the cohort of students who came to Form One in September 1968 had to continue their course without the headmaster who selected them from across the country to come to the school. We ended up in Form Five with very few masters. This situation, although unfortunate, provided three opportunities. My classmates and I learnt to study on our own, researching through books and acquiring knowledge wherever we could find it. The second opportunity was the ability to teach and help each other move forward in our educational careers. The third and biggest opportunity was the sacrifice made by a number of students in the three universities in Ghana at the time to come over to our school and teach us during the Easter vacation in preparation for the West African School Certificate O-Level Examination. This was for free and all that they needed was for the school to feed them three times a day. It was my first time of seeing real voluntary service in action. These young undergraduates taught us with a passion throughout the days, at weekends, in the night, and still made time for personal teaching and coaching.

The support visit from the undergraduates from the three Ghanaian universities had a very high impact on my life. For the first time, I started thinking beyond Manga. I wanted to become an undergraduate in one of the universities like them. The idea of becoming an agricultural technical officer suddenly became too small and disappeared from my horizon. This was the rescue mission that also enabled the 1973 year group in Ghana College to set what has been claimed to be an academic record that had never been seen before in the school.

Twenty of us obtained Division 1 in the West African School Certificate O-Level examinations. When the results came I was very excited that I had qualified to go to Sixth Form, but my desire to do so met with disapproval and condemnation from my family back at home. If I had not gone to the secondary school I would have completed my education as a Form 4 middle school leaver in 1969. Going to secondary school had delayed that completion by four years. Now that I had 'completed school' at long last, I was planning to go back to school. This was unthinkable. My beloved father was nowhere to defend my progress in education. With moral and financial support from three prominent people, Musah Mahamah, my cousin Osman and an Agricultural Technical Officer called Kofi Dartey, I nevertheless succeeded in going to Sixth Form in Navrongo Secondary School. This started a completely new experience in my life.

In the first place, Navrongo Secondary School was about 5 km from Navrongo town centre and there was no public transport between the two. My first experience of walking to the school with my suitcase on my head was a very frustrating one. One colleague of mine from Manga arrived in the town to find me sitting with my suitcase waiting for a taxi, and he opened my eyes to the fact that I had to get up, carry my suitcase and walk to the school. The sight of Navrongo Hospital after about a kilometre gave me some hope that was dashed immediately I realised that the school was further ahead. After another kilometre and a half or so, the sight of Saint John Bosco Training College raised my hope again only for me to discover that this was not the school. The next institution, the Agricultural Training School, raised my hopes yet again and once more I found that I had to go beyond this. We finally got to the school when I stopped expecting to end my journey.

The culture of the school was completely different from what I knew in Ghana College. The number of students was over three times the population of Ghana College. Students were identified by numbers, called folio numbers, instead of their names. The numbers that Sixth Form students were given were based on the sequence in which students arrived. There must have been a deliberate effort to give certain folio numbers to girls in Form 1 to 5 in order to put them in particular classes. The school had a dedicated chapel for Christian activities, a very rare situation in Ghanaian secondary schools. It was here that I met Mr Neil Cameron, Mr. and Mrs. John Turl and Mr. Colin Macdonald who became my life long friends. Colin Macdonald is one of the legends of Navrongo Secondary School. Stories about him could fill a book. One memorable story was his ability to remember the folio numbers of all students from Form 3 to Upper 6. Another was his daring purchase of the materials which had been used to construct a pavilion at the Trade Fair site in Accra, transporting them to Navrongo and reassembling them to make an assembly hall. The construction was accomplished by Mr. Macdonald himself, assisted by students working voluntarily, resulting in minimum labour cost. Mr. Macdonald introduced an 'agric' sixth form in Navrongo Secondary

School. This was a programme that enabled students with GCE O-level qualifications to come to the school and study agriculture as a vocation. The students studied the use, repair and management of agricultural equipment and accessories such as tractors and their implements. They also studied other subjects such as farm management, basic bookkeeping, and other business techniques that would help them in their businesses as professional farmers in the future. I have talked to several past students of this course and they are all in agreement that there was no other secondary school in Ghana that offered this opportunity. In 1973/74 he facilitated a process that enabled the students in this course to farm and produce 860 bags of paddy rice. He brought in a rice miller, attached it to a tractor and milled all this rice to feed the school.

Another innovative addition to the school was the maintenance workshop. This was a workshop where vocational skills such as carpentry and masonry were taught to form 1 and 2 students. Chairs and tables that got damaged in classrooms were taken to this workshop, repaired and returned for use in the classrooms at no cost to the school.

Throughout my career, every single thing that I have learned has always found some of its roots and foundation in Ghana College and Navrongo Secondary School.

CHAPTER 8

GOING TO THE UNIVERSITY

It was one morning in October 1975. I cannot remember why I was walking in Bawku town early in the morning. I met this friend of mine on a motorbike near the Bawku district council offices. He stopped briefly and said 'congratulations'. I asked him why he was congratulating me. He said he had seen my name in one of the daily newspapers of the day before among the list of students that had been admitted to the University of Cape Coast to read Chemistry, Physics and Mathematics. I told him that the newspapers for the day before normally arrived today but the State Transport Corporation (STC) bus which normally brings them had not come on that day. So how did he gets the papers? He explained that somebody came from Accra in a private car and brought the papers for him. I agreed to go and wait at a fuel station near his house and when he came back, he would show me the paper. After I had waited for about 45 minutes my friend arrived and invited me into his house to read the daily paper he was talking about. He could not find the paper and when he asked his wife she said she had used it to make fire. Oh my! This was becoming like a drama. He went to the kitchen and found some of the papers that had not been used. It was still there! We hurriedly found the page that had the list of students admitted into the University. The paper had been torn through the list. It somehow went through my name. But I could see letters BRAI. I was convinced that this was part of my name. So I went and sat at a friend's shop contemplating what to do next.

I finally arrived at home after 4:00 pm. Mothers will always be mothers. My mother realised right away that something was on my mind. After trying all the usual manoeuvres and tactics to avoid answering her directly I finally told her what I believed was good news – my admission to the University of Cape Coast. Not long after that, one of my sisters arrived in the house and heard the news. Immediately I found myself caught in a crossfire of comments and questions. Getting them to pronounce the word 'University' was a major problem. None of them had heard about Cape Coast before.

From Manga, anybody travelling down south beyond the Volta River at Yeji, was either going to Kumasi or Accra.

My mother and sister pointed out to me that I had already wasted seven years in this so-called secondary school and I did not have "anything" to show for it. As far as they were concerned, my General Certificate of Education (GCE), O-level and A-level results were not 'anything' I could show for being in secondary school. How does one explain grades in Chemistry, Physics and Mathematics in Bissa to the people who love you but do not understand these subjects? They asked me to point out one person from the community of Manga who had gone to this so-called university and the 'profit' he had made out of it. I tried to cite the first person from the Bissa ethnic group in Manga who had just completed his degree course at the University of Science and Technology, Kumasi. I was quickly told that his elder brother in Bawku town had a big compound house and thriving tailoring business as well as three corn mills but he had never gone to school. I was given the example of a classmate who had remained in Manga Middle School, completed the school and now had a job. He owned a motorbike and had built a 'square room' for himself, roofed with corrugated iron sheets and he was sleeping on a wooden bed. He had also married and had one child. I, Dubinyale, was still sleeping on a mat in a round mud room roofed with grass.

These were all legitimate sentiments expressed. I could not explain that I was aiming to be higher up the ladder and be competitive higher up in the job market. I could not explain that I wanted to be able to contribute to the development of my country at a higher level. The idea of a time machine has always remained in the fiction books. If this were not the case, and if I could have afforded the fare, I would have taken my parents and travelled from 1975 to the year 2020 and shown them what I hoped would become of this gentleman who completed his course in 1975.

Although I won the battle with my family and proceeded to the University, the argument in itself poses several legitimate questions. If the purpose of education is imagined to be the acquisition of property and material resources then we may be missing the point. If one can contribute to the development of the country, could this not be considered to be an acceptable outcome for education? Is not the urgent pressure to gain quick material returns for education one of the causes of corruption? On the other hand, after a good education if one works hard throughout his career and retires in poverty what would be the benefit of one's education? The debate between education and acquisition of wealth is a very complicated and delicate subject that will continue to be revisited by development workers in Africa.

This narrative shows the conflict I had to endure before going to university. I am aware that many people have had similar experiences and many were not successful. With the assistance of the three people who supported me to go to Sixth Form, I went to the University of Cape Coast.

In October 1975 I arrived on the university campus. I then had to go through another stage of transition. Everything was different. The Headmaster was called the Vice-Chancellor. The classrooms were called lecture halls and the masters were called lecturers. The dining hall was called the refectory or the cafeteria (a system which has been abolished in Ghanaian Universities since the late 1980s). The assembly hall was called the auditorium. The student dormitories were called halls of residence. The university had its own security system called Campus Guards. There were buses that carried students between some lecture halls and some halls of residence. This bus system has been modernised and students now pay for internal university campus transportation. Nobody rang the bell as we did in secondary school. We were now supposed to be adults and could decide to wake up at any time we wanted. We could also go to bed at any time we wanted and there was no time for "lights off". That was the most interesting part of my new life.

I was given accommodation in Oguaa Hall room number 366 and was really delighted when I found out that I was going to share a room with a Christian, K. D. Kessi. I learnt a lot about the Christian Life and discipline from this Christian brother and friend throughout the four years of studies in the University of Cape coast.

I settled down to my new life with enthusiasm. Then I realised that students from the Northern and Upper Regions formed less than 4% of the university student population. Indeed the number of students from the Bawku District starting from the Red Volta all the way to the Burkina Faso and Togo borders was only eight. In spite of this I was encouraged by the fact that 4 of us were from the Bissa ethnic group and one of the Bissa students, Dominic Payida Sore, was pursuing a master's degree in physics. I began to ask myself, what were the factors that influenced the entry of northern students into the University? Reflecting on this now I have been able to note several. There is the question of the three hurdles one must overcome to get into the university, namely, passing the Common Entrance Examination to go to secondary school, passing the GCE O-Level Examination to go to Sixth Form and passing the GCE A-Level Examination to go to the university. At all these three stages, there are stories of brilliant students who could not proceed because of family conditions and financial constraints. Then there is the question of pressure to work to bring some income into the family. This factor was complemented by the fact that with a middle school leaving certificate, or an O-Level or A-Level certificate one could get a job. In those days, another factor was the unawareness that one could rewrite both O-Levels and A-Levels more than once and use the best results over two or more years to gain admission into higher institutions.

Then there was the issue of studying to pass examinations as against studying to acquire knowledge. Many of our counterparts in well-established schools in Accra and Cape Coast studied under teachers who were examiners who marked the examination papers. These students had the advantage of being taught by more experienced teachers than their counterparts in Northern Ghana. Indeed, students from the south of Ghana who came from rural areas, who were first-generation literates and did not attend the big schools, were even more likely to be victims of some of the factors outlined above. I know a colleague in the south who went to secondary school only after passing the Common Entrance Examination for the fourth time. But for his persistence and the external pressure on his parents, this intelligent boy would never have gone to secondary school, let alone to the university.

Another factor that influenced the number of northern students in universities was that not many aspired to go. In my case, I never thought about going to a university until the second term of Form 5. One cannot aspire to become what one does not know. I have heard of a situation where a student who did not attempt to go to university for six years after completing school because he did not know that his grades were good enough until this was pointed out to him when he was working. Such a person obviously had nobody ahead of him in education to advise him – a very common situation among northern students at the time. Then the question of proximity to the universities comes into play. At our time the higher institutions of learning were all in the south. Undocumented observations show that the number of northern students in Ghanaian universities has increased since the establishment of the University for Development Studies and its campuses in Northern Ghana.

My financial difficulties continued whilst I was in University. Sometimes it was cheaper to remain on campus than to travelling all the way home and back. I took advantage of these times to stay on campus and study. During one of the vacations in 1978, I decided to travel home although I had very little money to do so. I travelled from Cape Coast to Accra and left my suitcase in the care of a security guard at the bus terminal of the State Transport Corporation. I then walked nearly three kilometres to a suburb of Accra to pass the night with a friend. The following morning I walked back again to the terminal. All that I had was enough money to pay for the ticket from Accra to Bawku and a flask of porridge. Throughout the journey, which lasted from 6:00 am to 11:00 pm, all that I did was to read a book and drink porridge. All the four stops on the way for passengers to eat meant nothing to me.

It was in the university that I initiated the building of my three personal libraries namely my Science, Maths and Education library, my Christian library, and my fiction and contemporary English literature library. In the first of these, I stocked books such as Inorganic Chemistry by David Cotton, Organic Chemistry by Prof. Hendrickson et al., Systematic Identification of Organic Compounds, Practical Organic Chemistry as well as Mathematics and Education textbooks.

The libraries I established in my room were complemented by the various departmental libraries as well as the central library. These provided avenues for further studies as a follow-up to what lecturers gave us in the various subjects. Long hours of practical sessions in the science laboratories as well as coaching in research work both in the chemistry department and the faculty of education built on the practical in secondary school, and also established a foundation for advanced studies.

The University Christian Fellowship provided one solid environment for Christian growth. It was here that lessons learnt from my Christian library could express themselves in reality. I stocked literature such as church history, a Bible concordance, a Bible dictionary, thought provoking Bible study guides and daily devotional guides such as Search the Scriptures. I also had books on apologetics and basic Christian living. This library enabled me to make an in-depth study of Christianity that affected practical living. My involvement in the leadership of the Ghana Fellowship of Evangelical

Students (GHAFES) between 1976 and 1979 played a significant role in my Christian development. GHAFES was made up of Christian Fellowships from the three universities in Ghana as well as the higher institutions in Winneba (which formed the core for the establishment of the University of Education in Winneba).

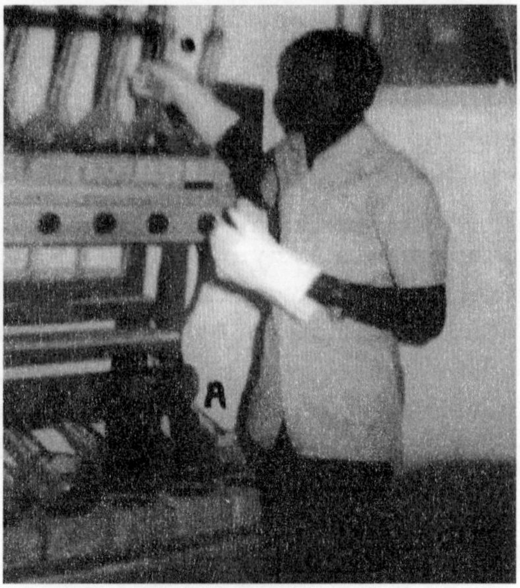

Figure 9: Carrying out research in the chemistry laboratory in the University of Cape Coast

The third library I built contained books of fiction, English literature and political science. I had books such as Earl Stanley Gardner's Perry Mason series, The Saint series by Leslie Charteris, and John Creasey's Department Z and Dr Palfrey series. I stocked classics from William Shakespeare to Agatha Christie. I used the central library to read literature on political science including the scientific socialism of writers such as Karl Marx. This enabled me to follow political discussion in the University. Delving into these books helped to improve my English language and gave me a broader view of the world.

The advent of internet search engines has provided an opportunity for anybody to look for any information on any subject. This is a powerful tool which every researcher greatly appreciates. I see search engines as being complementary to physical libraries and not a replacement. I have seen large bookshops in international airports in Johannesburg, London, Amsterdam, Washington DC, New York, Nairobi, and indeed all over the world. These bookshops are always full of travelling passengers in search of a good read. There is still a huge interest in building physical libraries that cannot easily be replaced by electronic books.

My time in the university from 1975 to 1979 appears to be one of the most turbulent times in the history of Ghana. This was the time when President Acheampong tried to introduce the Union Government concept. It was the period in which the Peoples Movement for Freedom and Justice

(PMFJ) came to be (January 1978), and in which there was great unrest among university students calling for good governance in the country. An internal coup d'état resulted in the formation of the second Supreme Military Council (SMC II). The attempt by Flt. Lieutenant Jerry John Rawlings to overthrow the government on May 15, 1979, brought things to a head. Rawlings was found guilty of treason, sound today Ussher fort prisons and waiting to be sentenced, but was freed on 4 June by a group of junior officers and staged a successful but violent coup leading to the formation of the Armed Forces Revolutionary Council (AFRC). The AFRC led the country to elections and handed over power to a democratically elected government in September 1979. Another coup by Rawlings in 1981 was less tumultuous, and permanent democracy was finally established in 1992.

I mention these events simply because they happened during my time in university. I have stayed away from making any political commentary as this is beyond the scope of my writing. At a personal level, I must say there were also several significant events in my life. It was in 1979 that I started my national service, for the first time earning money as a full-time worker. My happiness about starting work ended in the first week of December when I was informed that I had not passed my final examination for graduation and I had to repeat a full year in the University. I remember that this news kept me awake all night as I sat and contemplated my future.

I finally got the courage to go back to the university and sit in the same class with students who were one year behind me to complete my course in chemistry and mathematics. I had to engage a lecturer, pick up a research topic and carry out a research project, concluding with a long essay that was submitted by June 1980. The determination to gather myself after the setback in 1979 has been a major lesson in my life, on never giving up the pursuit for excellence. Graduating out of the University was a major milestone in my life and launched me into the real world.

My sister who engaged with me in the debate on whether to go to the university or not passed away during childbirth at the end of my first term in the first year of my university. She never lived to see the results of my education. By the grace of God my mother lived for 26 more years and saw my contribution to development across Africa.

My time in the University allowed me to build academic, professional and Christian networks in Cape Coast, Winneba, Accra, Kumasi, Tamale and Bawku. Many people in these networks have played significant roles in my education, professional career and Christian life. I will forever be thankful to God and grateful to them for the roles they have played in making me who I am.

CHAPTER 9

IMBIBING THE PRINCIPLES FOR SERVICE AND PURPOSEFUL LIFE

One of the most common words in development today is the word resilience. Development workers use this word to mean the ability of a community to survive difficult times successfully. I now realise that while battling for survival and confronting poverty as a child, I was also building resilience and learning the principles of service and purposeful living. As farming was the predominant occupation of the people in Manga and surrounding villages, this also provided the easiest way of looking for money. I tackled this from several angles. Dedication and hard work on the family farms ensured that I contributed to the production of enough food harvested from these farms for family consumption all year round. I also helped my mother, sisters and cousins to work on their farms thereby increasing their crop production and putting them in a better position to help me when I was in need. The other major farming activity I engaged in was going to people's farms and working for them to be paid a fee.

One day during the middle of the rainy season I decided that I would use about five hours the following day to complete some weeding on my mother's rice farm. The following day I picked up my hoe and left the house and was greeted by the sweet smell of the flowers on the vegetables around the house. The cries of early morning birds filled the sky. Bats returned from their nocturnal hunting expeditions to struggle for space in their sanctuary on the Shea Nut tree near Akolgo's house. Cattle egrets ended their night and began flying out from the tree near our house to go in search of areas where they could get little grasshoppers and other insects to eat. I walked through the early morning dew, destroying spider webs that crisscrossed the road, and was in the rice farm by 5:30 am. The smell of the riverside mud replaced all the different smells that accompanied me from home to the farm. The sounds around me were an uncoordinated blend of croaking from the frogs and toads, chirping from the grasshoppers and crickets and all the other noises I could not identify. At about 6:15 am I heard the rumbling of thunder. When I looked up there was a thick black cloud in the east that signified an imminent heavy rain. By

7:00 am it had arrived, heavy and continuous. I just ignored it and continued weeding.

As the rainwater poured from all angles I rolled the soil and covered the weeds while humming a tune to give me some rhythm. Sweat rolled down my face mixed with rainwater but I really did not care. By 10:30 am the rain was gone but my rhythm did not break. I finished my job by 12:30 pm and walked home with pride to tell my mother that the job on her rice farm was done. My mother asked me whether I did not see the rain coming. I told her that I had decided to finish the task today, in rain or sunshine and I had done just that.

One of my sisters had a rice farm nearly 3 km away from home. I dedicated 10 to 14 days every year to help her during the rainy season. I would normally wake up early to be at her house by 5:00 am. Usually, by then she would have prepared the food we needed while on the farm, and we would do the 3 km walk to the farm and start work by 7:00 am. We had a break at about 9:30 am to eat breakfast and at about 1:00 pm to eat lunch. We would normally leave the farm by 4:00 pm and hope to get back home before 6:00 pm. I remember doing this repeatedly between 1965 and 1972.

Working on people's farms for a fee was the other common thing I did. One of my clients had a rice farm that was swampy all year round. I did two major things on this farm. He nursed some rice on higher ground with an area of about 4 x 4 meters. I then had to spend several days uprooting the rice that had grown to a height where it could not be submerged in the water and transplant into the swampy area. The second thing was that I would go back into that swampy area after about a month and a half and pull out weeds to enable the rice to mature and the grains to be harvested. The biggest problem with this farm was that it was heavily infested with leeches. Yes! Leeches - the dreaded water creatures that could stick to the body of anybody in the water and suck blood until they are full or interrupted. So many young boys looking for farm work avoided this particular farm. For me, this was rather an advantage to increase the amount to be paid for working on a difficult farm. I would normally take 50% of the fee as an advance payment. I would then buy shea butter and put it in water in a bowl to prevent it from melting under the scorching heat of the sun. I took this to the farm and placed it on dry ground. I would then rub my legs with the shea butter all the way up to my knees and walk into the swamp. There, I would work continuously for about 30 to 40 minutes. In the beginning, the leeches would have difficulty in sticking to my skin. By the end of 30 to 40 minutes when I walked out of the water the effect of the shea butter would have reduced and I would see a few leeches sticking to my skin. I would just pull them off my skin into the hot sun, apply some more shea butter and get back into the swamp. Walking back into the swampy farm knowing that the immediate and extended family members of the leeches I had just destroyed, as well as their friends and neighbours, were in the swamp waiting for me, needed a certain amount of courage. It normally took me about 2 to 3 days of relentless battle with the leeches to finish weeding the farm. This was the biggest farming challenge I have ever had in my lifetime and I always won. One person I know has told me how he and a group of friends ventured into Manga in 1965 to look for work and earn some money. They ended up in a rice farm infested with leeches. He said the leeches he got on his feet after only 10 minutes of work were a really scary experience. He decided to leave that field by the second day.

In the middle of the rainy season of 1974, I was given a job on a farm in a village called Nafkoliga, about 16 km from Manga. My job was to be on the farm between 5 am and 9 am and between 3.30 pm and 6 pm to chase birds away from pecking the developing rice grains that were not yet solid. This meant that I had to sleep at a location from where I could get into the farm by 5 am. The only place I found to be able to accomplish this task was Nafkoliga Primary School. The teachers kindly agreed to give me and two other friends from Bawku who were working on their farm, the keys to the school. I brought cardboard thick enough to improvise as a mat and slept in the school every day for 3 weeks. Chasing the birds in the mornings and evenings required running around the farm area making as much noise as I could by clanging two aluminium bowls together and supported by several scarecrows I designed and planted all around the farm. The evenings after 6 pm were occupied by burning some bushes to produce smoke to repel mosquitoes and other insects and also sitting around and telling stories. One of the farmers from Bawku had a transistor radio with which we could listen to news from the Ghana Broadcasting Corporation (GBC) in Accra and British Broadcasting Corporation (BBC) in London, thus keeping us abreast with the rest of the world.

The owner of the farm I was working on, and his labourers, came from Manga every morning and brought us some food but our main evening meal was *gari* (grated dried cassava) soaked in water and sweetened with sugar. Once in a while, we strayed into the village nearby and bought some curdled cow's milk to increase the nutritional value of our 'dinner'. In the third week of my job, very heavy rain fell and filled two of the major streams between Manga and the farm, thereby cutting off the daily visits by the farmer and his labourers and any other form of communication. I had to devise other means of survival during these three days, including trapping partridges in the long rainy season grass and walking to the Fulanis in the nearby village for milk, which I drank, this time without any solid base. On the third day, when we realised that the water was not receding, my two farmer friends from Bawku and I decided to walk all the way back home. Our strategy was not to walk fast and on 3 occasions we sat by the roadside on the grass under trees to rest. Then we had to wade through the streams on the way with the water, at times, rising to our waist level. By 4 pm, I was at home, exhausted, hungry and needing a bath and rest.

These battles on the farms ensured my survival and extra money for a few 'luxuries', that is if one extra shirt and singlet can be called luxuries.

Fishing was a whole different ball game. There are several ways of catching fish in a stream or a river. In single hook fishing, you attach a thread to a hook through a triangular piece of calabash that acts as the sinker. The other end of the thread is attached to a stick. Bait is attached to the hook and dropped into the water. The fisher now sits on the bank of the stream with the stick in hand waiting for the fish to take the bait. When the sinker disappears in the water the fish is yanked out. This is repeated several times until the fisher decides he has enough or his time is running out.

With multiple hook fishing, several hooks are attached to a mainline at about 30 cm intervals and hanging about 15 to 20 cm below the line. I quickly found out that a box of hooks contained 144 hooks. Before the advent of the Aliens Compliance Order of 1969, when all non-Ghanaians (particularly Nigerians) were given a deadline to leave the country, Yorubas in Bawku market were the most reliable suppliers of hooks. Bait is then attached to every hook and a whole line planted to cross the stream in a zig-zag fashion in the evening. The fisher would go back to the stream very early in the morning and harvest the fish that had taken the bait

Cross net fishing is very similar to multiple hook fishing. The difference is that this type of fishing used a long net with pieces of lead attached to its lower end to hold it down instead of hooks.

The fourth type of fishing is done using a cast net. The net is woven in such a way that when it is cast, it spreads into a cone and pieces of lead attached to its bottom pull it down to the bed of the stream, trapping fish in its area of coverage. For some reason, I have never been successful in using the cast net.

The fifth type of fishing is carried out particularly in the cold dry season when water from the previous rainy season begins to recede. This is basically group fishing and it needs careful organisation, teamwork and speed. This method of fishing requires a team of about 12 to 16 children split into two groups of 6 to 8. The teams approach streams and use stones and boulders to block a section of the water upstream and downstream leaving what looks like a lake. The distance between the two blockages would be between 6 and 10 metres. Water is then collected quickly from the 'lake' and thrown into the downstream section of the stream using all types of available containers including buckets, broken calabashes, thereby rapidly reducing the trapped water. When the water reaches a level where the fishes are clearly visible, the children catch as many fish as they can, then break down the barriers to allow the water to flow. Once again this type of fishing requires teamwork, tenacity and speed.

There is yet another type of fishing carried out at the beginning of the rainy season, this is fishing for mudfish that have hibernated in the mud throughout the dry season. As a kid, I could locate the presence of mudfish underground by looking on the ground after the first two heavy rains. I would then dig the spot, locate the fish and stick my hand in to pull it out while being careful not to allow my finger to get in the mouth of the fish as this would spell disaster. It is known that a finger caught in the jaws of a mudfish can only be released by cutting off the head of the fish and slicing and opening the jaws by force. Mudfish were one of the biggest sources of income but also one of the most delicious meals at home as it was practically boneless below the head.

There is one more type of group fishing done mainly by adults in which I never participated and therefore am unable to describe clearly.

I carried out fishing for two major reasons: for sale to get money to respond to a few needs and to ensure that my mother had some protein for family meals. It is interesting to note that despite the presence of domestic birds such as chickens, guinea fowls, ducks and pigeons and animals like goats, sheep and cows in households in the rural community, these are hardly ever caught and slaughtered as protein for meals. The slaughtering of domestic birds and animals is usually done during festivals such as *Samanpiid* for the Kussasis and *Torta* for the Bissa and during occasions such as funerals, outdooring ceremonies and sacrifices to deities as advised by traditional spiritual leaders.

The violation of taboos can also lead to their slaughter, for example when a cock stands on a wall and crows in the Kussasi home, it is immediately caught and slaughtered. When chickens mate at the gate of a Bissa house, both cock and hen are slaughtered. These are simply taboo and no explanation is given for why they are taboos. In fact, domestic birds and animals are actually the savings of community members and sometimes have a sentimental relationship with their owners. Increased numbers of birds would result in the birds being sold to buy small animals. For example, the owner of guinea fowls may decide to sell several of them to buy one or two goats. As the goats multiply, the owner may decide to sell several goats and buy a cow or a donkey. Livestock forms the reserves to which community members turn to respond to either food shortages or sudden financial demands. A rural community member will appreciate counting the number of goats he has and estimate the increase in the next two years rather than relate to interest rates in the bank. This is the reason why fishing is so important in supplementing the protein needs of the family.

I have heard claims in the last few years about the presence of mercury in water bodies in the Upper East Region emanating from illegal small scale mining activities along the rivers. This has led to the death of domestic livestock, bush animals and fishes in the river. Development workers may want to consider a careful balance between increased veterinary support to reduce the risk of the loss of domestic animals to epidemics than the introduction of rural banking as a method for saving surplus resources.

As a child and throughout my development into adulthood, I had to understand these local social-cultural and economic principles in the rural community. Development workers in Africa also need to understand these traditional economic principles to ensure that the development interventions are relevant to the local community.

In carrying out all these activities, I did not stop going to school. They were done at weekends and during school vacations. Some development workers may refer to these activities as child labour. In my opinion, if a child does work in this way to earn money, it should not be considered as child labour. Interestingly, children in movies and talent shows coming from the western world are not considered to be engaged in child labour and yet their counterparts who use weekends and school vacations to work on farms are told that they are engaging in child labour.

With hindsight, I now realise that these activities helped to develop my principles for full-time work and a purposeful life. It was during this period that I learned determination, teamwork, coordination, timeliness and focus. I am aware that when my father was alive, he supervised me from a distance and this supervision continued with relatives. I will be forever grateful to my father and other relatives who allowed me the liberty to venture into all types of risky situations for survival and daily living. This period of my life established and entrenched the principles that have influenced the rest of my career.

CHAPTER 10

A GLIMPSE OF EUROPE

The date was the 31st of July 1980. I sat at the departure lounge of Kotoka International Airport in Accra, Ghana, and waited to board my flight on British Caledonian Airways to London in the UK. The flight was finally called and I made my way with the other passengers into the DC-10 Aircraft. I sat on the window seat on the left-hand side of the aircraft as I was directed by the cabin crew. In no time, we were airborne and as the aircraft turned to realign its flight path northwards, the night lights of Accra receded into oblivion.

As we reached our cruising altitude of 33,000 feet above sea level, I sat quietly reflecting on the events of the previous months and whether this first flight into Europe would actually succeed. Earlier in the year, my friend Neil Cameron had started communications inviting me to join him to manage a Scripture Union Youth Camp in Scotland. This flight was a result of that invitation. I got my first passport earlier that year. An attempt to get a British visa failed and I was told that I could fly into London without a visa and my fate would be decided by the Immigration Officers at the airport. In those days one did not need a visa to board an international flight. This is now a requirement on all international flights out of Accra.

I sat in the DC-10 aircraft cruising at almost 900 km per hour, heading for London, not knowing what my fate would be. In a worst-case scenario, I would smell the air in London and get returned to Accra. I prayed for a miracle. At about 6:10 am, we landed at London Gatwick Airport. This was supposed to be a six-hour flight and we had left Accra at 11:00 pm. Then I got some education – the cabin crew informed us that British summertime is one hour ahead of GMT which is the time zone used in Accra.

As we disembarked through the boarding bridge and out to the immigration area, I noticed the separation of passengers into nationalities. There was a place for passengers with UK passports, then one area for passengers with European passports and the final zone was for other passports. This zone was for passengers from Africa, America, Asia, Australia and New Zealand. A very large number of passengers went to the area for UK passports but this line diminished in a few minutes as passengers simply showed their passports to the Immigration Officers and walked past. I finally got to our officer after nearly 40 minutes in the queue. He asked what I was coming to the UK to do, where and how I knew Neil Cameron, whether there was any communication between Mr. Cameroon and me, did I have a valid ticket to fly back to Ghana, how much money did I have, where was I born, where did I go to school? The questions were just endless. I provided the appropriate answers for them all. I was taken away into a separate room and a second officer came to ask me many more questions. Then a third officer gave me a cup of coffee and some biscuits on a plate. I noticed that all three asked the same questions, sometimes framed differently. However, if one is telling the truth the number of times the questions are asked cannot change the answers.

I later learnt that the Immigration Officers tried to contact Neil Cameron on the telephone number I gave them. Unfortunately, this was the telephone number for British Nuclear Fuels where he worked. They waited for normal office hours in the UK and called the number. His boss answered the phone and told Immigration that Neil Cameron was on leave and then gave them his father's number. Immigration then took the time to call Neil's father to ask whether he knew about my coming. The old man responded in the affirmative and this was what opened the way to my entry into the UK. I wonder if Immigration Officers across the world do the same thing today. Finally, I was given an entry visa as a visitor and this visa was valid for three months starting on 1 August 1980.

This marked my entry into the UK and for that matter into Europe for the first time. I walked out into a 'warm' sunny London at a temperature of 14°C. In Manga, 18°C is considered freezing. Now, I was being told that 14°C is a 'warm' sunny summer day. I then tried to call Neil's father from a public telephone booth into which the caller put coins into a slot to be able to talk. The first 10 pence coin I pushed into the telephone slot got me enough talking time to introduce myself. While Mr. Cameron was trying to direct me on how to come to Helensburgh in Scotland, the telephone was asking for more money. I had no idea that the telephone bills were higher during peak hours (between 8:00 am and 12:00 noon). I therefore hung up the phone and tried to figure out how to work my way from Gatwick Airport to Helensburgh. Somehow, I managed to get on British Rail from

Gatwick Airport to Victoria Station in London and then make the necessary connections on the London Underground to Euston Station where I got on British Rail to Glasgow and then to Helensburgh. The cold was biting and in the absence of warm clothes, I was beginning to shiver. For the first time, I was in a British Rail Intercity Train powered by electricity and speeding at nearly 190 km per hour through the countryside of the UK. Rural British farming communities flew past us as I noticed cattle grazing in farmlands and hay being collected for storage. I arrived in Helensburgh at about 4:30 pm. Apart from a few sandwiches that I had on the train I had gone nearly 24 hours without eating a real meal.

I stood on the platform waiting for Neil's father. After a few minutes, a gentleman walked up to me and said "Welcome, Sammy". I asked "How did you know I was Sam?" and he responded "Do you see any other black person around here?" Amazing! He immediately attended to my two most pressing needs, that is warm clothes to protect me from the cold and food from a fast-food restaurant to deal with my hunger. Then he drove me to the campsite at Blavaich Campsite. I had missed the first few days of the youth camp, but was able to join the leaders to help manage the last four days. I was very impressed by the enthusiasm of the youth to learn scriptural information. These were eager Scottish teenagers delving into scripture to understand their Christian faith.

The major events during my two months stay in Europe included sailing with my friends off the west coast of Scotland, climbing Ben Nevis (the highest mountain in the UK) to the top, travelling through France to Switzerland and back through Germany and Belgium, and living with Neil Cameron in Preston in the UK.

One beautiful summer morning, I sat with Neil in a small coffee shop in a village called Luss on the shores of Loch Lomond with Ben Lomond in the background (lakes are called Lochs in Scotland, valleys are called Glens and mountains are called Bens). I have said over and over to many Scottish people I have met that Luss is probably the most beautiful small town I have seen on the planet. We were on our way to Mallaig to start our one week of sailing. The lady at the coffee shop in Luss cheerfully served us with a lot of enthusiasm as we enjoyed the beauty of Loch and Ben Lomond. The most striking thing in this experience was the brightness of the sun which however was not warm at all. Sailing on the west coast of Scotland took us to islands such as Staffa, Iona, Eigg, Muck. Living on a boat at sea for seven days can have a telling effect on the human body. By the time we came back to land, I found the land moving up and down and had to keep staggering to keep my balance and not fall. I am told that this was because I had got 'sea legs'. The feeling of the land moving was actually an effect of the change from the movement of the liquid in my inner ears during my time at sea. One of the most touching experiences during the sailing time was meeting the priests and monks of Iona Abbey, the monastery where some dedicated young people had decided to spend their lives.

Sailing off the west coast of Scotland gave me many new experiences. The skipper on the boat on which we sailed was Colin Macdonald who had just completed his service in Ghana as the headmaster of Navrongo Secondary School. There were seven of us on board. We had to listen to the weather forecast twice a day in the morning and the evening. This was to enable us to know the speed and direction of the wind at sea in order to decide on our next destination as we sailed in the cold North Atlantic Ocean. Colin used the basic tools of navigation. These included an enlarged map of the area, a compass, a ruler, and other instruments. Some of us who had never been to sea learned the rudiments of navigation for the first time. It was during this time that I understood the feeling of agoraphobia, the fear of open space. I learnt this word from Ian Fleming's James Bond books. For once in my life, when we got to a part of the sea where there was no land visible to the naked eye, I really felt a certain fear which would translate into my experience when I found myself in the Sahara Desert during my development time in the Republic of Niger.

Travelling with Colin to Scottish cities such as Edinburgh, Dundee, Saint Andrews and Fort William gave me the opportunity to see the beauty of Scotland. He drove a car whose price doubled whenever we filled it with petrol. In Saint Andrews, I met his mother, who taught us a few moves dancing to Scottish bagpipe music. With Colin and three other Ghanaian young men, we camped at Fort William and then climbed to the top of Ben Nevis. The climb took nearly 4 hours and then coming down took about 2 ½ hours. I must say this was the most strenuous part of my visit to the UK. At Loch Earn, I was introduced to the sport of windsurfing which was a complete failure. I spent more than 45 minutes in the cold Scottish water without being able to balance my body on the surfing board for up to one full minute. I concluded that windsurfing was not a sport I could learn and master.

My visit to friends in Switzerland was the next biggest thing on my agenda. I first tried to get a Swiss visa from the Swiss Consulate in Manchester which was quite easy. I then tried to get a transit visa from the French Consulate in Liverpool but this failed. I left Preston on my way to Switzerland without a transit visa through France with the hope that I could get this in London. In London, I failed to get the transit visa to travel through France by train. Against all logical thinking, I decided that I would take my chances and travel without a visa in the hope that I could be given one on arrival in France. I had my train ticket to Dover that was also valid for travel by ferry to Calais in France continuing by train to Zürich in Switzerland. I was doing this and with a prayer that God would work a miracle in this journey. I set off on my overnight journey, leaving London in the evening and arriving in Dover at about 9:00 pm. The ferry from Dover to Calais took about an hour. As the ship moved into the English Channel the lights from the shoreline of Dover were a beauty to behold and as it moved further this beauty was replaced on the other side by the beauty of Calais. I walked out of the ship in anticipation of trouble. I did not know whether this was a lack of faith or just a normal human reaction to a difficult situation. There was no French immigration, and so I walked straight into the waiting train that headed for Paris. I found my seat and was happy to relax for the first time. I fell fast asleep. According to my ticket, I was supposed to get off the train at Lille and take another train that would take me to the Swiss border.

When I woke up from my sleep it was almost 40 minutes after the time I should have made the change. I asked my travelling companion in the same cabin whether we had arrived in Lille and he said we already passed Lille more than half an hour earlier. So I just relaxed and enjoyed the ride to Paris. I got off the train at the Gare du Nord (northern railway station of Paris). Everybody seemed to be in a rush and it was difficult to stop and ask anybody for help. In my predicament, a policeman was the last person I wanted to ask for help. An African approached me and asked in French whether I needed help. I could not speak a word in French so I explained myself in English. He held my hand and took me to a spot and explained in rapid French that I had to take the Metro (the Paris underground system) to Gare d'Est (the eastern railway station), and then went as far as purchasing the tickets for me. He was from Ivory Coast and I was from Ghana, neighbouring countries, and yet we could not communicate with each other, thanks to our colonial masters. I thanked him profusely, and with smiles on our faces we parted company. I wondered whether this was an angel of God.

I spent the rest of the day waiting for my departure time and managed to buy sandwiches from a small shop. The train from Paris to Zürich left in the evening. This was a typical French TGV (Train à Grande Vitesse) that zoomed out of Paris. As we got to the countryside, rural French farming communities seemed to go into a mad rush back towards Paris as the TGV cruised at a crazy speed towards the Swiss border. No French Immigration were on board the speeding train. The first stop must have been near the Swiss border. Immigration Officers came on board and from the many novels I had read, I recognized they were Swiss Immigration by the Swiss flag on the uniform. They asked for my passport which I happily presented and although I asked for a two week stay in Switzerland, they gave me a 3-month visitor's visa - another miracle in my life. I told this experience to Christian Youth Groups in three schools, in two church meetings, to the German embassy in Zürich and to the Swiss Railway Company that was trying to reroute my ticket through Germany and everybody just stared at me in amazement. The lady who was rerouting my ticket through Germany told me that what I was saying was impossible but my ticket showed that that was exactly what happened.

Figure 10: Resting on the way down from one of the Swiss hills

As in the UK, the rural communities of France and Switzerland caught my attention. Beautiful farmhouses with the farmers making hay and domestic animals moving around within confined and fenced areas. The big difference was the bells hanging on the necks of all the Swiss cattle. My hosts in Switzerland were Drs Claire and Peter Glauser, medical doctors who had spent 12 years of their lives in the Bawku Presbyterian Hospital. They knew me from Manga and knew exactly where

I lived as a child. It was a pleasure to meet them again after their departure in 1979. Ten days in Switzerland was what I had to enjoy the beauty of that country including the rides on cable cars and open-air chair lifts between two mountain peaks as well as climbing some hills.

The drama of my return to the UK via Germany came to a climax in Cologne. On my ticket, I was supposed to arrive in Cologne at 14:02 and leave at 14:04 but this looked to me like an impossibility. I was assured by the lady who issued the ticket to me that the train would arrive at 14:02 and that my connecting train would be on the next platform on my side. The train actually arrived in Cologne on time, and I got off and into the next train. We departed at exactly 14:04. I have told this incredible story dozens of times but that seemed to be German precision at the time. I am told this accuracy has been compromised over the years and trains sometimes arrive up to 5 mins late. These speeding, accurately-timed trains took me to Oostende in Belgium and by ferry to Folkestone harbour in the UK and back to Scotland.

From then most of my days were spent in Preston, where I got some understanding of the United Kingdom. The experience that remained with me for most of my life is a visit to a big supermarket. I was bewildered looking at the array of shelves laden with all types of goods. I will describe only three sections of the supermarket – those for milk, sugar and bread. On the shelf holding milk, there were four different brands of milk and each brand had pasteurized, skimmed, semi-skimmed and full cream. Now, I thought back to the reality in Ghana. At that time, the most popular brand of milk was Ideal Milk. Many people who had to use milk would open the tin of milk, use a tablespoon to measure and add to whatever beverage they wanted to drink and then peel off the label, fold it and use it to close the open holes to prevent the contents from going bad and being invaded by ants. The milk would normally be kept in the fridge. If one did not have a fridge, then the most appropriate thing to do was to put the tin in a bowl of water to prevent ants from getting into it. Here in Preston most of the milk was delivered at the doorstep of households by the milkman. In the section for sugar, there was cubed sugar, granulated sugar, brown sugar, and so on. Bread covered large shelves that looked endless.

In contrast to the affluence, I also saw a different picture of poverty. In Victoria and Euston Railway Stations in London there were periodic notices on the electronic boards warning passengers that "thieves and pickpockets" operated on the platform and passengers should, therefore, take good care of their personal belongings. At Victoria Railway Station, a woman rushed up to me asking for 50 pence to add to her money to buy a train ticket. I brought out several coins from my pocket and gave her 50 pence and then she started asking for more. It was then that I realised that it was a scam. I also noticed a number of people rolled up in blankets at various railway stations.

We do not have homeless people in Manga; nobody sleeps in the street. And you are most unlikely to be tricked into giving out money. Manga definitely does not have streets as beautiful as the streets in the UK but the social network will hardly allow anybody to be homeless. I asked myself what it really means to be a developed country. Is development always plagued by an increase in crime, poverty and dishonesty? These were some of the realities that made me think that it was better to return to Ghana and contribute to the development of my country. I had had a glimpse of Europe, but I felt I belonged in Africa.

CHAPTER 11

GROWING WITH MUSIC

Music has played a major role in my development as a child, throughout my education, in my life as a Christian and in my development work across Africa. My early memories of music go back as far as when I was between 4 and 6 years old. I would wake up early in the morning still lying on my mat (my childhood version of a bed) and the music would drift into my ears from the kitchen where my mother would be grinding millet for the day. She would normally sing a song to provide the rhythm that would accompany the grinding on the stone. During that same stage in my life, local stories told to the children in the night usually had a song to accompany them. Usually the same story would be told several times with the same songs and we would always find them funny and laughed until we were in tears.

From the age of 6 years onwards, I became more aware of the music produced by praise singers (*Baambaam* in Kusaal and *Laalorr* in Bissa) during funerals and festivals. The Bissas play a two-stringed guitar that is built on a specially shaped calabash and skin called *Konni* while the Kusaasi play a single-stringed violin called *Duruung* also built on a calabash and skin. It is played with a string attached to a bowed stick. Although the string of the *Duruung* looks as if it is single, it is actually made from several strands of horsetail. The Kusaasis also had their own version of *konni*. The praise singers tune their instruments and ensure that it is in the same key as their voices. The most unusual situation that I marvelled at was a Bissa musician who played the *duurung* and sang in Kusaal. Praise singers generally sing in their mother tongue. In my maternal uncle's house near Bitou in Burkina Faso (Upper Volta in those days), I saw several musical instruments and went to gatherings where these instruments were played and accompanied by the singing of praise singers.

Praise singers (or Griots) can be found across West Africa. They are oral historians who can narrate the histories of families and clans. They are also gifted at singing the praises of anyone they encounter and are paid to perform at events and functions. In the past, and now in the twenty first century, they played an important role in the community because they are a repository of history and tradition.

One of the praise singers who impressed me and had a deep impact on my life was called Doma. He seemed to know the history of every clan and could narrate family histories with amazing accuracy. He could play the local musical instrument and sing for hours on end, starting in the early hours of the evening and continuing until sunrise. With music all around me, I automatically wanted to acquire skills in playing a musical instrument no matter what I became in future. In 1963, I came home from my uncle's house and persuaded my father to make a traditional Bissa musical instrument called *Jengira* for me. This instrument is made by bending a stick that is about a metre long and holding it taut with a wire connecting both ends. Earlier generations might have used a string. The bottom of a small calabash is then attached about 25 centimetres from one end of the bent stick with the open end of the calabash facing in an opposite direction to the side of the stick with the string. The open end of the calabash is placed on the abdomen to help produce the deep sound emanating from the instrument. Unlike the modern guitar, the longer side of the stick should be on the right-hand side of the player. With the right hand, the musician then plucked the string with the middle finger. The stick runs across the right palm of the musician. The left-hand changes the sound of the instrument by placing the left forefinger and thumb on and off the string.

I realised that nobody else around the community knew about this instrument. At the same time, on the shepherd grounds with the other boys, while looking after sheep and cattle, I learnt how to make a wind instrument using clay. The Bissas call this *Feerr* while the Kusaasi call it *Wiig*. It can be likened to a clay flute that can produce up to six different notes. There is actually a wooden version of this instrument made by craftsmen but I never got the chance to own and use one. Then there was another wind instrument made from the stalk of sorghum. The length of the stalk is usually such that it had only one joint between both ends. This instrument is called *Bungkaare* in Bissa and *Nankpak* in Kusaal. It is usually made at the end of the third part of the rainy season, that is around October to November, but it will normally be abandoned and broken by the beginning of January the following year. I know a few people who were able to keep their instruments for more than a year.

In 1965 I built my first two-stringed *konni* (guitar). I quickly found out that this instrument could be tuned to play with 5 notes. I managed to learn several categories of Bissa music including the hunter's dance, the war dance, and funeral dirges. I used to sit in my mother's yard and play all these types of music while my half-sister danced to them with pride. I perfected the use of this instrument throughout my education and for much of my life. My last two-stringed *konni* must have been thrown away in the year 2003 when my family was moving out of Ghana.

It is interesting to note that some traditional musical instruments were used for other purposes apart from entertainment. For example, the wooden flute was used by some ethnic groups such as the Kasenas in Navrongo and the Bissas in Burkina Faso and the Upper East Region to send messages of approaching danger or pleasant news from one community to the other.

When I was in Ghana College in Tamale, I discovered the harmonica. I quickly learnt how to use this instrument and became proficient at playing different Christian songs. I became so attached to the harmonica that I took it into an examination hall in Navrongo Secondary School in 1975. The invigilator could not accept it and it was taken away from me. It was some time before I got it back.

The Western style of music broke into my childhood sense from many sources. The first was the houses of Agricultural Technical Officers based in the Manga Agricultural Station. Indeed, there was one Agricultural Officer who owned a guitar and he would normally come to our house when my mother had the local alcoholic brew called *Pito* and play it. This instrument fascinated me. Then there was music from movies shown in the single cinema house in Bawku. The other source that influenced my life was music taught in school by my teachers from Primary One up to middle school Form 3.

In school, we learnt Kusaal songs and Kusaal translations of English songs. The most amusing one was the translation of "Mary had a little lamb, its fleece was white as snow". This was translated to "Assana Mori upebilla Ka u pelgi gat sakuga" (meaning Assana had a little lamb and it was whiter than hailstones). The linguistic ingenuity of the teachers enabled them to "translate" Mary into "Asana" and snow into hailstones. Amazing indeed. How on earth would one translate a name! Most of the songs we learnt in school were the English nursery rhymes, their translation into the local language, or Christian hymns. For example, I learnt songs such as "How sweet the name of Jesus sounds in a believer's ear" in primary school.

It was in the year 1964 that I saw an accordion for the first time. I was really fascinated by the clarity of the sound it produced. It was played by one of the teachers in the middle school. He taught his class the song "They were in an upper chamber. They were all with one accord. When the Holy Ghost descended. As was promised by our Lord." I just followed the tune with amazement and never knew the meaning of the words until I became a Christian.

My small world of local and foreign music established in Manga exploded into a new world of contemporary music in 1968 when I arrived in Tamale. The shops along the streets of this town displayed record players and record changers on their windows and played loud music that came from huge loudspeakers standing outside their shops. This was brought to reality in Ghana College on Saturdays that were designated for the "Record Dance Nights".

The music of those days was dominated by artists such as James Brown, Wilson Pickett and these were equally matched by singers with smooth voices such as Jim Reeves, Marvin Gaye, Otis Redding, Aretha Franklin and the like. There was also the reggae music from prominent Jamaican musicians such as Bob Marley, Jimmy Cliff, Peter Tosh, Burning Spear and Johnny Nash. As the years rolled on, Africa was not left out of the show. In Ghana we had highlife music promoted by musicians and musical groups such us Nana Ampadu, K Gyasi and the Okukuseku Band and Ramblers International Band. Congolese music was also a big force with the famous Ok Jazz. Emerging African musicians included Alpha Blondy, Salif Keita and Lucky Dube. Then musical groups such as ABBA, Bonny M as well as The Beatles made their contribution to the contemporary music scene. Christian musicians of the time included Andrae Crouch and Jamie Owens.

I took my time to assimilate all these genres of music over the years and picked up lessons from their lyrics as well as their performances. For example, Bob Marley says "in the abundance of water the fool is thirsty". This is a philosophical thought that points to the fact that one needs more than resources to respond to a need. It requires intelligence and wisdom to recognise the resources around you that will respond to your need. Such philosophical thoughts spoke a lot to me and enabled deep reflection. Beyond the lyrics, I was also deeply interested in the melodies and harmonies produced by musicians even if I did not understand the language in which they sang. I remember playing Congolese music although I did not understand the songs. I also played Nigerian Juju music particularly the work of Ebenezer Obey and Sunny Ade. My interest in listening to different instrumental combinations drew me deep into the love for classical music especially that of composers such as Mozart, Beethoven and Handel.

In the year 1968 in Ghana college in Tamale, I saw a piano for the first time. My first thought was that this was a giant accordion. This was also the first time I was taught by the music master, Mr Thompson (a British volunteer). In those days, it was very difficult for a Form One student to attempt to play on that piano, particularly if he or she did not know anything about music. I can say that I grew up surrounded by all types of music and playing all types of musical instruments.

Becoming a Christian and going to Scripture Union meetings and also attending church services significantly increased my use of music in all forms of Christian worship. The weekend Scripture Union meetings and monthly conferences at the Presbyterian Youth Training Centre in Vitin, near Tamale, provided huge opportunities for learning several songs. I remember that Sunday evenings after such conferences were really opportunities to showcase the new songs we learnt as we were brought back to the school. One particular driver called Ziblim took pride in driving us back to the school as we made a lot of noise, sang new songs and pounded on the side of the wooden truck (Boneshaker) that he brought to carry us.

Although I became a Christian in 1970, I have persistently refused to throw away music that does not contain Christian or biblical lyrics. I believe that life's lessons are not limited to the Bible or Christian songs. One can learn from Christians and Non-Christians because we all have common grace. Wisdom and knowledge is not the exclusive domain of Christians. Music as an art form, helps us appreciate life experiences in all its various forms in a unique and important way.

I got my first radio cassette player in 1977 when I was in 3rd year at the university. It was a 1977 version of a Trident CX model sent to me by a friend, King David Amoah, who was studying Veterinary Medicine at the University of Ibadan in Nigeria. With this cassette player, I gradually built a library of cassettes of all types of music but mainly Christian music, reggae and other types of contemporary music that I liked.

The biggest drama in my musical life happened in 1984. I sat down in the congregation in my local church in Tamale and watched in disbelief when three young men who were the main instrumentalists of the musical group in the church decided that they were no longer going to play the instruments. They were the bass guitarist, the lead guitarist and the keyboard player. Nobody else in the group knew how to play these instruments. This meant that the group had to abandon the use of their instruments and start training new people to play them. The group was called "Redemption Singers" and was the first group of its kind to be formed in northern Ghana. This interruption of the work of the group really surprised me. I narrate the history of the Redemption Singers just for the documentation of historical facts and because my short experience with the group has had a profound influence on my life and will remain deep in my memories.

Redemption Singers as a Christian musical group was started in 1978/79 by Ransford Kojo Boakyi and about 10 other Christian musicians. Their first instruments were made up of a set of drums, a keyboard with its accompanying amplifier, a bass guitar and a lead guitar. They were purchased from an Assemblies of God missionary called Reverend Arthur Hokett. Funds for the purchase of these instruments came mainly from personal contributions from the group members and the Christian community at large. Some of the contributors were not members of the local Assemblies of God church.

At one point, in their efforts to move the group forward, the leadership of the group decided that it should become independent of the church and run on its own. The church on seeing the determination of the group members decided to back them up and own the group. I believe that there might have been external influences persuading the leaders to want to become independent of the church. The decision was not unanimous as some members preferred to remain as a church-based musical group. It was in this standoff position that the instrumentalists decided not to play the instruments again.

For nearly two months, church services went on without the use of modern musical instruments. During this time, emerging young leaders decided to train to play the instruments. The three people I can remember were Daniel Ali, Ebenezer Tetteh and Joseph Kalari. A talented Muslim instrumentalist and musician, Ahmed Issifu, agreed to come and train the new hands from scratch. At the time, this appeared to me to be simply ridiculous. For Christians to abandon service and a non-Christian to have the heart to step in and provide support seemed really incredible. Ahmed was also a multi-talented musician. Although his main instrument was the lead guitar, he could also play the bass guitar and the keyboard and he understood the musical parts sung by the singers and guided them. He trained the team relentlessly and after two months these young people were back on the stage to accompany the congregational singing of the church. Ahmed became a Christian while working with and supporting the group. He is now a lecturer in the University of Development Studies (UDS) in Tamale.

It was during this struggle of the group to re-establish themselves that I asked myself the question "What is really so difficult about playing the keyboard?" I had grown up playing all types of instruments, had listened to all types of music and had developed a keen musical ear. This was the beginning of my learning to play the keyboard. The three young men Ahmed Issifu, Ebenezer Tetteh and Daniel Ali agreed to help me learn. They taught me the basic chords that accompanied congregational songs in general, and songs sung by the group in particular. My eagerness to learn how to play this instrument was only surpassed by their determination to teach me.

I can remember some late nights when I had Ebenezer sitting on my left-hand side, mimicking the sound of a bass guitar while Daniel sang a song and clapped his hands and I tried to play along with them on the keyboard. My mistakes were many but their perseverance was solid. Ahmed taught me all the tricks of playing the right chords without the need for written music. He quickly recognised that I had a musical ear. I remember the first time I played what is known in music as a chord inversion he stopped and looked sharply at me, asking who taught me this. I told him that I found out by myself.

It was Ahmed who taught me the minors, the majors, the 7th and 9th chords. Nobody in the group knew about my earlier musical exploits as a child playing local instruments or as a student listening to all types of music and now as a worker wanting to become part of a musical group that was made up of mainly younger people. My engagement with the Redemption Singers lasted until September 1988 when I was transferred from Tamale to Accra. During the four-year period when I played the keyboard for them, I spent personal resources taking them to Assemblies of God Youth camps in Yendi, Bolgatanga, Bawku, Tenkudugou in Burkina Faso and to a famous crusade in a village called Arigu near the White Volta organised by Reverend Samuel Tigah who was a pastor in the Wulugu Assemblies of God church.

During this time, we had the awkward situation of having to sleep on mats. Some members of the group who had never had this experience before were impressed that I could quickly adapt to the practice. They had no clue that I had lived in worse conditions during my childhood. The group provided musical support in other Christian functions including funerals, weddings and special events organised by other groups.

I will never forget a programme organised by a new Christian musical group called "Stewards Incorporated" in the forecourts of Tamale Cultural Centre. Members of the "Redemption Singers" arrived for the occasion in white T-shirts and black trousers for the men and black skirts for the women. The host group came on the stage with both men and women gorgeously dressed up in northern Ghanaian regalia made up of heavy gowns sewn from traditional material. It was a real display of pomp and pageantry. Then the "Redemption Singers" were invited onto the stage. We walked up onto the stage rather timidly. I cannot remember whether we played two or three songs. I just remember that the last song was entitled "Jesus Christ died for me". On the keyboard, I played the introduction to the song using a tone called "bells" very slowly. The lead singer then followed by singing slowly. Then we all stopped for just four beats. The four beats seemed like an eternity with the audience all waiting in anticipation. The drummer performed a series of "rolls" on the drum set and went into a quick highlife beat, joined by the singers and instrumentalists, and everybody sang the song in a highlife style. We got every member of the audience on their feet and dancing. It was difficult to stop playing at the end of the performance because of all the dancing. Finally, it ended and the applause went on and on.

I have always reflected on the issues that led to the difficulties that confronted the Redemption Singers and the local church in Tamale and come to the following analysis. Development workers engaged in conflict work usually carry out what is known as conflict analysis. In this process, it is generally true that every conflict situation has underlying causes that remain dormant and the actual conflict normally arises because of a trigger. In the case of the conflict that arose between some members of The Redemption Singers musical group and the leadership of the local church, the underlying causes could be related to the attitude of church leaders towards young people who offer their skills in music to the church. Church leaders tended to look at such young people as "kids". Even when adults joined musical groups in the church they tended to be treated like children. Although I was a member of the leadership of the church, the moment I joined these young people to play an instrument, I could feel the perception that I had compromised my maturity. This was the underlying cause of the problems in the church. External influence on these young people could have been the trigger that brought about the conflict. This perception has gradually changed over the years and musical groups in churches, with members that are professional workers in their own rights, are now taken more seriously.

Learning how to play the keyboard from these young people significantly influenced my development work for nearly thirty years. I have had the opportunity to play in several environments across the African continent including a musical band in the French Cultural Centre in Zinder, Niger, a musical group to entertain hotel residents in Serekunda in the Gambia, a Ghanaian church in London, UK, a local group in Bujumbura, Burundi, and a group of Tarab musicians at the White Sands Hotel near Dar es Salaam, Tanzania. In all these circumstances, identifying with the entertainers always brought me closer to the common people who are always overlooked in society and made me appreciate the problems confronting them.

When I was transferred from Tamale to Accra and had to part ways with the Redemption Singers, my last meeting with them was very emotional. However I encouraged the members to build the group around their belief in God, rooted in the local church and not around an individual. Thirty-two years down the line, the evidence is that the Redemption Singers still stands strong as a group in Tamale. Many of the older members have dispersed and are in various businesses across the world. About 10 of them are now in full time Christian ministry. All of them are in touch to encourage each other and support the current generation of singers. This all came from the original initiative of Ransford Boakyi. Some important lessons derive from my experience with this group. Firstly, leadership of musical groups should work to train several people to play musical instruments. This will ensure that a few people will not take the group hostage. Secondly, the leadership of musical groups should be convinced about their calling into the music service and ignore the question of status. Thirdly, church leaders need to understand that being a musician has nothing to do with maturity.

I thank God for enabling me to be part of the music ministry to the church. Above all, I thank God that my two sons have developed musical skills and play at a higher level than I did. My daughters also sing beautifully and serve in the church with their voices.

PART 2: DEVELOPMENT EXPERIENCES AND LESSONS

CHAPTER 12

CONSERVING LIFE-SUSTAINING GAINS AND FOODS

I hardly have any conversation with childhood colleagues without bringing up memories of my childhood work on the farms to produce grains for preparing the foods we ate in those days. These grains are the basic source of food and nutrition that sustained us and still sustain a majority of the Ghanaian population.

Most people who grew up in the savannah belt of West Africa will always remember the thick paste made from the flour of grains such as millet, sorghum or maize called Tuo Zaafi (TZ) in northern Ghana or Nigeria. In the francophone countries, it is generally called Patte. The Bissa and Kusaal names for this food are *Wu* and *Sa'ab* respectively. Different languages in the savannah belt will have their local names.

After talking to 30 farmers in over 20 communities in the Upper East and Northern Regions, the general observation is that millet and sorghum production is gradually being replaced by maize in northern Ghana. This observation is being confirmed by reported practices in households particularly in the Upper East Region. One farmer told me that he prefers food prepared from millet or sorghum but he cultivates maize and sells it to buy the grain he wants. There are several reasons for this trend.

The yield per acre of maize far exceeds the yield per acre of millet. For economic reasons, most farmers will therefore prefer to cultivate maize instead of millet. Population growth has put pressure on land, thereby decreasing the land area available to the average family. The cultivation of millet is also more labour-intensive than that of maize. One farmer in the Bolgatanga area called maize farming "the lazy man's farming". Furthermore, the changing climatic conditions, resulting in the decreased number of months with adequate rainfall, make it easier to cultivate maize which matures more quickly than millet, particularly late millet.

Farmers have complained about the attacks of birds on their early millet. Research into improved production technologies is funded mainly by development partners such as multilateral and bilateral donors (the UN system, the World Bank, the European Union, development corporation offices of the different embassies) and they focus mainly on maize, soybean and rice. Agricultural scientists therefore have to use whatever extra funding they have for other research activities to carry out research on millet and sorghum. Some consumers prefer the sensory qualities of TZ made from maize (which is whiter than that made from millet) compared to millet or sorghum, without consideration of the superior nutritional value of the two grains. Despite all these reasons, it has generally been accepted by rural farmers and scientists that millet and sorghum are more nutritious than maize.

The idea of farmers moving from subsistence to commercial farming was started in the early 1960s when several tractors were brought to the Manga Agricultural Station to provide services to farmers in nearby villages who thought they were in need of them. As a matter of fact, it looks as if nobody considered that deep ploughing using tractors would damage the soil in the Upper Region. The ploughs that were used on these tractors were developed for European soil structure. In the late 20th and early 21st-century, development facilitators started encouraging community farmers to think beyond subsistence farming and approach farming as a business that could earn increased income to respond to household needs and grow their wealth. It is most likely that the current trend of replacing millet with maize is in response to this call for agriculture as a business. If this is the case leaving millet behind compromises nutrition for wealth.

Whenever I talk to research scientists from the Council for Scientific and Industrial Research (CSIR) - Savannah Agricultural Research Institute (SARI), I get blown away by the technical know-how of the scientists and the amount of research that has been done so far. In putting together information on life-sustaining grains, this is what I found when I talked to the Director of the CSIR-SARI sub-station in Manga, Dr Alhassan Sugri. After a period of research and experimentation, several varieties of millet have been released between 2016 and 2020. These include, to use local names, Akad-kom, Afribeh-Naara, WAAPP Naara, Kaanati, and Naad-Kohblug. They have the following qualities:

Drought resistance to water stress.
Higher yield over conventional varieties.
Early maturing to respond to changing climate conditions.
A variety that has bristles to resist attack from birds for early season production.
A variety with bigger size and cream seed colour grains.
A variety with increased micro-mineral (Iron and Zinc) contents.

The fact that researchers are working to produce varieties of millet in response to changing climatic and economic conditions is indeed very commendable and gives the hope that millet is not a crop that will vanish in northern Ghana. I am however not sure about how the development of these varieties will translate into actual production by local farmers there. In the first place, successive Ghanaian government agricultural promotion policies do not target millet. Secondly, seed companies do not find it profitable to adopt new varieties of millet and produce them in large quantities for sale to farmers.

It is reassuring that these improved varieties of millet are available at CSIR-SARI Manga Sub-Station. The cost of improved seed will however be higher than what farmers will find in the open market and these farmers are not likely to be prepared to pay more for the improved seeds. Indeed, what farmers buy in the open market is usually not seed but grains for consumption. If these grains are planted without careful selection of seeds the probability that they will germinate is heavily compromised. It is disappointing that several years after independence and nearly 90 years of the Manga Agricultural Station, farmers still want free inputs to increase the productivity of their crops.

Replacing millet and sorghum with maize that has a lower nutritional value in the preparation of TZ could have a negative impact on the health of community members in the long run. Something needs to be done urgently to maintain and indeed increase the production of millet and sorghum to the levels observed in the 1960s and 1970s.

Three possible lines of action include policy-level, field-level and donor-motivated interventions. At the policy-level, a policy that makes available a certain percentage of the national budget for research into millet and sorghum will ensure that research by CSIR-SARI is not dictated by bilateral and multilateral donor agencies and by non-governmental organisations. If such donors are allowed to provide the money for research, the Ghanaian government will have little say in deciding the crops on which research should be carried out. This kind of policy will help reduce dependence on donor funding for research and ensure that the very competent and well-trained scientists in the country research into foods that will benefit rural Ghanaians. At the practical field-level, government departments of agriculture can do more to bring the outputs of research to the common farmer in the communities. For example, when I was a child, in the 1960s, the technical officers came to my father and asked for 20 square meters of his farm, preferably at the edge of his land, on which they could plant improved seeds. They then visited the plot every week throughout the farming season to ensure that he was following their instructions in weeding and chemical application. At the harvesting season, my father clearly saw the difference between the output of the improved seeds and his traditional variety of seeds. Adoption of the improved variety was guaranteed at that point. If this practice could be restarted, it would go a long way to bring the results of scientific research to local farmers. Finally, Ghanaian development workers should make an effort to advocate strongly for donor funding for advancing the cause of millet and sorghum. Non-governmental organisations need to provide leadership in advocating for funding for research and community engagement in this cause.

Early millet takes about 58 to 64 days to mature and be ready for harvesting. This millet matures early enough to create the bridge between the period of food shortages and the harvesting of all the other crops. One common scenario I remember was to be crowded with my siblings in my mother's household kitchen, called in Bissa the *Genla Che*. This was a room with a traditional fireplace made up of stones fixed to the ground that combined with the wall to form a tripod on which a cooking pot can be placed and fire made under the pot. A platform is erected to occupy about a quarter of the room against part of the wall and raised over a metre high on which grinding stones are fixed and used for grinding grains. The common practice was to gather into this room particularly during the middle of the rainy season when the rains drizzle for very long periods, and roast early millet to eat.

Until recently early millet and late millet have been the predominant grains from which TZ is prepared and for preparing several life-sustaining snacks. The easiest snack to prepare is called *Nyaasi* in Bissa. It is prepared by kneading roughly ground millet with a little amount of water, sometimes with the addition of shea butter and pepper, and moulded into balls not bigger than a clenched fist. Water is poured over it to create a foamy liquid that leaves its mark on the upper lip of the drinker. The fact that this snack does not need heating at all means that partakers get the best nutrients from the millet. The water is generally called *Nyaasipi* in Bissa. By the late 1980s, this drink had been commercialised in Ouagadougou, Burkina Faso. The drink is now available during ceremonies all over Ghana particularly in northern Ghana and settler northern Ghanaian communities in Accra and Kumasi.

The second easiest meal to prepare from millet is called *Baambuurey* in Bissa. It is prepared by pouring the millet flour into a small amount of boiling water and stirring it until it cooks. This is eaten hot after adding shea butter, salt and pepper. Other Bissa foods prepared with millet flour include *Tunto Nyaasi, Duubaambureh, Pumpunni, Beyisga, Pipirr*, and *Kariyaama.* A detailed description of these foods is beyond the scope of this narrative. A recipe book for these foods would be a great way of preserving Bissa culture. I have referred to these foods as snacks because they are normally taken during the daytime whereas the main meal for households would normally be in the evening and would be on most occasions TZ.

While flour from the different varieties of sorghum can be used for the preparation of TZ these grains are also normally used for the preparation of the local alcoholic drink called *pito.* As stated earlier the use of flour from maize for the preparation of TZ is a recent development in the 21st century. I remember that when maize was first introduced to Manga, a neighbour's wife came to my mother to find out how she was able to grind these big grains on the grinding stone. My mother advised her to crush the maize in a mortar to reduce the size before taking it to the grinding stone. Although corn mills were available in Bawku it would have cost extra money to take the maize to town for grinding.

Other life-sustaining grains in the savannah belt of Africa include rice, groundnuts, and the different kinds of beans such as Bambara beans and black-eyed beans. Soybean is a new commodity that has come to the fore in the 21st century. Apart from simply cooking the black-eyed or Bambara beans and then adding shea butter, salt and pepper to eat, beans are also used for the preparation of a variety of foods. The most common food prepared from black-eyed beans is called *Tubani* in Hausa and *Gawur* in Bissa. Other foods prepared from beans include *Koosey, Kansa, Zare Pumpunni* (names in Bissa).

There is an annual Bissa festival held around Easter in Kulungungu where these Bissa foods are prepared and displayed. Any development worker in Burkina Faso or northern Ghana who visits this annual festival will go away with a lot of knowledge about life-sustaining foods.

Rice has been the most common food used for occasions and festivals such as funerals, weddings, Christmas celebrations and other religious festivities. It is prepared either as rice balls with soup, Jollof rice or plain rice with sauce. It can also be combined with black-eyed beans to produce what is commonly called *Waakye* in Hausa, a delicacy in big cities and a common breakfast for the average Ghanaian worker.

The gradual disappearance of life-sustaining grains and foods is worrying. Unless the call to reverse this trend is heeded, the consequences in the next 40 to 50 years could be disastrous.

CHAPTER 13

VALUABLE FRUIT TREES FOR LIFE

While living in Zinder in the eastern part of Niger, between 1996 and 1998, I made several journeys into Nigeria. During one of these trips, I went into a traditional restaurant (commonly called a chop bar in Ghana) in Kano, northern Nigeria, with my driver for lunch. I requested to be served with tuozafi (TZ) and baobab leaf soup. TZ is a meal made from grains such as millet, sorghum and maize or from the powder of dried cassava and looks very much like kneaded dough. The consistency depends on the kind of grain and the technique of preparation. Similar preparations can be found in other parts of Africa with different names e.g. *ugali* in Kenya and Tanzania and *shima* in Zambia, Zimbabwe and South Africa. The food was served on a table slightly higher than the bench on which I sat. The baobab leaf soup had the right condiments to make a great taste. I bent over and enjoyed it as if I was back in Manga.

After lunch when we got back into the car, the driver told me about the comments he had from the women in the restaurant. He said while I was enjoying my lunch, I became the centre of interest for the women. They said this man knows exactly the value of baobab leaf soup. The lesson I learned from this experience is that women without formal education are aware that sometimes they know better than so-called formally educated people. It also makes me ask the question of whether we know the value of the fruit trees that we encounter in our daily development work in rural areas. Although I can count nearly 15 valuable fruit trees in northern Ghana, including the familiar mango and guava, which are relatively recent imports, I have chosen in this chapter to focus on what I consider to be four of the most important, namely the Baobab, Shea Nut, Dawadawa and Tamarind trees.

The shea nut tree (botanical name: *Vitellaria paradoxa*) called *kourr* in Bissa and in Kusaal *ta'aŋ* (singular) or *tamis* (plural) is the tree I have climbed most in my childhood and probably the most valuable tree in northern Ghana. This is a shady tree that blossoms mostly in the hot part of the dry season. It bears green fruits which unlike many fruits do not change colour when they become ripe. The green flesh of the food is eaten leaving a brownish nut. The nut is collected, boiled, dried and then cracked to remove the seed. The seed is then crushed into smaller pieces, roasted and milled to produce a paste that is processed into shea butter. The tree provides shade for community members who sit under it during the hot dry season. Apart from providing that needed open-air ventilation, this daily habit provides an opportunity for community cohesion and the passing on of oral traditions, history, values and norms. It is also under the shea nut tree that village news and rumours circulate freely. A large percentage of the community history and traditions I know were learnt under the shea nut tree.

It is in this environment that children acquire 'home sense'. For example, the younger generation receives teaching on taboos and best practices. Children are taught not to greet, eat or do anything respectable with the left-hand. When walking on the village path one should step aside and give way to other people who are coming on the same path. They are taught the culturally appropriate way to announce death, birth or any news. They should never look straight into the eyes of an elderly person to whom they are talking as this shows disrespect, in contrast to practice in the western world, where not looking into the eyes of an elderly person would be interpreted as a sign of dishonesty. It is under these shady trees that I learned to play several games. For example, a game played with 12 holes , six in front of each player, using stones called *yirr* in Bissa and *beeri* in Kusaal. The holes for this game were usually dug on the hard ground and stones were used as counters. It is in southern Ghana that I found that the board for this game could be carved out of wood, and seeds used instead of stones

The sweet green flesh of the fruit can be eaten and helps to fuel the very energetic activities of children. As a child, I saw the arrival of shea nut fruits as a midday hunger reliever while I waited for the evening meal which was honestly the only meal one could be assured of at this time of the year. Competing with us for the shea nuts were vipers and other snakes on the ground and bats in the air. I have heard stories of community members who were bitten by snakes while picking shea nuts in the early hours of the morning. Somehow, I never encountered these venomous creatures under the shea nut tree. The season when this fruit is produced can thus be a season with an increased number of snakebites. Any development worker going into an area where shea nut picking is a major community activity will need to think of the provision of anti-snake venom serum as an intervention.

When the nut is cracked to remove the seed, the shell can be used as fuel to make fires in local kitchens. The shell from the nuts has the special property of burning easily even when it has been soaked by the rain. Smoke from burning the shells has insect repellent properties that keep mosquitoes away.

When the bark of the tree is punctured with an axe it produces a sap that dries up to become like chewing gum. This gum is used for repair work, such as sticking together a broken calabash and for mending holes in a bucket. The bark of the shea nut tree has medicinal properties and is used by local herbal medicine sellers. As is the case for many African trees, chemical analysis to determine the active ingredients present in the bark of the tree is an important field for scientific research.

The residue after the production of shea butter is called *nyimbu* in Bissa and *buruma* in Kusaal. When it settles, the thicker part is moulded into round balls, dried in the hot northern Ghanaian sun and used to make fires in the local kitchens. The liquid part is used to sprinkle on the ground in local compounds to prevent the formation of spirogyra in the rainy season. Shea butter in itself is currently marketed widely across the world with a market size estimated at 1.12 billion US dollars as at 2018. It is used both for the production of cosmetics and as oil for food. My mother would always have a piece of shea butter dropped into vegetable soup and sometimes placed on the TZ to give it a special flavour. As a cosmetic, nothing can fight the effects of the dry harmattan on the skin better than shea butter. It is indeed surprising that many people turned to western lubricants for this purpose, when the local alternative is so easily available.

The African Locust Bean also called the Dawadawa tree (botanical name: *Parkia biglobosa*) called *karr* in Bissa and in Kusaal dʊɔɔ (singular) or dʊɔɔ'h (plural), is another valuable fruit-tree in northern Ghana. This tree starts to blossom in the cold dry season and the production of its fruits dovetails into that of shea nuts. The dawadawa fruit is a slender pod that contains the powder in the seeds. When ripe, the fruit turns black and the powder is yellow while the seeds are black. All that one needs to do is to pour water on the yellow powder and mix it into a smooth paste and it is ready to eat. I am not sure about the food value of this powder but it fills the stomach of the children in the community while they wait for the major evening meal. When this powder and the seeds are removed, the empty pod is usually pounded and cooked over a very long period and the extract is used to strengthen the plaster on mud walls, where it acts as a binding agent. It would be interesting for researchers in building materials to carry out a study on this extract and come out with ways in which it can be used to strengthen building materials. The pounded pod is called *kansannereh* in Bissa and *am* in Kusaal.

When I was a child this tree was considered so valuable that landowners who gave land to my father to farm reminded him that he can farm around the trees but the trees do not belong to him. I know of situations where people have been arrested and sent to the Chief's house to be fined for attempting to harvest dawadawa that belongs to somebody else. The bark of the tree also has medicinal properties. The dry branches of the tree are used as firewood. Dawadawa is a widely used condiment for preparing soup, mostly in northern Ghana, but now all over the country and indeed the world. I have eaten soup with dawadawa in New York, Manchester, Sheffield, Reading, London, Ouagadougou, Kano and Nairobi while visiting Ghanaian families in these places - evidence that Ghanaians living outside Ghana still hold onto dawadawa as a precious ingredient for cooking. My mother used to say that a woman who cooks soup without dawadawa is really poor. The inability to afford dawadawa was her indicator of poverty. One of the easiest sauces to prepare to accompany TZ is dawadawa mashed in water with salt and pepper and quickly heated with a bit of shea butter. My mother turned to this when she was in a hurry to feed us and there was no soup immediately available. And this almost instant preparation saved me on numerous occasions as a child from hunger. I was quite surprised when I first noticed that the same thing is done by the Kusaasis, the Moshes, the Mamprusis and the Dagombas. Ongoing research work in Ghana and Nigeria on the nutritional value of this very important food ingredient is bringing up interesting results that may be exploited for its improvement and commercial value.

In 1989, I visited projects in Senegal. It was there, in an area called Thiès, that I saw the highest concentration of Baobab trees (botanical name: *Adansonia digitata*), called *poh* in Bissa and *te'ig* in Kusaal. This tree is one of the most valuable trees in northern Ghana. The leaves of the baobab tree are arguably the cheapest ingredient for soup in northern Ghana. The leaves can be cooked fresh, or dried and pounded into powder before preparing the soup. They have been shown to be high in vitamin A. It is more appropriate for a development worker sitting in a rural community in West Africa to refer to baobab leaves than to carrots as a source of this vitamin. The fruit of the baobab tree when cracked contains a white powder and black seeds. The powder is very rich in vitamin C. In fact, one can find baobab juice well packaged for sale in Senegal and Mali.

The Tamarind tree (botanical name: *Tamarindus indica*) called *ferr* in Bissa and *pusik* in Kusaal bears fruits that look like pods. The pod contains brownish flesh and seeds. The flesh tastes sour but is very rich in vitamin C. It can be mixed with water to make a drink, and there are reports on social media that when taken at regular intervals, it controls high blood pressure as well as cholesterol in the blood. Many local people will buy the tamarind flesh rolled up into balls, soak them in water throughout the day, and drink the extract while replacing the water from time to time until it loses the sour taste. In the absence of soup, TZ mashed in tamarind extract has a really pleasant sour taste. In December 1973, I came back from school and noticed on the third day that some rashes were appearing all over my body. My mother quickly identified this as chickenpox. A local herbalist asked us to get hold of the flexible branches of the tamarind tree. These were folded into several rolls and placed in a pot. Enough water was added to cover the rolls and then boiled for nearly an hour. I was given a small calabash of the resultant liquid to drink at a lukewarm temperature in the evening. By 6 o'clock the following morning, every inch of my body was covered in chickenpox rashes. The same liquid was heated and I was made to bath with it. In four days the chickenpox was gone and the scars were peeling off. This is my personal experience of the medicinal properties of the tamarind tree.

All these fruit trees can be found in the savannah belt of West Africa, from Senegal through Mali, northern Ivory Coast, Burkina Faso, northern Ghana, northern Togo, northern Benin, northern Nigeria all the way to northern Cameroon. Indeed, I have seen baobab trees in Tanzania and Mozambique.

There is so much to get from fruit trees in Africa that there is the need to think carefully about how plant-based medicines in Africa can be combined with chemically produced medicines and vaccines to deal with health issues.

CHAPTER 14

DISAPPEARING PRACTICES AND EMERGING ALTERNATIVES

In the middle of one of those sweet childhood dreams where I was holding so much money I couldn't count, my mother tapped me on my back to wake me up. I lay awake for a few minutes. It was not yet daybreak so what was this early rising all about? I moved my feet gingerly and came to a sitting position. I was sleeping on a mat made from the stalks of elephant grass. When your bed is a mat made from such materials you do not make sudden movements of the feet otherwise a piece of the mat will stick into your leg and you will have to spend a few minutes extracting it, leaving a wound that you put shea butter on to heal. Yes, shea butter. It was everything from skin moisturizer through medicine for all types of cuts to an addition to all types of foods as a seasoning. I took off my cover cloth that was actually old flour sacks cut into various pieces and stitched together again to form the cloth. The inscription "Takoradi Flour Mills" was still written somewhere on it but who cared? The cloth never came out of the bedroom anyway. I used this type of cloth until I was going to secondary school and I vowed that I would not take that to a boarding school. After sitting for a few minutes I remembered that that day was the day for communal support for my mother on her rice farm.

I jumped up, went outside, got a calabash of water to wash my face and a 'chewing stick' to clean my teeth. A chewing stick is a small twig from a tree (in this case the Neem tree) that is chewed until one end becomes frayed. The frayed end is then used to clean the teeth. Sticks like this provide some medicinal value that guarantees good dental care. It is why you can still find some old people in villages with good dental health. I got hold of my hoe (the reliable local farm tool) and headed for the rice farm. I had to be there before sunrise so that neighbours coming to the farm could identify where it was. By 7:00 a.m. we were all gathered at the farm. We were about fifteen men with ages ranging from ten to fifty and working shoulder to shoulder in a straight line, we gently turned the soil over burying the grass and exposing the undersoil. Slow and shallow streams of water ran all over our feet just above the ankles. This was clear water and it was running, therefore minimising attacks by leeches.

A few minutes after 9:00 a.m. my sisters arrived with breakfast. This was in 1965 when I did not have a watch so how did I know it was a few minutes after 9:00? Simple - in the rural community, one had to learn how to approximate the time by looking at the position of the sun in the sky. In Manga, there was the added advantage from the Agricultural Station where a bell was rung at 9:00 am for the labourers' breakfast break. The bell, an old piece of metal from the crossing of a railway line and hung on a tree, had just been rung. Talking about watches, many people at the time put on wristwatches as part of their dressing. In fact, we were aware that the majority of these watches did not work. Asking somebody wearing a watch for the time was common and so was the ability of the person to look at the sun in the sky and look at his watch and tell you the time. It was never clear whether the time he was telling you was from the wristwatch he was wearing or from the position of the sun.

So breakfast arrived and we broke up into three groups and sat around what was served to us. It was a simple snack called *Nyaasi* in the Bissa language. Basically made up of roughly ground millet kneaded into balls the size of a clenched fist, spiced with pepper and shea butter and water poured over it. Each person in the three groups took their turn to drink the flour-water (*Nyaasi'pi*) from the same calabash. Of course, we were sitting but how could we sit in a wet rice farm? We simply moved to higher ground, pegged the metal parts off our hoes on the ground and sat on the wooden handles – thus converting them into seats. This was a normal practice in the Manga of our time.

We finished breakfast and went back to work. The pace of work was slow enough for conversation between the workers. I learnt a lot of local history and acquired 'home sense' during such communal working times,. meaning how to conduct oneself correctly in the community, for example, how to show respect to elders or treat visitors. By 11:30 am, a good guess from the position of the sun, we finished work then moved to attack my father's millet farms around the house which was far faster than in the rice farm. By 1:00 p.m. all the farm work was over and lunch was ready. Lunch was *Tuo Zaafi* (TZ) and a rich sauce made up of a combination of vegetables and groundnut soup. The shea butter on the TZ and in the sauce was evidence of a rich meal. This was the end of the communal support on my mother's rice farm and the family farm around the house.

This kind of communal support is called *Yawre* in the Bissa language. It is the way the community members in many parts of northern Ghana supported each other. The Bissas also make use of this peer support to thrash late millet, winnow it and store it in granaries before serving it out to women in the house from time to time throughout the year. The same communal spirit comes to life when a family decides to settle in a given community. The person would usually choose a plain area where there was no building and ask permission from the owner of the land to build his new house in that location. The traditional owners of the land would normally come and pour libation asking the ancestors to accept the newcomer and bless the family. After this, almost all members of the community came around and helped the new settler to construct the whole of the house from foundation to roofing level. The women would fetch water as part of their support for moulding the mud for the construction while the men moulded the mud and did the construction of the walls. The men wove the grass and then roofed the rooms with it. The women plastered the walls and carried grade one gravel from nearby pits to floor the compound and make it pleasant for sitting. It is here that young men learn how to build using mud for the walls of the house and how to weave grass for roofing as well as the roofing itself. I reflect on the series of activities in rural communities and proudly claim that there is a strong communal spirit in Manga, in Ghana and all over Africa.

But alas, I may be talking about the past and not the present. It seems this communal spirit has significantly reduced and indeed, is gradually disappearing.

Weedicides for maize and rice are gradually taking over manual farming. When the owner of a farm wants workers to carry out manual work on his or her farm, the workers charge a fee and ask for payment upfront. This was only done by a few big farmers when I was a child. The evidence so far is that increased maize production coupled with chemically enhanced maize production technologies and monetisation of labour could be the main cause for the decreasing trend in communal peer support in agricultural activities.

The vast tracts of land that existed in Manga and the surrounding villages that made it possible for families to move in and settle and benefit from communal support has significantly decreased. The land is now divided into plots which are sold at competitive market prices. New settler families now purchase plots and construct their houses with cement blocks using the expertise of professional masons and carpenters. This is definitely a sustainable emerging alternative that will make the houses stronger and more durable.

Rapid urbanisation and the availability of improved construction materials, as well as community understanding of spatial planning, seem to be the main reasons for the decline in communal support for house construction.

I believe that my generation who were born in the 1950s have lived to traverse the widest spectrum of technological evolution. We have lived through the times when telephones were not common. The second fastest means of communication was the telegram using Morse Code. I have asked several youths of today whether they know what Morse Code is and many of them have had to go quickly onto Google and find out what it is. On the subject of telegrams, the prices of the messages sent were based on the number of characters.

In my school days, I remember messages such us "Father dead. Please proceed." received by telegram. Then came the telex machine which enabled the sender to type their message on their telex machine and the same message would appear on the telex machine of the receiver. The telex machine gave way to the fax machine where we could send images of any document from the sender to the receiver. Currently, anybody with a smartphone can scan a document and send it by email or by WhatsApp. These are very powerful communication tools that have occupied the communication space in the last 40 to 50 years.

In the rural community, when I was a child, the common means of communicating messages was verbal transmission, when children are sent to deliver important messages concerning funerals, weddings and the like. Now, all that one needs to do is make a phone call to communicate a message. While this is a significant improvement in communication methods it also means that whereas young people used to go around physically and communicate these messages, they now get less exercise and therefore could become prone to lifestyle diseases. It must be said that many Ghanaians still consider the verbal delivery of certain kind of important messages as more acceptable than the use of telephones. For example, an important member of a family, like the family head, would normally receive important messages verbally and in-person.

Long-distance walking to the market and to other villages has also been replaced by the use of tricycles in almost every corner of northern Ghana. All that one needs to do is to walk a few minutes and there will be a tricycle around to jump on at a very small fee and get to where one wants to go. Once again this has significantly reduced the energy used for walking long distances but has also reduced physical exercise. Obesity, high blood pressure and lifestyle diseases may begin to emerge in rural communities in the north of Ghana due to reduced physical activity.

For students in boarding schools, the panic moments experienced in the last two weeks before vacation waiting for money for transport home is over. Parents and guardians simply send money to their wards via 'mobile money'. Mobile money allows people to send money to each other via their phones. The physical cash can be retrieved from a mobile money agent. This is a huge improvement with pleasant emotional benefits. Mobile money frauds are however lurking around to take advantage of the naive and innocent.

Libraries were places that I used extensively for research and general reading, a common practice during my years of study. These are being replaced by the use of the search engines on the internet where a lot of research material has been catalogued and made available. The internet has become one of the most powerful means of communication and knowledge gathering tools that has emerged in the latter part of the 20th century and has advanced to levels that could not have been imagined 40 years ago. One of the growing challenges of the internet is that which requires the ability of a user to differentiate between falsehood and truth.

One major disappearing practice is the naming of children based on the circumstances surrounding their birth. The strong influence of Christianity and Islam has introduced a pattern where children are given names with Middle Eastern roots without consideration for ethnicity. This is gradually making Ghanaian ethnic names disappear. We may have to learn from our neighbours in Burkina Faso who have a way of giving Christian and Muslim names and yet keeping their local ethnic names. It is encouraging to note that the trend is reversing particularly in urban areas among the middle class where parents think carefully and give names to their children which reflect the birth circumstances.

In this 21st century, there has been an amalgamation of northern and southern Ghanaian cultures with a clash of religious influences. Funerals, weddings and naming of children provide the best examples. For example, originally, northern Ghanaians did not wear dark clothes to funerals but this has become the norm across the country. Wedding customs especially within northern Ghanaian communities in the south have taken southern trends with some heavy religious underpinnings. The taking of cows as a 'bride price' has seriously been reduced and monetised or replaced with alternative items such as pieces of wax print. It is now more common to use traditional cloths.

In a continuously evolving world, development workers in Africa need to observe local community practices and identify those that are disappearing as well as alternatives that are emerging. They will therefore be in a position to decide when to help community members retain valuable practices or let obsolete ones go and embrace the new. Indeed, some emerging trends could be a very significant indicator of development.

This narrative represents a sample of disappearing practices and emerging alternatives. Many more examples include tribal marks given to children at birth for identification with particular ethnic groups, groves that protect groups of trees, initiation ceremonies, and unwritten dress codes for funerals.

CHAPTER 15

CHALLENGED TO SERVE A NATION AND START A FAMILY

I walked into the upper sixth form class with a chalk box and a duster in hand, ready to tackle the task of the day, the beginning of the first term of the 1980/81 academic year and indeed the start of my national service. Started in 1973, the Ghana National Service Scheme is a one-year mandatory employment programme that gives all graduates of tertiary institutions an opportunity to serve the nation for at least one year before going into any other employment. I was in Bawku Secondary School as a national service teacher to fulfil my duty to the country. I introduced myself to the class as their chemistry teacher and then upon asking several questions, I found out that they had not had a chemistry teacher in their lower sixth form. This meant that I had to teach the two-year chemistry syllabus in one year. I told the class that I could see among them, potential medical doctors, engineers, pharmacists and all categories of scientists. I assured them that I had come to contribute to making them what they wanted to be. The task of completing the two-year syllabus in one year was quite daunting but if they were ready, I was prepared to do all that I could to make them get the best results that would take them further in their different careers. This was most likely the best motivational speech I had ever given to any group of people in my life.

I tackled the job of teaching these young people, some of whom were actually the same age as me or older, with a lot of enthusiasm and energy that was only surpassed by their determination the study. I had to organise and teach the students beyond the normal classes that were provided for on the timetable. Working with the students, I held classes in the night, during weekends and at any other free times we could find – *at no extra cost*. In this twenty-first century, parents of high school students in Ghana have been compelled by circumstances to pay fees for extra classes for their wards. The practice of teachers to make pamphlets of notes and to sell these to students has also evolved to the extent where the profits become a significant supplementary income.

Meanwhile I was preparing to get married in December of the same year. The journey to my marriage started in 1973, when I met Rachel Roda Sogene in Navrongo Secondary School. We both attended the Protestant Church services in the school chapel as well as the Scripture Union, where we served as executive members in the 1974/75 academic year. In 1976, just before the beginning of my second year in university, I went to Kumasi, where she was on vacation with her sister, to propose to her, but for some reason, I lost my tongue. I ended up going back to the University of Cape Coast and sending my proposal in a letter to her. It took three years for her to respond to me and although we exchanged letters talking about other subjects, we never communicated about my proposal. I patiently waited three years to hear from her. Those were the days we wrote letters, put them in envelopes, put stamps on the envelopes, posted them and waited for several weeks and sometimes months for a reply. The waiting for incoming letters and worrying about when the next letter would come created a lot of anticipation and excitement in those days. Instant messaging and evolving technologies of the 21st century seem to have taken the excitement out of the experiences of yesteryears. Our courtship hit a snag when the time came for me to get introduced to her family. From a previous disappointing experience, Rachel's father, Rev Sogene Pagashida, the Pastor of the Binaba Assemblies of God at that time, was worried about allowing his daughter to get married to a Bissa from Manga. This obstacle was only overcome by the intervention of two senior Pastors of the Assemblies of God Church to my relief.

Preparing to get married while making use of every available time to teach a group of enthusiastic students who needed extra tuition was a challenge for me - to serve the nation and start a family at the same time. The events leading to the wedding were characterised by the drama and miracles that have become associated with my life. During this time, Rachel worked in the dispensary stores of the Bawku Hospital and lived with friends of mine, Mr. and Mrs. James Yambor, who were nurses in the same hospital. I lived in a house in the secondary school, about 5 km away.

Wedding invitation cards are the main means of informing friends and relatives about the occasion. While in Preston in the UK in the month of August and September that year, I played with the idea of printing wedding invitation cards in the UK and actually made a draft on plain paper. The idea never materialised and at the end we had the invitation typed on a stencil and duplicated on ordinary paper in Bawku and then distributed to friends that we could reach while all other friends were informed by word of mouth. It is important to state that invitation cards were sent to 'bulk receivers' such as churches, and persons we would call very important people. For example, invitation cards would normally be sent to a church and read on the pulpit and this invited everybody in the church. The majority of people came to weddings without any invitation and this was not a bother to anybody.

One of the main components of a wedding is the engagement of a photographer to preserve memories of the day. We approached a photographer in the town to arrange for this important function but we did not have the money that was required to secure his services. We asked whether he could just take eight to twelve photographs of selected parts of the programme, a proposal he politely declined. So, the idea of having a photographer during our wedding was thrown out of the window. Three days to the wedding, I received a message from Tamale that my friend Neil Cameron, who lived in the UK, was in the country and on his way to Bawku. Neil brought along a camera and ended up as the wedding photographer although he did not anticipate this role. I wanted to know how he figured out the date of the wedding since I did not send him any invitation and he explained that I had left the draft of the invitation card in my room in Preston when I left on the 30th of September to fly back to Ghana. Unknown to us, Dr Rolland, a Swiss medical officer in the Bawku Hospital also came to the wedding with a camera and took photographs. Both of them used colour films and had to process the photographs in Europe and this meant that we did not see our wedding photographs until two months after the event. Twenty-first century mobile phone technology has put a camera in the hands of anybody who can afford a decent cell phone. Indeed, I have received photographs of wedding couples while the ceremony was still in progress.

In Ghana, the entertainment of guests by feeding them is an important part of any wedding ceremony. My mother came up with a 90 kg bag of paddy rice and this formed a significant portion of what we needed for guests who would be travelling from afar for the wedding. Three days before the wedding, I received ten four-litre bottles of concentrated Barona Squash, one of the common fruit juices of those days, from a friend of mine, James Tiigah, who lived in Accra. Diluted, this became the main drink that was offered to our guests. Rachel and I as well as a few others on the 'high table' were privileged to be served Fanta and Coca-Cola. The day before the wedding, the most important guests, Rev Sogene, his family and members of the Binaba Assemblies of God church, arrived. One of my friends came to inform me that he had seen an old man called Ashaki Awin who had come for the wedding and if this man was part of the contingent, then the whole congregation had come. Miraculously, with support from unexpected sources, and contributions from friends we managed to cope with this large number of guests. The wedding was attended by nearly 300 people. We concentrated on feeding the guests who travelled from outside Bawku as the majority of people from the town were only interested in witnessing the ceremony and not in the 'entertainment'. Interestingly, I found a close-up photograph of Ashaki Awin's face displayed on a wall in Neil Cameron's house in Keyingham in 1992.

On the day of the wedding, I stood by my bride, dressed up in what could be described as a mixed bag of clothes that constituted the wedding apparel. The white shirt I wore came from a second-hand shop in the UK. The tie, belt and cufflinks were borrowed from James Muale, an accountant friend who worked for the Bawku Hospital. The shoes were a second-hand pair from Switzerland. The three-piece suit was the only brand-new item I wore and it was made by a tailor called Sulley. Rachel's wedding gown was made from a cream cloth decorated with flowers that was bought for us by a young lady in Winterthur, Switzerland, called Ingrid Rubli-Locher in August while I was visiting Drs Peter and Claire Glauser. Ingrid was a high school teacher and I met her when I had the opportunity to speak to youth Christian groups in high schools in that country.

At the end of the wedding, Drs Schneider and Rolland made their car, a red Peugeot 504 saloon car, available to drive us around for the first 3 days. On the evening of the day after the wedding, Neil Cameron drove us to Manga, my traditional home, where the Bissa community in Bawku performed traditional dances to entertain us. Then we made what looked like a honeymoon trip to Cinkassé in Togo, once again, driven by Neil Cameron who had to remind himself constantly that in Ghana and Togo, we drive on the right-hand side of the road. It is amazing that all we could buy during this 'foreign' trip were basic items such as sugar, milk and soap. Neil and I looked at each other knowingly and reminded ourselves about the supermarkets in the UK that were filled with every imaginable grocery that we could not find in Ghana.

Rachel and I tackled the daily chores of a household with enthusiasm. We had to fetch water from a hand pump fitted onto a borehole about three hundred metres from the house and Neil Cameron was really amused to find us performing our water fetching activity just a few days after our wedding. I reminded him that this was not the UK where water flowed out of all taps in all houses. Rachel carried a large pan of water on her head while I held a bucketful in each hand. Neil did not hesitate to get hold of his camera and take some memorable photographs. Rachel and I have never bothered about how this photograph would be captioned as we were just doing what we had to do to live.

The icing on the cake of the events surrounding our wedding happened one week after the ceremony. At about two o'clock in the morning on that day, I had a dream that engaged me in what I will describe as a spiritual battle. In the dream, I was trying to get hold of a cow's tail that had a golden handle but there seemed to be a spiritual force that was preventing me from getting a hold of it. I was praying while making my attempt to get hold of the object and my prayer became so audible that my wife woke me up to ask what was happening. I woke up sweating profusely, something that is uncommon in December in Bawku at that hour of the night, but I actually succeeded in getting the object before I was woken up. I told my wife about my encounter and we took time to pray about it and went back to sleep. The following morning, we narrated the encounter to Neil Cameron and while we were still trying to figure out what the interpretation of the dream could be, my mother arrived from Manga. She said she could not sleep during the night but never told us the details of what happened to her. All that she said was that she had decided to become a Christian. This is the genesis of my mother's Christian life that started in December 1980. Many people do not understand that conversion to Christianity is accomplished in the spiritual realm but manifested in the physical - the experience is not an academic exercise. Neil and I have gone over this story several times and it has given us a deeper understanding of conversion.

On the 8th day after our wedding, Neil, Rachel and I embarked on a trip to Binaba to greet my in-laws. This time, we did not have a car to carry us around and we walked over 4 kilometres to Bawku town and boarded a Binaba-bound wooden truck with an open top and filled with goods of every kind in jute sacks. The women sat inside the truck on the sacks of grain that were destined for the Binaba market while the men sat precariously on the wooden edges of the truck. During some parts of the journey, the men sitting on top had to time carefully branches that hung over the road and duck quickly to avoid being knocked off. It was amazing how Neil Cameron managed to learn and adapt to this branch-dodging game until we arrived at our destination. Indeed, we had no option and had to forget the fast intercity trains and buses of the UK and deal with the slow inter-market trucks which was the reality. The return journey was full of uncertainties as the market trucks left before we were ready to travel back home. A minister of the Anglican church kindly helped us from Binaba to the Bolgatanga-Bawku Road where we waited for several minutes before we could get on the next available bus. Neil and I have on several occasions remembered these events and mused about the challenges we went through.

The Year 1981 started with a lot of anticipation as we tried to start a family and I worked to accomplish my objective of completing the two-year chemistry syllabus in one year. The first challenge was for Rachel to get to work every morning and come back to the secondary school every evening. This translated to nearly ten kilometres of walking each day for five days in a week. News about bicycles that were made available by the government for workers to purchase at 600 cedis each, which was equivalent to 220 US dollars at the time, gave us some hope. A worker could buy a bicycle, pay half of the price at the time of purchase and spread the other half over a six-month period. If we could buy one of these bicycles, it would enable me to travel the five-kilometre journey every morning and carry Rachel to work as a passenger on the carrier located behind the seat of the rider. I would then come back to my own work and go in the evening and bring her back. Although this made a lot of sense, we realised that we could not afford it. We thought it through and arrived at a second option. We rented a room close to the hospital and Rachel lived there from Monday to Friday and then came to the secondary school on Fridays to spend the weekend. With this practical arrangement, we eliminated the weekly fifty-kilometre walk and gave our best at our workplaces as a young couple. I consider my time during this period as the beginning of my efforts to impact human lives and facilitate development.

My work as a National Service Teacher was interrupted by two accidents that have been described in detail in the chapter entitled '*Accidents, near accidents and survival*'. I was in hospital for the treatment of burns on my body during the A-level examinations in 1981. After each paper the students came to the hospital to give me an update of what they had written and always said that there was no question on a subject I had not taught them. I took this as a measure of my ability to complete the syllabus and prepare these young people for the A-level examinations.

Many lessons emerge from our 1980/81 experiences. One common piece of advice given by marriage counsellors to young people preparing to get married is that they should avoid getting into debt by trying to organise a wedding that costs beyond their means. In other words, they should try and live by the English saying 'cut your coat according to your cloth'. The temptation to spend beyond one's means during weddings could possibly be driven by the desire to have a wedding that equals or surpasses others, as if life is a competition. Counsellors have given examples of couples who have spent more than a year paying the debts incurred during their weddings. Rachel and I had the courage to be different and not be put under pressure to borrow money and do what everybody else was doing, and the Lord was on our side with miracles to accompany our single-minded determination. Current social media and television programmes display wedding ceremonies that are beyond reality and many youth tend to attempt to match their reality with the exaggerations on social media and television, leading to difficulties in their actual married lives. Rachel and I have worked as marriage counsellors for more than twenty years and during this period we have encountered situations where young people have avoided getting married because of their inability to finance an expensive wedding. Unless church leaders find a way of helping young people to escape the exorbitant cost of marriages, this phenomenon will continue for a long time to come.

CHAPTER 16

INITIATION INTO DEVELOPMENT WORK

At 7:45 am on 3rd August 1981, I stood in front of the big 'storey building' in Nyaniba Estates in Osu, Accra, waiting to enter the offices of World Vision International, Ghana. I was supposed to report for my new job in this organisation as the new Projects Coordinator for Northern Ghana on the first of August. However, this was a Saturday so I ended up reporting on 3rd August. I waited patiently at the reception. By 8:00 am all the staff had trooped in. That entry into the offices of World Vision International in Ghana marked my entry into the development world where my career would continue for three and a half decades. This narrative is my contribution to the documentation of the history of World Vision in Ghana.

The processes leading to my entry into World Vision International in Ghana started in 1980. I received a message through my Christian network to get in touch with the organisation in Accra. Upon my return to Ghana from the UK at the end of September 1980, I decided to visit the offices of the organisation. Here I met Kofi Hagan whom I knew from Tamale in the early 1970s. I was also able to meet the National Director of the organisation. My visit coincided with the Kofi's plans to go to the north of Ghana and he agreed to give me a ride to Tamale. It was during this long drive that Kofi told me a lot about what World Vision was doing in Ghana and all about development work. I learnt much from his description of what was needed in development work but at the time I still believed that I could do more as a Chemistry teacher. At the end of our journey I asked for time to think through the possibility of joining the organisation. I wanted to spend one year teaching advanced level Chemistry during which I would be able to decide what to do next. In February 1981, I came to Accra from Bawku and confirmed that I would join the organisation at the end of the academic year. I needed to ensure that the A-level students I had started teaching were prepared for their final examinations. These events culminated with my entry into World Vision International.

I was supposed to go through orientation and induction in Accra before going to establish the office of the organisation in Tamale. This helped me to learn the history of World Vision International, to meet and know the staff of the organisation in the Ghana office, to learn the basics of development theory and practice, to understand and perform community dialogues leading to the production of project proposals and documents, to understand the fundraising strategy and methodology of the organisation and to learn how to drive properly.

World Vision International was started by Robert Pierce in the early 1950s at the end of the Korean War when he raised funds from American churches to respond to the needs of children who had become orphans as a result of the war. Since then, the organisation has grown in many ways. During my time with them, it was made up of three entities. These were the International, Support and Field offices. Fundraising was done by the Support offices which were located in developed countries in the west. Development projects were carried out in the field offices located in Africa, Asia and Latin America. The International office located in the USA acted as the liaison between the Support offices and the Field offices. I should say that this is an oversimplified rendition of the structure of World Vision International and the reality may be slightly different now.

World Vision International was brought to Ghana by George Nicholson. At the time I joined the organisation in 1981, the staff numbered less than 25. I am told that the staffing grew to over 500 in the first decade of the 21st century but as at July 2020 stood at 262. This must have been due to the usual NGO practice of developing a new strategy to reduce administration and overhead costs and increase spending on needy communities in the field. Commodore P. F. Quaye (a retired Navy commander) was the National Director. His Personal Assistant was Charity Agbeblewu and Jonathan Pratt was his driver. The Operations Department was headed by Kofi Hagan and the Coordinators were Gershon Adzokpa, Clement Odua-Mensah, Emmanuel Ayeh and Aaron Lawson. I was the fifth Project Coordinator. Florence Laryea (now Mrs Florence Kyei-Kwakye) was the secretary of the department.

The Administration Department was headed by Chris Bonuedi (a retired Flight Lieutenant of the Ghana Air Force) who worked with Clement Odoye, Suzie Koufi, Emmanuel Adayie and Samuel Addo and they were joined by Margaret Bediako (now Mrs Margaret Barnor) who started work on the same day with me. The Finance Department was headed by Kofi Asante-Ochere and assisted by Isaac Osei. The sponsor relations department was headed by George Ennin and the staff included Florence Ayitey, Adelaide Otoo, Ebenezer Okoampa, Florence Mortu (now Mrs Florence Aboagye), Jonathan Apecku and Joshua Boadu-Nkrumah. This detailed list is for the sake of institutional memory. Further growth of the organisation is fully described in a separate chapter.

The first development literature I was exposed to was "Development Ethos" and contained mainly the writings of early development thinkers and practitioners such as Paolo Freire, the famous Brazilian development practitioner, and other World Vision development educators. I acquired a large component of my initial development knowledge and skills sitting at the feet of the Operations Staff who preceded me as well as from those who came after me. Clement Odua-Mensah, particularly, taught me the basics of community dialogue and proposal writing as well as data collection and reporting.

My first day in the Ghana office of World Vision International was met with an emergency. The news was rife on the airwaves and the national daily papers about the ethnic conflict between the Konkomba and Nanumba ethnic groups in northern Ghana. I was immediately sent out with Clement to fly by a Ghana Air Force aircraft to Tamale to assess the emergency relief need to which World Vision could respond. I just followed Clement and had my first lessons in assessing emergency needs after a conflict. After arriving in Tamale we continued to the conflict area around Bimbilla via Yendi using public transport. The findings of the assessment revealed that the most pressing needs of the communities were salt and fish. Our relief assistance to the area consisted, therefore, of the airlifting of these commodities to Tamale and their transport to the conflict area.

I remember my first lessons in project proposal writing. Clement Odua-Mensah taught me how to write project objectives and said that they must be SMART. This acronym stands for Specific, Measurable, Attainable, Realistic and Time-bound. It was during his inputs into one of my first proposals that Clement helped me to spell correctly the word potable to mean water that is safe for drinking instead of spelling it as portable. I have remembered this over the years and corrected such spellings several times.

This narrative highlights the support I received from colleagues and friends as well as the challenges I faced when I worked to establish the development initiatives of World Vision International in northern Ghana. It identifies my naivety and inexperience in administration, logistics and procurement procedures as the main reasons for my initial challenges. It also suggests alternative policy and operational actions that could have helped avoid or minimise the challenges.

Although my work of pioneering the interventions of World Vision International in northern Ghana started during my orientation in Accra, I settled in Tamale in December 1981. On 10th December 1981, my wife and I with our three-month-old baby packed our small personal belongings into a Toyota pickup that had been converted into a passenger vehicle. We set off from Bawku, where we were residing and headed for Tamale. As we left Bawku town and drove past the secondary school where I had taught chemistry for one year, the reality of my departure from the teaching profession and my entry into the development field dawned heavily on me. The journey took longer than we expected but we finally arrived in Tamale at about 6:30 pm at the house we had rented earlier through a friend - off the third road in Kalpohin Estates We offloaded our luggage into the dusty rooms and were confronted by what would become a daily problem in Tamale – lack of water. The taps were simply dry. My wife and I found our way to a friend's house on the first road in the estate. There we had enough water to bathe the baby. We spent our first night in our new home without water to take a bath.

For the rest of December, I tried to build my network in Tamale, settle my wife and baby in our new home and look for opportunities to build the work of World Vision in the north. On 31st December, we woke up to the announcement of a coup d'état that overthrew the government of the People's National Party (PNP) led by President Hilla Limann. The leader of the coup said it was a revolution and not a coup. The usual sentences that accompany such upheavals were on the radio waves. "The constitution has been suspended. Parliament has been dissolved. All government officials should report to the nearest police station for their own safety ..." So here was a new job, a new home, a new baby and now a new government. It dawned on me that I had a very high, steep mountain to climb. Two days after the coup d'état, the Tamale central market went up in flames. After three weeks of diligently showing my wife where to find what in the market, it was reduced to ashes by the fire. We were back to where we started.

Pioneering work can be very challenging and it becomes more so when one is confronted with a new political era. The dusk to dawn curfew that was introduced by the new government presented its own difficulties. In order to make progress, I started with the basic principle of going from the known to the unknown. Since World Vision International is a Christian organisation, the partnerships for development had to be established with churches. My first network consisted of leaders of churches who had branches in rural communities. This enabled me to focus on the leadership of the Baptist and Assemblies of God Churches.

I was given the initial task of identifying and renting a house in Tamale that could serve as both a residence and an office. I ended up in a house that did not qualify to play either role. The window between the office and the living room of my residence was completely wide open without louvre blades. We bought and hung polythene material to create a physical separation between the two rooms. The office and household furniture I ordered from a carpenter three months before our arrival actually arrived a month late. I had to sit on the living room armchairs without cushions until August 1982 before I could purchase cushions from Burkina Faso to complete the furnishing. From this inadequate base I had to find a way of getting to rural communities on public transport until the middle of February 1982 before a motorbike was sent to me from Accra.

In my desperate search for support, counsel and direction I found a minister of a Baptist Church called Rev. Abu Mahama. I remember how he diligently introduced me to communities with Baptist churches in the Dagomba area around Tamale. It was difficult getting to these communities. For example, in trying to get to a community called Tarikpaa I took public transport from Tamale to Savelugu. I got off the truck at the junction to the community just about 1 km from Savelugu. I then walked on foot for a further 6 km to get to the community. After nearly 2 hours of meeting with the community members, I was faced with the next task of walking back to the main road to get on board any public transport to Tamale. Two young men in the community saw my plight and came to my aid. They gave me a bicycle to ride and one of them took the other as a passenger on a second bicycle. We rode these bicycles all the way back to the main road. Then I had to wait with the young men for about an hour and a half until I got an articulated truck heading for Tamale. Was the driver of the truck simply kind enough to stop for me? Not really! He was interested in the lorry fare to Tamale which I gratefully paid, even though there was no seat and I stood on my feet throughout the nearly 20 km journey. I made similar journeys to communities using public transport.

The Tamale sub-office of World Vision International was the first office from which one could work outside Accra. With hindsight, it would have been operationally better to send an experienced logistician who knew procurement procedures to go ahead of the incoming Project Coordinator designated to carry out the pioneering work, and rent accommodation. The idea of renting one place that would serve as both residence and office was not the best. Such an arrangement puts unnecessary pressure on the family of the person supposed to carry out professional development work and also interferes with the professional work of the staff. Combining a residence and an office in one building also posed a security risk and did not allow for work/private-life balance. The arrangement at the time must have had budgetary advantages but did not facilitate maximum efficiency and effectiveness.

I worked alone in Tamale from December 1981 until March 1984. I was the Regional Project Coordinator but I also performed the functions of an Administrator, an Accountant, the Secretary, the Driver and a host of other functions that needed to be performed in the sub-office. I very much appreciate the confidence placed in me during this time by the authorities in Accra. However, this arrangement stretched all the elements of my integrity and honesty. As I was working for a Christian organisation, I understand that my recruitment was based on the trust the organisation put in me and my Christian faith and principles. However, in my humble opinion, I think that no organisation carrying out pioneering work should send out staff to begin the work alone. The example of Jesus Christ in the Bible (Luke 10:1) is clear; he sent out the extra 72 disciples on a mission in pairs. Starting pioneering work with at least two or more people provides an opportunity for teamwork, mutual support and synergy. It is a valid principle that two people working as a team will accomplish more than the combined results of the same two people working separately as individuals.

The project car, a Peugeot 504 caravan, was delivered to me mid-May 1982. Ideally, a project vehicle should have been procured and a driver assigned to it before the start of work at the sub-office. In the beginning, World Vision provided these caravan cars for fieldwork. The organisation soon found out that this was not the most appropriate vehicle for rural work. There was a shift to use Nissan Patrol four-wheel-drive cars that were more appropriate for access to rural communities. This further evolved to the use of Toyota four-wheel-drive vehicles. I had to read the manual from cover to cover to understand how to manage the vehicle, including basics like putting the light on and off. The rudiments of driving I picked up in Accra became the foundation on which I built my driving experience. It brought back memories of learning from my driving instructor in Accra. My driving education took six weeks made up of three lessons a week. The instructor taught me all the details about managing a car at home as well as the basic rules of driving in traffic and on the highway. He timed me changing a tyre and worked out my reaction time that showed the minimum distance I should stay behind a car in front of me at any given speed to avoid hitting the car in case of a problem. When I hear people say they learned how to drive in two days I wonder what they were taught.

I also had memories of the period of my orientation in Accra when I had to take my driving skills beyond the driving school. During a project visit to conduct community dialogue in a community called Akyem Awenare, I was on my way back to Accra with Clement Odua Mensah. As we reached the Kumasi-Accra Road and turned to face Accra, Clement stopped the car. He then asked me to come to the driver's seat and drive the car all the way to Accra. This was my first time driving a car on the highway. I managed to concentrate and drive the car all the way to the outskirts of Accra, respecting all the driving rules I had been taught. This included signalling before overtaking a slow car in front of me, slowing down to follow a long chain of cars in case the road ahead of the car in front of me was not clear such as the crest of the hill, a curve or oncoming vehicle etc. I wanted Clement to take over the car at the outskirts of Accra but he insisted that I manoeuvre my way through the traffic of the city to the offices of World Vision International. I consider this as a major milestone in my life and give the credit to Clement Odua-Mensah who had such firm confidence in me.

Back in Tamale, my first long drive alone was from my house to the airport to take the driver who brought the car to me to catch a flight to Accra. I drove back home alone sweating and mastering the act of driving. For the next few months, I drove to rural communities around Tamale and two communities around the Walewale area. Then the real test came in the first week of August 1982. I received a visitor from the international office of World Vision International in the USA called Sam Voorhies. He came by air to Tamale and we proceeded to visit several projects over a one-week period.

He looked at the project document and compared them to what he saw on the ground. He looked pleased but had several questions to ask. For example, in the project document, I had written that the project would support the construction of deep ground wells to provide potable water. Sam asked me what I meant by deep. Then it dawned on me that I could look into a well and tell whether it was deep or not but I did not put a description on paper that would give any person in the US and who had never seen a well in Ghana an idea of what I was talking about. At the end of Sam's visit, Ghana Airways flights from Tamale to Accra were cancelled for two consecutive days. We therefore decided that I would drive him on the third day all the way from Tamale to Accra. By 5:30 am we were out of Tamale on our way to Accra. The roads were not as good as they are now, so I hit my maximum speed of 120 km per hour on the good patches and came to a crawling speed when it was full of potholes. By 4:30 pm we had just gone past Nsawam. Sam then asked me how long I had started driving on my own. I said I had been driving on my own for less than three months. Sam told me in later meetings that when he heard my reply, he nearly had a heart attack.

In Accra, one problem followed another and instead of going back to Tamale after two days, I was there for two weeks. Communication between my wife and me was nonexistent. There were no telephones at home. The only solution was for my wife to go to the offices of Ghana Institute of Linguistics, Literacy and Bible Translation (GILLBT) and send a radio message that would be written down and brought to me in the World Vision office and for me to do the same in reply. On day 10, my wife managed to send such a message. The reality was that inadequate communication made life very difficult.

One of the challenges faced by World Vision International in Ghana in the aftermath of the 31st December coup d'état was the balance between modesty and visibility. Sometime in the early 1980s, there was a publication in the Ghanaian Times Newspaper that focused on the operations of World Vision International in the country. The publication described World Vision as a so-called American development organisation with offices obscurely located in Nyaniba Estates. It said that they did not have any markings on their cars and that projects were in rural areas out of Accra without signs to show the presence of World Vision in those communities. The organisation was headed by a former Navy Commander, who was a member of the National Redemption Council that ruled the country after the overthrow of the Progress Party government in 1972. It then added that the Africa Regional Director was a former Chief of Defence Staff in the Ghana Army and became a liaison between the Armed Forces Revolutionary Council (AFRC) and Government Machinery in 1979. It then indicated that this could be an undercover CIA operation. While the facts about the personnel were true, the conclusion that World Vision was a CIA operation was completely false.

This misunderstanding raises the question of how to manage the delicate balance between modesty, that can be misread as undercover work, and visibility, that can be misread as trying to blow your own trumpet. The cost of some of the giant billboards of NGOs could easily meet certain development needs. However, if they do not do this they may be accused of low visibility and having something to hide.

I hope that any organisation with plans for thematic and/or geographical expansion that would lead to pioneering work will learn from the lessons in this narrative. I am grateful for the support I received from the World Vision team in Accra during these hard times.

CHAPTER 17

WORKING IN TOUGH TIMES

Lying awake in my bed, I was silently planning the activities of the day in my head. The dry north-easterly winds of the harmattan whistled through the mosquito netting. My thoughts were rudely interrupted by a siren from Tamale town centre that signalled the end of the 10 p.m. to 5 a.m. curfew to which we had become accustomed. I jumped out and got dressed very quickly before even washing my mouth. My wife asked me why I was out of bed at 5:00 am. I told her that I was going to the NRDC (Northern Regional Development Corporation) to buy bread. She wished me good luck. I am not sure whether this was a sceptical wish based on experience or a genuine one based on faith.

I drove to the compound of the NRDC. The build-up of the queue to buy bread could be likened to a movie with the fast dispersal of soldiers in line played in reverse. I got out of the car and joined the queue. There were at least thirty people in front of me and less than five minutes later, there were over thirty people behind me. We waited patiently, chatting among ourselves about the difficulties of the time. At 6:00 am, the window for the sale of bread opened. I realised that some people were buying up to five or six loaves of bread. I kept checking in my pocket to make sure my money was there. As I got closer to the window I became a bit anxious. At the point when I had only three people between me and the window, the lady selling the bread stuck out her face and announced that the bread was finished. We all stood there trying to make sense of this situation. Standing there and wondering did not change anything. I drove slowly back home. My wife came out to ask me where the bread was. I tried to explain that I was only a few steps to the window when the bread got finished but this was irrelevant information. Whether I was the third person to the window or the fiftieth person did not make any difference. I tried to stop the tears coming to my eyes. I remembered the piles of different brands of bread on the shelf of the supermarket in Preston in the UK in 1980. Here was I, without bread after over an hour of standing in a queue in the cold dry season of 1983.

The period from 1982 to 1984 can easily be described as the toughest time in the history of Ghana. A brutal combination of natural, economic and political calamities had mercilessly struck the people of Ghana with devastating effects. The first was the dry, long, devastating drought that swept across Africa from Senegal in the extreme west, all the way to the horn of Africa in the east. This drought did not leave out Ghana. Then there was an outbreak of bush fires that swept through the country all the way from the north through the thick green forest belt to the coast. The implementation of the Structural Adjustment Program (SAP) proposed by the International Monetary Fund (IMF) to respond to the economic crisis in Ghana was in full swing. This programme resulted in the devaluation of the Ghanaian currency. At the beginning of 1982, one US dollar was equivalent to 2.75 Ghanaian cedis. By the beginning of 1983, one US dollar was more than 135 cedis. The IMF programme resulted in the privatisation of state-owned enterprises such as factories under the Ghana Industrial Holding Corporation (GIHOC) and hotels under the State Hotels Corporation (SHC). The rationalisation of the number of staff under the public services resulted in the layoff of thousands of public servants. There was a massive shortage of fuel resulting in long queues of cars in petrol filling stations waiting for fuel without knowing when the next consignment would arrive. To add to all this, 1.5 million Ghanaians were forcefully sent back home from Nigeria. These "returnees" arrived back in Ghana through all the entry points on the eastern border of the country by road while some arrived by air through Kotoka International airport and more arrived by sea at Tema Harbour. The year of 1983 will never be forgotten in the history of Ghana.

The deportation of Ghanaians from Nigeria was an effort of the Nigerian government to reverse the influx of Ghanaians into that country during its oil boom period of the 1970s. The Nigerian currency (Naira) was so strong that it was valued at 1:1 with the British pound. It is claimed by some that businesses in the UK accepted the Naira as legal tender. Professionals from Ghana, including doctors, engineers, teachers and nurses flocked to Nigeria to work and earn salaries that were two to five times the salaries of their counterparts in Ghana. Non-skilled Ghanaians found themselves on the streets of Lagos doing menial jobs for monies they would never have earned in Ghana for doing similar jobs. Agege was a suburb of Lagos and the expression "going to Agege" meant going to Nigeria. By the beginning of the 1980s, the economy of Nigeria began to deteriorate. This led to the implementation of austerity measures including the deportation of thousands of Ghanaians. Some have interpreted it as a retaliation for the expulsion of Nigerians from Ghana in 1969.

The drought and bushfires in Ghana resulted in massive shortages of food in the market in the latter part of 1983 and in 1984. I know a farmer in Tamale who harvested 1,600 bags of paddy rice in 1982 and on the same area of land and using the same inputs and implements in 1983, he realised that he was going to harvest less than 100 bags. He therefore abandoned the field for nearby community members to glean whatever they could get. The firm estimated that the cost of using a combine harvester in the farm was going to exceed the income from the quantity of rice that he would have harvested. The food shortages were countrywide and affected everybody in the social spectrum of the country. People worked hard, ate little, lost weight and ended up with visible clavicle bones that became known as "Rawling's chains", a name derived from that of the Head of State at the time. Men punched new holes in their belts to compensate for the diminishing circumferences of their waistlines.

The leadership of World Vision International in Ghana designed multiple interventions to respond to the interrelated problems created by the events of the time. The different problems dealt with included communication, the food shortages in the country, the fuel crisis that affected transportation, the return of Ghanaians from Nigeria and how to deal with the shortage of goods in general. As a result of the devaluation of the local currency, staff were required to come back to the office in Accra and rewrite budgets for projects that had already been submitted. This meant that the project staff had to find out prices of supplies and use these to rewrite and submit revised budgets. The exercise had to be repeated more than once to cope with the constantly changing exchange rate of the cedi to the dollar and it took away precious time required by staff to supervise projects in the communities.

With the food shortages, the organisation had to respond to strategies in communities where there were projects and also respond to the food needs of staff. For the latter, a caterer was engaged to bring lunch to the office every day. This enabled staff to buy the food and spend a short time eating during lunch break, instead of wasting precious time looking for scarce food in Accra that could cost a fortune. Writing about the food situation across the country would be difficult without illustrations. I remember trying to get dinner by going into the house of a member of staff whose mother sold kenkey, the common local maize meal in Accra. By the time we got to the house, the *kenkey* had finished. We found out that customers preferred to buy the raw *kenkey* and take it home to cook. This was most unusual but became the norm in Accra. I remember driving around Accra trying to buy any type of food I could get on the street. The only available food I got fined was fried cassava.

In response to the shortage of food in communities where World Vision was working, there was a massive importation of rice and biscuits which were distributed to project communities. The interesting thing about this distribution was the fact that World Vision staff who had very little to eat at home were not at first included as beneficiaries. This meant that staff supervised and distributed food to project communities and came back home with little or nothing to eat themselves. The difficulty was resolved when the leadership took a second look at the situation and made provision for staff. With the provision of lunch in the office, some staff bought food during the lunch break but dared not eat it in the office and rather carried it home to their children.

In every language, new words appear based on evolving circumstances. In Bawku and surrounding towns in the Kusaasi area, the term "*Ayaayual*" emerged to describe this period of acute food shortages. The term comes from the way cereals were measured by market women. In normal times, the bowl used to measure cereals was held in such a way that the cereal would overflow into the palms of the person holding the bowl at the sides, thereby taking along extra grain. This meant that one could get extra bowls of cereal when buying several. During the period of the food crisis, the measurement was made and the bowl picked up carefully with the fingers to ensure that no extra cereal followed what was purchased. So, the word means "take it out exactly as it is". People who did not live through these hard times may never hear this word and if they did, they would never understand what it meant.

The fuel crisis, that was a manifestation of the economic crisis, hit World Vision very hard. This is because field staff needed fuel to travel to project communities, and project staff from the communities depended on public transport to come to the field office. The organisation had to resort to several strategies for getting fuel and travelling to project communities. I remember some staff driving cars to various fuel stations around Accra and parking them in queues in anticipation of the arrival of fuel. There were times when drivers had to leave their cars in the queue for several days and sometimes even weeks. During one of these occasions when a car was thus parked for several days, a chicken entered into the open space between the engine and the splash shield below and laid eggs. At this time, every car had a jerry can in it to carry fuel as well as a length of rubber hose to syphon fuel into the car in case the need arose.

Back in Tamale, I had my own coping mechanisms. In addition to struggling at public fuel stations, I was supported by collaborators such as the Ghana Institute of Linguistics, Literacy and Bible Translation (GILLBT) and the Northern Regional Administration (NRA). I had six jerry cans and a rubber hose. In the worst-case scenario, I could get fuel in Burkina Faso. This meant driving nearly 200 km to the border, filling the fuel tank and buying six jerry cans of petrol. On one particular occasion, I was in the queue at the regional office to buy fuel and all of a sudden there was an explosion in the room where the fuel attendant was working. He managed to break a window and jump out with burns all over his body. For the first time, it was more convenient to be further away from the selling point. Customers who were near the selling point scrambled to get their cars out of the way. It is a miracle that throughout these times no World Vision staff member was caught in a fire. There were actually incidents of domestic fires in the country resulting from people keeping containers of petrol in their houses.

The communication challenge was very daunting. This was decades before the advent of the mobile phone, so the fastest means of communication at the time was by landline telephone. However, International Direct Dialling (IDD) telephone facilities were difficult to come by. The next fastest means of communication was by telex. However, to send a telex out of Accra one had to go to the International Communications Office of the Post and Telecommunications Corporation that was located off High Street towards the sea. The sad fact was that one could go there at about 9 am and join the queue and still be unable to send a telex by 4pm. At one point it was faster to drive to Lomé in Togo to send a fax and be back in Accra before 3 pm. The extra advantage of going to Lomé was that the person could buy very basic items such as sugar, milk, tea, coffee, soap, and the numerous things which were not very easy to find in Accra. Indeed, standing at the Ghana side of the border post and looking across into Togo was like looking into a completely different world. The difficulty in communication seriously affected the work of World Vision International. The situation was so bad that the director of World Vision in Germany at the time, Manfred Kohl, travelled to Accra with a telex machine as hand baggage to rescue the Ghana office. It took several weeks before this machine could be installed and be functional in Accra because of the difficulties in subscription of a dedicated number for it, but we finally had our own telex machine and did not need to go all the way to Lomé to send telex messages.

World Vision bought bicycles for volunteer workers in project communities. The organisation also made provision for bicycles in the field office. These bicycles became a means by which staff compensated for the difficulties in transportation due to the shortage of fuel. I remember one dramatic situation when a project worker in a community called Wawasi, rode a bicycle from the community to the Accra-Kumasi road at a junction near Suhum and then cycled all the way to Accra to submit a project report. The distance from Suhum to Accra is about 63 km, and he had to ride all the way back to his community. He said he did this because he could not get public transport on the Kumasi Road to come to Accra because of the persistent fuel shortages. The dedication of these volunteer project workers was exceptional. The turn to the Republic of Togo for transactions that would facilitate the smooth running of World Vision went beyond communications to include banking as well as the purchase of cars and vehicle spare parts. The organisation was forced to open a bank account in Lome in which money could be deposited and withdrawn for the transactions mentioned above.

The food crisis swept across Africa. In 1984, I travelled with Kofi Hagan and Akwesi Agyeman-Dua together with Roger Walker, a member of staff of the World Vision Australia office, to Burkina Faso to assess the relief needs in that country. This was to enable us to provide support to our partners, Fédérations des Églises et Missions Évangéliques (FEME) in Ouagadougou. During this trip, we had to fly on a light aircraft from Ouagadougou to Dori and then to Djibo before returning to Ouagadougou. When we got to the airport, I noticed that the four-seater, single-engine aircraft was held to the ground by ropes tied to cement blocks on both sides to prevent it from being moved by the wind. Kofi and I plus our Australian visitor and the pilot took up the four seats, and we managed to squeeze our counterpart called Jacques into the back of the craft, but he could not sit up straight. Before we took off from Ouagadougou, Kofi called Akwesi to the side of the aircraft and told him that in case anything happened and we did not return, he should tell our families that we perished in pursuit of helping the poor.

In Dori, we came across a group of children numbering about 15 to 20 between the ages of 3 and 15 sitting very quietly at the edge of a gutter. It is very unusual to see children of this age bracket sitting quietly and not playing. These children were simply so hungry that they could not play. We were told that some of them had not eaten anything for nearly a week. The signs of hunger were written all over their lean faces. One could easily count the ribs of those who did not have clothes on. Back in Ouagadougou (we survived the return flight!) that evening we went for dinner in the restaurant of the hotel where we were staying. We looked at the menu and Kofi Hagan said that after all he had seen that day it did not make psychological sense to eat. We drank a bottle of soft drink each and went back to our rooms without eating dinner. The sight of those children in Dori has remained in my mind over the years. When I see little children running all over the place and parents trying to stop them from running, I remember the scene and tell the parents that children running around is a sign of good health and nutrition.

In the same year of 1984, I drove a photographer called David Ward to photograph the situation in project communities in northern Ghana and in Burkina Faso. Sometimes we worked all day without food. In Burkina Faso, we visited one community near Koudougou. In this community, we had the privilege of being served with rural community roast chicken for lunch. This meant that we could not eat the sandwiches that we carried along from Ouagadougou. The following day we travelled to another community near Yako in the north of the country. This time we did not take any packed lunch. The community did not think that we needed lunch and so we worked until 5 pm, being sustained by the breakfast we had taken in Ouagadougou.

When we finished our work and wanted to leave we noticed that one of the tyres of the Peugeot pickup that we borrowed from Christian Services Committee in Tamale was flat. We did not have a spare tyre. When the community members noticed our predicament, they came up with a pump that is usually used to pump the tyres of a Mobylette. Every effort to pump air into the tyre with this device failed. Somebody then had an idea. The chief of the next village which was about 5 km away had a similar car. Two people were therefore sent to the village to go and plead with the chief to give us his spare tyre that would be returned the following day. David Ward and I sat down and waited and waited and waited. Our host came up with hot millet meal (TZ) and vegetable soup. David and I ate hungrily even though there was no trace of protein in the soup. A hungry man will eat anything. This was not the time for nutritional lessons. Finally, the spare tyre arrived, carried on a Mobylette. We changed the tyre and headed for Ouagadougou. By 10 o'clock in the night, we were back in our hotel. These experiences of 1983 and 1984 remind me that when one is committed to development, one can work in the toughest of conditions.

One of my coping mechanisms in Tamale was to learn a new trade from which I could earn additional income to supplement my salary. I found an experienced photographer called Samuel Boadu. I took my time in his library to learn the basics of photography. I read several chapters on the combination of aperture and shutter speed at different light strengths that can produce a good photograph. I learnt how to unload a used film from the camera in a dark room and to develop, fix, wash, and dry the film, using chemicals that I had bought and prepared myself. I then learned how to load the film in an enlarger under 'safe' light and similarly process the photographs. My background in chemistry came in handy in this venture and I was able to show my photography tutor how to read volumes correctly in a measuring cylinder. To support this new skill, I created a darkroom in my house and then used the fixed focus Konica camera, given to me by Sam Boadu, to pursue photography business in the village//s around Tamale during my spare time. This became a major income earner throughout most of my career. The popular cameras used by professional photographers during those days included Nikon, Canon, Minolta Olympus, Pentax and Yashica. In 1992 I upgraded my camera to a Nikon FM2. Common photographic materials at the time included products from Ilford, Kodak, Agfa, Tura and Fuji. The current inclusion of cameras on almost every mobile phone has rendered this skill irrelevant in the 21st century.

One interesting scenario all around the country was the phenomenon of queues to buy what became known as 'essential commodities' such as sugar, milk, soap, tinned mackerel, etc. While driving through town in Tamale, when I saw a queue of people in front of a shop, I would stop my car, join the queue and then ask the person in front to tell me what was being sold at the head of the queue. 'Conditional sales' became the order of the day. This term may be unfamiliar to readers who did not live through the tough times in Ghana. You would go out to buy 1 or 2 kg of sugar, and then find a queue in front of a shop. When it came to your turn to be served, you would be presented with a sachet containing about 5 different items. The items could be half a bar of soap, 4 tins of milk, 2 kg of sugar, a can of Vim, and a packet of Typhoo tea. All that I needed would be the sugar and the milk and probably the soap but I would be compelled to buy the Vim and the tea as a condition for buying what I wanted. I would end up with several tins of Vim in the house that I did not really need.

One day, at the time of these shortages, I watched as my wife washed the napkins of our daughter. In those days, there were no disposable diapers, so families had to use cotton nappies and then wash, dry and reuse them. The commonest soap one could buy in the market was so badly made that it remained sticking to one's hand and this gave it the name 'don't touch me'. From my chemistry, I understood that they had got the saponification constant wrong, but who was in the factory that produced the soap to get it right? When washing the nappies with 'don't touch me', the soapsuds disappeared before the job was done and the nappies were not as clean as we wanted. The following day, I drove to the northern Ghana Bible Institute of the Assemblies of God Church where I borrowed 100 US dollars from a missionary called Rev David Vespa. I then drove over 200 km to cross into Burkina Faso where I changed the money into CFA francs, bought soap, sugar, milk and the basic things we called 'essential commodities' in Ghana - and petrol of course - and then drove back to Tamale. Life was tough.

In response to the sudden influx of returning Ghanaians from Nigeria, World Vision imported a large number of medicines and made these available at the three major entry points, i.e. Kotoka International Airport, the Ghana-Togo border at Aflao and Tema Harbour. This also required calling field staff back to the headquarters to prepare the necessary proposal and budget for the exercise. Efforts were made to identify Ghanaians returning from Nigeria who arrived in project communities and to help them resettle.

Former staff of World Vision International and indeed any organisation should be proud that they were able to hold the organisation together during these tough times. The staff of World Vision International who never experienced these tough times should always remember that they are building on a foundation that was laid in hardship and toil. Anybody wishing to be a development worker in Africa must be prepared for tough times. The context and the severity may be different but the need to be tough would remain the same.

CHAPTER 18

THE IMPETUS TO GROW

This narrative is mainly for the purpose of institutional memory and readers who are not related to World Vision may not find the list of local names of particular interest.

Mothers who go to postnatal clinics with their babies for weighing once a month understand that one of the evidences of healthy life is growth. Any organisation or institution that is alive and healthy needs to grow. This narrative documents the evolving situations and thinking that led to the growth of World Vision International in Ghana up to the time I left the organisation in 1994. I am told that the organisation grew until there was a total of over 500 staff. The operations department alone had 350 staff. But this has been reduced to about 262 in the year 2020. The massive growth and subsequent reduction could be attributed to changing strategies that required increases in human resources at one stage and decreases in the same at another stage.

Led by the National Director, Commodore P F Quaye, the growth of World Vision in Ghana took place in several dimensions. This included human resources, technology, fundraising methodology, geographical expansion and overall development approach. In terms of human resources, the growth was basically the increase in the number of personnel to respond to the evolving needs. In terms of technology, the growth was in response to the evolution of technology itself. For example, manual typewriters gave way to electric typewriters that were gradually replaced by computers.

I believe that Kofi Hagan, who was the Operations Manager, significantly influenced thought processes and strategic actions that facilitated the growth. He identified, appointed and nurtured leaders in various positions. He then identified the various technical areas that were needed to facilitate in-depth growth in the development interventions that would engage the most relevant stakeholders and leave a permanent impact in the fight against poverty. The areas included audit, agricultural extension, water and sanitation, public health and nutrition, food security, leadership and evangelism, construction and women in development (WID) as it was called at the time. Kofi left Ghana in 1985 to become the National Director of World Vision in Uganda where his ability to nurture people into leadership positions has been documented by people he managed and who wrote recommendations for him. From Uganda, Kofi became Africa Regional Director for Leadership Development for the organisation before he took up the position as the National Director in Rwanda. He has since retired to work as a management and leadership development consultant. The massive increase in human resources was managed by Chris Bonuedie, the Head of Administration, before the setting up of a dedicated Human Resources Department.

In addition to Commodore Quaye as Director, who was later succeeded by Doctor J. W. de Graft J Riverson, the staff of the National Director's office included Charity Agbeblewu, Beatrice de Graft-Johnson, Kofi Gyima, Emmanuel Aye who was taken from the operations department and John Quaisie.

The operations department grew to cope with the increasing number of projects in various geographical areas. By the time I left the organisation in 1994, the staff members who had worked in the department included Kofi Hagan (left in 1985), Gershon Adzokpa (left in 1993), Clement Odua-Mensah, Emmanuel Aye (moved to the office of the National director), Edward Opare-Saforo, Aaron Lawson (left in 1985), Samuel Asare, Alfred Owusu, Theodore Afari, Stephen Nkrumah, Harry Akama, Emmanuel Oppong, Robert Djangmah, Victor Adom, Peter Sefogah, Eugene Asante, Jane Kwao-Sarbah, Jacob Kotin, Alidu Dason, John Yankson, Hebert Brako, John Quaisie, (who managed projects in other West African countries where World Vision did not have an office and was later sent to the National Director's office) Dora Owusu and John Antwi-Bekoe. I was in this department throughout my work with the organisation and became the Head of Operations from 1993 until my departure in March 1994.

In order to implement development projects, World Vision guided project communities to open bank accounts in the nearest banks they could access. Funds, usually in the form of cheques in the name of the project, were sent to these banks and the project staff accessed the funds to implement their development initiatives. In those days, electronic bank transfers were still new. This project funding mechanism required a basic understanding of financial management, including the banking process and how to keep simple financial records, in order to be able to report to World Vision on how funds were disbursed. This meant that the Project Coordinator had to understand the basics of book-keeping in order to train at least one project volunteer to keep records of financial transactions. The organisation decided that the best way to handle this was to recruit auditors who would relieve Project Coordinators of this task, provide training for the community volunteers who worked for the project, and at the same time audit the project books. The first two auditors to be recruited were Jerome Ofori and Emmanuel Osekre and later Ken Konu joined them. This definitely took the burden off Project Coordinators as anticipated and is a good practice to be emulated by NGOs. The arrival of the auditors initiated and entrenched the principle of segregation of duties in financial management. It ensured that the Project Managers and Project Coordinators who approved funding to project communities and supervised disbursement of the funds were not conflicted by becoming the auditors of the books at the same time.

The unexpected intrusion of food shortages into the lives of Ghanaians in the 1983-1984 crisis introduced a new dimension that management had to cope with. The idea of a relief team to lead the process of supporting project communities came up and the team that started this work was made up of Charles Amaning (a retired Colonel of the Ghana Army), Ebenezer Okoampa (who was taken from the Sponsor Relations Department), Paul Akorofi, Charles Duodu, Fred Anim and Mahama Tampuri. This department was called the Large-Scale Development (LSD) Department. The department later managed the massive transportation of relief food purchased by World Vision International from Ghana and transported to Mali through Burkina Faso and Niger.

A new initiative relating to food termed Food Aid Test (FAT) was started in 1989 headed by Jacob Ansah and assisted by Gloria Kwateng. The initiative sought to explore avenues for using food aid in development, monetisation of food for development and responding to the food deficit of the country without negatively affecting food production and prices. In the monetisation of food aid for example, development partners wanted to send significant quantities of wheat directly to flour milling companies in Ghana who would pay cash to World Vision and the money could then be used directly for development initiatives in rural communities. Apparently, the idea of FAT did not work out and was abandoned.

As the volume of financial management responsibility increased, the finance department also grew. The first head of the Finance Department, Kofi Asante-Okyere, resigned and was succeeded by Sylvester Gbewornyo. The finance team at the time of my departure included in addition Anthony Awortwi-Tandoh Salome Sapati, Isaac Osei, Jones Abdallah, Charles Mensah, James Nkansah Obrempong and T. T. Ayerson.

One of the common needs of people in rural communities is the agricultural technologies and skills required to increase food production. It became apparent that not all Projects Coordinators had a basic understanding of how this could be done. This then led to the need to recruit staff with a specialisation in agricultural extension. In response to this, the organisation recruited Agricultural Technical Officers or Agricultural Extension Officers to carry out this job. The team of Extension Officers included Peter Gyau, Samuel Laari, George Kumahlor, Alex Sackey-Addo, Anthony Kofi Odoom, John Yeboah Mensah, Ophelia Osei Yeboah and Augustine Yawson. The result was that the organisation grew in its capacity to implement agricultural projects with technical expertise. Jacob Ansah was recruited to provide strategic direction and operational planning as well as coordination of the work of the extension officers. Jacob later headed the FAT initiative mentioned earlier.

Another critical development intervention was Primary Health Care and Nutrition. While the project coordinators talked to project communities about vaccination, nutrition and other public health issues, they did not have the technical capacity to implement health and nutrition projects that were consistent with international standards. In response to this, the organisation needed a medical doctor with extensive experience in tropical medicine and public health. It is necessary for me to go back in history in order to appreciate this part of the story of World Vision International.

My first visit to the University of Cape Coast Hospital was in the first quarter of 1976 when I was a first-year student in that University. I was directed to see a physician called Dr Addo. He attended to me but I was upset by the fact that his consulting room was full of cigarette smoke. On my next visit to the hospital, I explained to the staff that I did not want to see the same Doctor I consulted during my last visit and I was directed to a different consulting room. The consultant in this room was Doctor Joseph William de Graft-Johnson Riverson. What looked like a coincidence turned out to be a longer relationship than I could have imagined. Dr Riverson's participation in Protestant Christian Church services and engagement to speak to the members of University Christian fellowship enabled me to identify with his personality and faith. This was the doctor who was recruited to implement the health and nutrition programme of World Vision and it was easy to reconnect with him when he arrived. My work with him became closer when he became the National Director of the organisation and I was the Head of Operations. He left his office wide open for me when I needed to prepare any documents for him. Doctor Riverson was particularly strict about the use of correct English grammar and I remember how he copiously reviewed the documents I wrote to ensure correctness in grammar and accuracy in content. It was he who taught me the correct use of the 'The Ministry of ....' and 'The Minister for .....'. He was one of the giants who contributed significantly to my professional growth as a development worker.

Upon his recruitment to start the health and nutrition team, Dr. Joe Riverson, recruited several public health nurses and nutrition technical officers into his team. The nurses were Suzie Ayeh, Sanatu Nantogma, Naa Maku Agyeman-Dua, Diana Dsani, Elizabeth Yarquah and Jemima Amanor. The nutrition technical officers were Genevieve Olympio and Esther Mannieson.

To remain consistent with the policy of working with churches in communities where World Vision International had projects, the Evangelism and Leadership department was started by Reverend Richard Asua-Sekyere. He was joined later by Rev. Konotey-Ahulu, Rev. Samuel Tigah and Rev. C. N. Aduamuah. The department was also responsible for the training of church leaders to understand and contribute to development processes in their communities.

In the early 1980s, the issue of development organisations focusing on the development of women became paramount. In response to this, the Women In Development initiative was started, with the first person in charge being Alice Yirenkyi. Eventually, Alma Adzraku joined and led this initiative.

The communications department was started by Akwesi Agyeman-Dua and he was later joined by Benny Ashare, Agnes Philips and Phyllis Nyanteng. As World Vision International's work in Ghana progressed into the 1990s the issue of Information and Communication Technology (ICT) and computerisation became critical. Issah Mohammed was recruited as the ICT Coordinator to lead the ICT work in the country and the West

Africa sub-region. Edward Akayesi and Alex Zanlerigu joined him later. This significantly improved the ICT capacity of the organisation.

The increase in geographical spread resulted in a corresponding increase in support between the Field Office in Ghana and the Support Offices. This automatically resulted in the need to increase the number of staff in the Sponsor Relations Department (SRD). The staff of the department at the time I left were Florence Laryea, who became the Manager of the Department after the departure of George Ennin, Florence Ayittey, Florence Aboagye, Adelaide Otoo, James Narh, Stephen Dodd, Stephen Owusu, Samuel Kyei-Kwakyi, Jonathan Pratt, Emmanuel Belon, Ebenezer Peters, Diana Owusu-Ansah, Jonathan Apecku, Joshua Nkrumah Boadu, and Christie Afful.

The increasing number of projects that required the construction of structures such as school buildings, health clinics, and Kumasi Ventilated Improved Pit (KVIP) latrines necessitated the recruitment of a construction specialist and Geoffrey Amegbey was recruited to meet this need.

The number of secretarial support staff increased greatly to meet the demand for documentation. Staff in this category included Gifty Ofori, Andrew Akom-Mensah (a bilingual secretary who later provided management support to World Vision in the Republic of Niger), Mary Odoom, Siegfried Matti, Freda Owusu, Verbena Dogbey, Novenia Lumor, Anthony Kofi Odoom, William Gomado, Mercy Dadson, Felicia Akuffo, Charlotte Mingle, Mercy Kpozah, Leticia Belon, Kate Osei, D. M. Yakubu and Theresa Quarshie. Although the secretarial staff have been lumped into one group, they were divided among the various departments.

The increase in staff outlined above required a dedicated Human Resource Department to take off the pressure from the administration department and this department was started by Florence Hutchful who was later supported by Kwakye Boateng. The administration department was managed by Chris Bonuedie and staff included Margaret Barnor, Alfred Aquaye-Badoo, George Noi, Emmanuel Afful, Samuel Addo, Emmanuel Adayie, Sussie Kofie, Christie Aryee, Ataa Nii, Baba Moro, Osabutey, Wisdom Damale and Paul Aboagye.

The single biggest growth in the organisation was the introduction of the Ghana Rural Water Project (GRWP). This project was planned and executed in response to the massive need for water across the country. It was a multimillion-dollar project that was financed mainly by the Conrad N. Hilton Foundation and involved the recruitment of the Project Manager and several well-drilling experts including hydrogeologists, geophysicists, water engineers and several categories of borehole drilling machine operators. It would be impossible to remember the names of this large team that arrived at the same time but prominent among the leadership was Colonel Charles Armaning, Bismarck Nerquaye-Tetteh, Col Kwame Mifetu, Mr. S K Sarpong, Harry Reynolds and Braimah Apambire.

In 1988, I was moved from the Tamale Sub-Office to Accra. By the time I was leaving the sub-office, the staff there were Jacob Kotin, Samuel Laari, Alidu Dason, Mahama Tampuri, D. M. Yakubu, Sanatu Nantogma, and Rev. Kanton. I was replaced in the Tamale Sub-Office by Clement Odua-Mensah.

It is important to recognise the evolving contexts that created the need for growth. The biggest lesson here is that organisational growth should result from the need to respond to evolving situations. What many development workers do not recognise is that when the contexts change there could also be the need to downsize as different skills may be required to respond to different changing contexts. In organisational growth, it is important to ensure that the incoming human resources align their skills, competencies and knowledge with the core business of the organisation. World Vision International is a Christian development organisation with a mission of carrying out integrated community development. In the increase in human resources, the organisation ensured that all incoming personnel understood this core business and realigned their skills accordingly. For example, secretaries were given to understand that they would be dealing with project workers from rural communities and project reports. They therefore had to take time to understand the rural community context. Auditors needed to understand that the audit work would not be in the public or the profit-making sector but rather the auditing of non-professional financial people in rural communities who were volunteering their services. Agricultural extension officers were helped to develop skills in rural community development facilitation and go beyond simple agricultural extension to also facilitate community transformation.

Growth may not necessarily mean an increase in numbers. Indeed, it could actually mean a decrease in numbers as the organisation replaces its nonessential skills with evolving new ones. Clearly, there may be a case where one person could easily do the work of five people. Although this could be growth in capacity, it could result in a decrease in numbers of staff.

With the sudden injection of computers into World Vision and the necessity for managers to be given laptop computers and asked to write their own reports on the computers themselves, secretaries who did not have computer skills became redundant although there was a growth in capacity.

The survival of any organisation depends heavily on the ability of the organisation to go through the thinking and repositioning exercises that would help them to develop a strategy to stay abreast with evolving contexts. Credit should be given to the first National Director who preferred the recruitment of national staff to respond to evolving needs rather than seeking short-term support from external sources. In the absence of many people with academic qualifications in development at the time, World Vision International recruited staff mainly from the public sector and avoided the transfer of human resources from one community to the other, and instead encouraged capacity building within communities. The trend has changed since then with the introduction of development studies in the universities.

The rapid growth of staff in the organisation created new challenges in staff orientation. In response to this, the Africa Regional Office of World Vision introduced the new staff orientation course in Nairobi, Kenya. A number of staff started to benefit from this programme from 1984 onwards. This growth, particularly in the Ghana Rural Water Project, tended to focus more on technical expertise than Christian commitment. There has been a perception that World Vision's Christian values were significantly compromised as a result. The biggest lesson in the growth of World Vision International is that the leadership of every organisation needs to have the courage to grow but with the awareness that such growth could result in a compromise of core values.

CHAPTER 19

FRUITS OF THE GROWTH

In January 2014, I sat on a bench in a shade near the Baptist Church in Tarikpaa, near Tamale in the Northern Region, with two of the young men who were part of the initiation of World Vision's work in the community in 1982. I had not seen them for nearly two decades. They commented on the grey hair that was all over my head and I reminded them that it was over 32 years since I first came to the community. I was impressed to see the changes in that community. Shops were selling second-hand clothes and a dressmaker displayed her products in another shop. An impressive 500-gallon overhead water reservoir stood nearby. More importantly for me, the borehole that was constructed by World Vision's Ghana Rural Water Project (GRWP) in 1986, stood solidly in place with women pumping out clean and safe water and carrying their containers home. I asked my two friends to tell me the number of community members who had Guinea worms. After a very long laugh, one of them said children aged less than 15 years in this community did not know about Guinea worm.

This brought back memories of January 1982. I was sitting in this same community with my mentor, Rev. Abu Mahama. We were in front of the Chief and several members of the community and discussing the most pressing needs that required development intervention. Among the list were potable water and medicine to deal with the prevalence of Guinea worm that rendered people unable to work on their farms, particularly during the rainy season. I tried to explain that the prevalence of Guinea worm is directly related to the continuous use of water from the pond nearby. The whole group burst into laughter. One of them turned to me and pointed at the visible blood vessels on his hand and told me confidently that this was Guinea worm. He explained that every human being has Guinea worm and that for some people it will develop into a swelling and exit the body. For others, this may never happen. This simply showed that I was a naive young man trying to throw dust into their eyes. When I asked for the number of people in the community who were suffering from Guinea worm at the time, they scratched their heads and told me that it was easier to count the number of people who did not have any Guinea worm and they managed to count about eight people from specific houses. This was very distressing. In the rainy season, many people got swellings in different parts of the body that burst and Guinea worms were extracted. The most distressing case for me was the appearance of the worm from the scrotum of one person.

Access to water in the community was very difficult. Women walked two to four kilometres to fetch water from what could only be described as a pond. The water was carried in metal containers of about ten to twelve litres. It was not something that anybody would like to drink, as it looked like tea with a small amount of milk – brownish and milky. The women would normally pour it into a big pot and then add some alum to it to get the mud settled and make it look deceptively clear. This treatment only left the water looking clean but not safe for drinking. I waited patiently for an opportunity to prove my point and this took more than four years. Finally, the drilling team of World Vision arrived in Tamale in grand style. This community was one of the beneficiaries of the drilling project. About 26 years down the line, the dreaded Guinea worm had all but disappeared. This was one huge fruit of the expansion and growth that took place in World Vision in the 1980s.

To enhance the sustainability of the water projects, several teams were sent out to the communities in a carefully thought-out sequence that resulted in community ownership of the boreholes and continuous maintenance of the pumps. The teams included facilitators, who were experts in community mobilisation, geophysical studies, borehole drilling, pump installation and maintenance. The community was left with a water management committee and a pump maintenance team that had been trained by World Vision.

This narrative from Tarikpaa illustrates the debate among development workers about whether external ideas and resources are necessary for the development of any community. The people of Tarikpaa were trapped in the false belief that Guinea worm had nothing to do with the source of their water. Whether they would ever have come out of this belief without external ideas and resources is an interesting question for development practitioners and academics. As a development practitioner I was in the community to collect information that would help me to prepare a presentation to be delivered at a conference of the Moroccan National Human Development Observatory that was held in Rabat later that year. Three other lessons that came up during my visit were related to the attainment of output, outcome and impact indicators. The output of the water project was quickly accomplished through the drilling of a borehole and installation of a hand pump that produced water for the community members. The outcome was accomplished when, after the installation of the hand pump, women had access to safe drinking water for their families close to hand and did not have to go through the laborious process of trying unsuccessfully to purify the water. The impact of seeing a population without Guinea worm however took several years to accomplish. The expectation of partners who fund development projects of wanting to see the impact of the project in three to five years may actually be too ambitious and make viable projects look as if they have no effect.

The introduction of the audit team as part of the growth of World Vision International in Ghana yielded fruits in different forms. In the first place, the work of the organisation required the transfer of substantial amounts of money and other resources to project communities. The auditors worked hard to bring together people from the communities with or without any knowledge of accounting at all and build their capacity in basic bookkeeping and financial management. They also communicated the principles of probity and accountability as part of basic Christian living. The auditors would spend several days and weeks in very rural communities, sometimes travelling in very rugged conditions. I remember travelling with Emmanuel Osekre from projects at very odd hours of the day. On one such occasion, I drove through a flock of wild guinea fowls that were crossing the road and killed one of them. We brought it back home for a meal.

The training of project workers in basic bookkeeping brought a huge improvement to the financial reporting by project communities. It also enabled project managers and project coordinators from World Vision to take their hands off project audits and focus on the planning and supervision of other project activities. Emmanuel Osekre remembers three people who received capacity building in bookkeeping and financial management going further to acquire professional qualifications in this area and become gainfully employed.

In order to enhance increased food production and ensure food security, Agricultural Extension Officers were recruited. Their main task was to support community farmers to cultivate food crops using modern agricultural techniques, and link this to the wider development agenda of the community. One of these officers, George Kumahlor, recounts a story from a community in the Volta Region. During one of his visits, he discovered the farm of a young man who cultivated commercial non-food crops. The young man claimed that cultivating food crops did not yield any benefits. George challenged him and other young people in the community to destroy the non-food crops and cultivate any food crops of their choice. He was prepared to guide them through scientific agricultural practices to produce and meet production targets the farmers would set. The young people in the community decided to cultivate maize. With the approved maize seeds, planting in rows, maintaining the correct distances between plants, weeding at the right time, and applying the right types of fertilizers in the right quantities and at the right time, the young people harvested more than three times their own estimated targets. This simple intervention turned around agricultural production in the community. Young people bought corn mills and built new houses from the proceeds of their farm products. Their contribution to development in the community became very significant. This was a major fruit of the growth of World Vision International.

In August 2020, I listened to the stories of Baba Alhassan and Comfort Sulemana with a lot of interest. Baba is a pastor of the Assemblies of God Church in Sowutuom, Accra. He recounted an evening in 1984/85 when he was a child. He was with the rest of the family shelling groundnuts when the new teacher in the village of Zangbalung Yipielgu, near Kumbungu in the Northern Region, came to the house to enroll one or two children from the family to the school that had been constructed with support from World Vision International. His father looked around and pointed at one of the children and told the teacher to write the name of this child called Baba. "He is very frail and is not strong enough to work in the farm for me." His mother broke down in tears because her child was going to be sent to school. Today, Baba has a first degree from the University of Cape Coast, is the Head Pastor of a Church and is the main breadwinner of the family.

In the case of Comfort Sulemana, also from Yipielgu, going to school was not as complicated as it was for Baba. Her father was a pastor in the community and knew the value of education. She now works mobilising funds for a rural bank in Tamale. From the Yipielgu Community Primary and Junior Secondary Schools, she went to Dalung Senior High School and later trained in Tamale Polytechnic. She now has a qualification in Accounting. I am told of Abubakar Ibrahim, a graduate of the University of Development Studies (UDS) in Tamale, from the same Yipielgu community, who is also currently teaching in a senior high school in Tamale.

I drove into Yipielgu in 1984 following a signboard to the church and this was the genesis of the project in the community. As in the three cases already given, there are several examples of the products of these schools all over the country in responsible private and public sector jobs. A young man studying for a diploma in monitoring and evaluation gave the growth of the day nursery that was started in 1988 in Bulpiela, a suburb of Tamale, as an example of successful community development work by World Vision. This was in the Ghana Institute of Management in Public Administration (GIMPA). After the lecture, one of his colleagues approached him and said: "I am a product of that school in Bulpiela". By the time I left World Vision in 1994, the organisation had supported the construction of educational infrastructure in at least 20 communities in northern Ghana and more than 100 in southern Ghana.

The work of the health and nutrition team had a major impact in project communities where they vaccinated children against the six killer diseases, i.e. measles, poliomyelitis, whooping cough, diphtheria, tuberculosis and tetanus. They also vaccinated pregnant women against tetanus. Through their guidance, World Vision supported communities to construct health infrastructure. In the north, I remember the construction of clinics in about 10 communities at the time I was leaving the organisation. I visited one of these clinics in 2015 and found out that it was now operating as a health centre manned by a qualified Medical Assistant.

The Communications department played a major role in telling the rest of the world what World Vision was doing in rural communities. By 1994 when I left, the department was producing periodic newsletters that wrote stories of success in rural communities for development partners. They also produced photographs of project activities for visitors to the World Vision offices in Ghana.

The growth in ICT saw the transition from manual typewriters to electric ones and then to computers. By 1994 all managers were computer literate, equipped with laptop computers and able to write their own reports. This enabled the staff of the organisation to stay in step with evolving technological advancement.

Through the consistent recruitment, training and capacity building of staff, World Vision in Ghana became a major human resource reservoir for the rest of Africa and indeed the world at large. This became so entrenched that in the year 2007, after one of the auditors, Emmanuel Osekre, retired he was still invited to work for the organisation in Haiti. I have counted more than 20 former staff of World Vision Ghana who moved on to play leadership roles in other World Vision offices and other development organisations outside Ghana.

The inclusion and growth of the Evangelism and Leadership Department (E&L) bore fruit in church growth in the communities where we worked. The E&L Assistance organised a series of pastors' conferences that built the capacity of church leaders in planning, organising and implementing Bible study and prayer programmes in their churches. This facilitated the process of enabling church members in the communities to establish a firm grounding in Scripture and achieve a greater understanding of their faith. The process further enhanced church growth leading to the same churches opening new branches in the same community to cope with the growth in numbers. The evangelism and leadership programme also enabled the pastors and church leaders to understand and engage in their roles in the development of the communities in which they were situated.

I must say here that the original Christian position of World Vision International as an organisation in Ghana was one reason for the significant impact in development in the country. Development was seen as a holistic ministry that engaged and was concerned about the spiritual and physical well-being of the person in the community. This approach is rooted in the Luke chapter 4 verse 6. "The Spirit of the Lord is on me, because he has anointed me to proclaim good news to the poor. He has sent me to proclaim freedom for the prisoners and recovery of sight for the blind, to set the oppressed free."

In 1993 and 1994, I worked closely with Emmanuel Opong and Victor Adom to refocus the development approach of World Vision to go beyond infrastructure development and facilitate community transformation. After working with the community of Oku Junction near Ejura in the Ashanti Region, World Vision supported the community to construct a primary school building. The events leading to the opening of that structure and subsequent events are among the best demonstrations of community transformation I have seen in my development career. Oku Junction is located in the Afram Plains of the Asante Region. One had to drive up the Mampong Scarp all the way to Ejura and drive down the mountain to the Afram Plains and then park the car and take a canoe to the eastern side of the Volta Lake. On this particular occasion, I was taken by the operations and technical support team of World Vision to Ejura where we passed the night. The following day we drove for three and a half hours to get to the river. We provided a car to bring the District Chief Executive to the project community.

The opening ceremony of the school was a spectacular affair. There were speeches by the community leaders, a representative of World Vision International and finally the District Chief Executive. The community leaders observed that since the independence of Ghana in 1957, this occasion was the first time a high-ranking government official at the level of a District Chief Executive had come to them. The only government officials that came to the community were tax collectors, officials of the electoral Commission and officials of their statistical services department coming to take the population census. After the ceremony, the community leaders requested a face-to-face meeting with the District Chief Executive without the participation of World Vision staff. They compelled the District Chief Executive to make the commitment that the district assembly would provide earth-moving equipment and civil engineers and the community members would provide the funds for the construction of a road from Ejura to the river. As a result of this initiative, within six months, it was possible to go from Ejura to Oku Junction in forty minutes. This was an actual demonstration of bringing the community members as rights holders to meet government officials who are duty bearers to discuss development issues. The transformation of the community from passive receivers of aid to active rights holders who actively involved every member of the community in their development and claimed their rights from duty bearers is one of the best fruits of the growth of World Vision International.

The Women in Development (WID) team organised workshops that brought women together to build their capacity to engage in cottage industries and earn money for their families. The skills learnt included food processing such as the processing of cassava to gari, bead making, the dyeing of cloth to make batik materials, processing of grains to produce highly nutritious blended flour for children. These were called Income Generating Activities (IGA), which is, however, a term I have never liked. I preferred to call them small business ventures because the absence of a business mind does not help in the profit-making of such ventures. Most of the women in World Vision Ghana enthusiastically got involved in these activities independently of their jobs in the organisation.

I have learnt that NGOs in Africa must see themselves only as facilitators of the development process who need to contribute resources to facilitate development. NGOs can never replace governments in any country. All that they need to do is support the government as duty bearers with resources and ideas and support communities as rights holders with resources and ideas and leave the development process to the two. The infrastructure and resources put at the disposal of the communities where World Vision had projects have all been handed over to district assemblies as duty bearers to enable them to continue the facilitation of development in these communities. World Vision also initiated the higher-level planning process for districts that engaged government ministries, departments and agencies, the private sector, civil society organisations and other stakeholders in the development of district plans. The evolution of development paradigms continues and every NGO is seeking to do its best in fighting poverty.

CHAPTER 20

PROJECT MANAGEMENT EYE-OPENER IN KENYA

I found my two work colleagues, Alfred Owusu and Stephen Nkrumah at the check-in hall of Kotoka International Airport, Accra, Ghana. This was in April 1985 and in those days, travellers could come into the baggage check-in area with as many people accompanying them as they wanted. Family members of Alfred and Stephen waited excitedly in anticipation as we checked in our baggage for an Ethiopian Airlines flight. We said our farewells, went through departure formalities and boarded the Ethiopian Airlines Boeing 757 aircraft en route to Nairobi. We were on our way to Kenya for project management training organised by the Christian Organisations Research Advisory Trust (CORAT).

We arrived in Nairobi by 6:00 am East African Time which was 3:00 am GMT. This was my first visit to East Africa and so many things surprised me. The first surprise was the weather. Unlike West Africa, Nairobi was very cold and everybody was dressed in a suit or a jacket. The second surprise was the skyline of Nairobi. There were these beautiful high-rise buildings crowned by the Jomo Kenyatta Conference Centre. We were taken to the Serena Hotel. Another surprise was the beauty of this hotel. I could not compare the hotels in Accra in those days such as the Ambassador Hotel, the Continental Hotel, and Star Hotel to Serena Hotel. (Continental Hotel is now Golden Tulip Hotel in Accra, Ambassador Hotel is now Movenpick Hotel and Star hotel is simply non-existent in this 21st-century.)

I asked myself several questions. Ghana was the first Sub-Saharan African country to gain independence. I know the three West African cities of Abidjan, Accra and Lomé. Of the three, I thought Abidjan was the best and most developed in terms of infrastructure and high-rise buildings. Nairobi seemed to be better than all three. But one has to ask whether infrastructure and high-rise buildings are the best indicators of development. This has been a debate in development study classes for decades. My six-week stay in Kenya showed that this was not necessarily the case.

We made our way into Nairobi city and got ourselves some warm clothes to guarantee our survival for our time in Kenya. The following day we were whisked out of Nairobi to Limuru where we were supposed to participate in the management training course. The travel to Limuru showed us a bit of the countryside of Kenya, another surprise for me. The farms were nicely demarcated and one could mistake the landscape and the farms for those in the United Kingdom. It was a meandering road with increasing altitude all the way to the training centre.

This six-week course taught us the key functions in project management including Planning, Organizing, Staffing, Directing and Controlling. We used biblical principles to understand each of these functions and used NGO development work as the practice ground for their applications. Since then, I have made the interesting discovery that every management function can be taught from a Biblical perspective. For example, the book of Nehemiah is the best teacher of the planning process, including Costing, Monitoring and Evaluation, Midterm Review, determination to complete the task ahead, the possibility of opposition while trying to complete the task and the need to divide the labour in such a way that the task succeeds despite every opposition. The visit of Jethro to the Israelites, who were in the desert on their way from Egypt to the Promised Land, is the best text for teaching delegation. During this visit, Jethro advised Moses not to do all the judgment of cases on his own but delegate people to handle less weighty cases (Exodus 18:14).

In group work, our various organisations' projects were used to understand the functions. There were participants from Sudan, Uganda and Kenya. I lamented that this was the course I should have been exposed to when I started my career as a development worker in 1981. I was four years behind time. Financial management was the other course that was done intensively by professional accountants. The use of examples from our development work back in Ghana in the group activities was the most valuable part of the training. Every evening ended with assignments and with Alfred and Stephen, we diligently worked on the assignments to enhance our learning and to be consistent in the presentation of the results to the facilitators. Day by day, as we went through different components of the course, I could identify the mistakes I had been making in starting the work of World Vision in Northern Ghana. It was too late but I definitely learnt many more skills to continue the rest of my career as a development worker.

The big lesson here for me is that any organisation that wants to get the best out of its employees must put training ahead of everything.

The food in the conference centre, particularly breakfast, was great. One of the surprising discoveries I made is the abundance of fresh milk in Kenya. This really enabled us to enjoy our breakfast and tea/coffee breaks. There was also a large supply of meat. Maize meal and vegetable stew (with lots of meat) became our most dominant meal for the course.

It was during this course that I wrestled with and internalised the meaning of integrity. After a long debate among participants, we agreed that integrity was the opposite of hypocrisy. With a high level of integrity, a person's words are consistent with his actions both in private and public. When the things we say contradict what we do, integrity is low and we tend to be hypocrites. This definition has stayed with me all my life. It was also in the training that I took time to study and have an in-depth understanding of accounting, financial management, reporting, bank reconciliation and the other intricacies of financial management of projects. The use of real-life project accounts from across Kenya made this study realistic and prepared me for subsequent areas of management in my development career.

Six weeks away from the hustle and bustle of development work in a quiet place like Limuru with two colleagues who were more experienced in life than myself was also a great opportunity to reflect and learn from others. That was one of the most precious times I have had in my life. One important product of the course in Kenya was the manuals and handouts that were carefully bound and given to course participants. These manuals have remained a part of my library collection and references anytime I want to go back and refresh my memory.

At the time that we were pursuing this training program, Kofi Hagan, the gentleman who convinced me to join World Vision International, was based in Nairobi from where he tried to establish the World Vision office in Uganda, which was at the time emerging from Civil War. A few weekends with Kofi's family in Nairobi enabled us to converse with him, enjoy the meals his wife provided for us, play with his children and to relax as Ghanaians in a foreign land.

Limuru was cold, indeed very cold by Ghanaian standards and there were no heaters in the rooms. This compelled us to wear several layers of clothing for going to bed as well as covering ourselves with two or three blankets. The mornings were so foggy that one could hardly see the tips of one's fingers on an outstretched hand. In same training centre, the staff of Barclays Bank from Nairobi were also having a training session. Smartly dressed young bank workers in the same place over a period of time is fertile ground for photography and my Manga survival instincts kicked into gear as I got hold of my camera with two zoom lenses and jumped into photographic work.

Those were the days when photography was done by photographers. Nowadays, as commented before, anybody with a mobile phone that has a camera can take good photographs. All the intricate settings we did in the 1980s are now done automatically. I started cautiously, taking photographs of participants of the CORAT course as well as participants in the Barclays Bank course. I then found my way back to Nairobi on the minibuses (called Matatus) that ran through the town and found a photographic lab where I handed over my film for processing. The following day, after the sessions at about 4 pm, I was on the minibus back to Nairobi to collect the printed photographs. In those days, colour photography was beginning to emerge in Accra but was the norm in Nairobi. My first photographs had drawn attention and kicked my photography business into high gear. Alfred and Stephen wondered how I managed to juggle the course with photography. I spent the break times and the end of sessions taking photographs of course participants. I adopted every position in order to get good shots with my zoom lenses – I knelt down, laid on the grass, squatted, climbed on top of chairs and employed every trick that I learned from Sam Buadu's studios back in Tamale. After fighting through leach-infected rice fields in Manga, this was definitely a better way of making money. This went on uninterrupted for six weeks. Six weeks of exciting management course and exciting photographic business were really great although tainted with the blistering cold of Limuru. On the very last day, before going to the airport to fly out of Kenya, I was still giving out photographs to clients.

The course organisers took us to Nairobi one day on a field visit to a slum area called Mathara Valley. Nothing has remained so strongly in my memory than this visit. We saw one of the poorest slums in Kenya and most likely in Africa. People used all types of materials to build shacks in which they lived with their families. I saw a one-day-old baby, wrapped in not the best of clothes, being laid on cardboard and tears came to my eyes. On television, I had watched photographers scrambling for space to take pictures of babies of celebrities. I asked myself what this baby did wrong to be born in a slum in Nairobi and what did the other babies do right to be born with silver spoons in their mouths. I concluded that we do not have any choice in deciding where we should be born, but after we have been born, we need to fight and struggle and accomplish something on this planet before we are called to our Maker. It was not my fault that I was born in Manga.

There are several lessons I learned during this training programme that have remained with me for life. One such lesson is that "he who fails to plan is planning to fail". This was a key principle used during the group discussions on strategic and operational planning. Another lesson is that "in staff placement, place staff in such a way that you make their weaknesses irrelevant and exploit their strengths for the best of the organisation".

The use of actual case studies from NGOs in Africa to facilitate group work had a special impact on me. In the first place, it demonstrated that our everyday working realities are indeed case studies. If all development workers looked at the realities as case studies, they would approach it with intellectual minds and not emotionally. If we all wrote our real experiences as case studies, there would have been a lot of resource materials to train upcoming development workers.

The training in project management in Kenya was an eye-opener for me. The examples and case studies from different organisations and from different countries demonstrated that project management has a commonality of issues across Africa. It also demonstrated that it is important to give all members of staff of development organisations some basic training before sending them off to confront the reality that is ahead of them. I remain so grateful to the facilitators and course participants who contributed significantly to open my eyes to development management.

My management practices and capacity building of other managers has benefited significantly from this course.

CHAPTER 21

TAKING STOCK TO CHART A NEW ROAD MAP

December 31st, 1988 will go down as an important night in my life. It is on that night I took the time to take stock of the whole of my life up to that point. The entire month of December is a vibrant month because of the Christmas festivities. Throughout the month, multiple activities are always going on, climaxing on the night of the 31st. Some of these activities include the buying of clothes (sometimes called "Christmas dress"), snacks and food items for entertaining visitors, firecrackers, toys and much more.

Food prices, especially the cost of chicken and meat, go up during this period, particularly in the last two weeks. This was the first time my family and I were spending Christmas in Accra. We somehow managed to survive the Christmas festivities and expenses until the last day of the month. At that time, a general trend followed by Ghanaians to celebrate the new year was either to watch different parts of the world on the television as they rolled into the new year or to go to church and pray into the new year.

In our home in Osu, Accra, we sat at home on the night of the 31st of December 1988 and did not go to church. The 14-inch television that we had bought a month earlier from the proceeds of the Honda 80 motorbike we sold in Tamale, sat in the corner waiting for us to switch on and follow the different parts of the world rolling into the new year. The first would be Australia, due to time differences, and then Tokyo in Japan and then on to Russia before coming to the European countries moving on to the USA and finally ending in Hawaii. Our church usually waited patiently for members to troop in to sing and dance, praising God for the past year, waving white handkerchiefs and praying into the new year. We did neither of the two.

I remembered the advice from my father. He said: "Never do things because everybody is doing them". This year, my wife and I decided that we were going to sit as a couple and take stock of our lives from the period we were single to the period we got married and look at our life as a family. We intended to develop a strategic plan with clear objectives that we could revise every year and follow for the next six years. I got hold of my notes on strategic planning that I had kept since 1985 from my course on project management in Kenya. At 8:30 p.m., we sat down to tackle the big issue of developing a family strategic plan.

This deviation from the normal annual routine was because of the events of the second half of the year 1988. In July 1988, I was informed by the headquarters of World Vision International, Ghana, that I was to be transferred from the Tamale sub-office to the headquarters in Accra. I was going to take up a new position while the regional manager of the western region sub-office, Clement Odia Mensah, was going to move from Takoradi to replace me in Tamale. The Greater Accra regional manager, Theodore Afari, would move from Accra to Takoradi. So in September 1988, I arrived in Accra with my family. This move was seen as strategic by the leaders of the organisation in Accra. However, it was seen by most of my friends, particularly outside World Vision International, as dramatic. For my family and me, it was a mixture of being dramatic, confusing and even catastrophic, but as a Christian family, we saw it as a "move" directed by the Lord and all we needed to do was to wait and pray patiently expecting that clarity would come and enable us to move forward. When a Christian is put into a situation which is seemingly against his or her will, there is a need to consider that this may also be God's way of leading into a new path in life.

As we moved into Accra, several things happened. The school fees for our two children went up sevenfold. Our house rent went up fivefold. Market prices went up by a factor that was difficult to calculate. Looking back, I saw that the situation I faced was like a well-fed lizard running up a tree being pursued by a hungry snake. The well-fed lizard was the market and prices around us and the hungry snake was my family. My wife left her job as a teacher in the Primary and Junior Secondary School in Bagabaga, Tamale and came to Accra where she did not have a job. The official car I used in Tamale was no longer available to me in Accra. I had the opportunity to drive my boss's car when he was away and I acted for him. Unfortunately, that car was taken from me immediately on a Friday night for non-official use. I was disappointed that I did not have the vehicle for the weekend. My seven-year-old daughter was deeply traumatised by this incident. I told myself that I was equally guilty of using an official car at the weekends for non-official activities. The bottom line is that the organisation did not have a clear policy on the use of official vehicles for private purposes.

I remember trying to walk from the office in Cantonments to my house in Osu. After Danquah Circle, a taxi nearly hit me when I forgot myself and walked into its way. The driver had to stand on his brakes to avoid ending my life. He jumped out of the car and rushed to find out whether I was alright. It looked as if I had acted like somebody who was completely out of his mind. He took my briefcase from me to his car, opened the passenger door and asked me to get in. I initially refused, but he did not seem to be giving me any choice. He asked where I was going and I mentioned the suburb. He told me he was taking me home and I did not need to pay. The gentleman drove me home and when I got out of the car, he did not even wait for a thank-you. Once again the Almighty God had come to my rescue.

My salary for August quickly disappeared before the middle of September. Then God once again came to my aid. A client for whom I had taken photographs for a project called and wanted me to produce 20 A4 copies of 25 photographs. I had taken these photographs a year earlier. This was a huge blessing from above. I had carefully kept the negatives of all photographs I had taken in a file. I spent the whole night locating this set of negatives. It looks as if the concept of photographic negatives has disappeared in recent times. This request prevented our immediate financial collapse but the recovery was quickly swallowed up by the 'climbing lizard'. With all this coming at us, we had no option but to sit up and think out of the box. There is a saying that doing the same thing over and over again and expecting a different result is equivalent to madness.

So on this final night of the year, we had decided to do something different. We started our planning process by laying down the various steps that would lead us to a complete strategic plan. My wife and I took time to reflect on the Biblical foundations of planning as documented in the book of Nehemiah. We also internalised the counsel of Jesus Christ to his disciples in Luke 14:28-30. Here Jesus asks which of them when planning to build a tower will not first sit down and count the cost before starting the construction. Otherwise, when he is midway through the construction he may not have enough resources to complete it and everybody would laugh at him. We also spent the time to pray for God's wisdom and guidance in the family strategy planning process.

We asked the questions such as: "Where are we coming from? Where are we now? Where do we want to go in the next six years? How will we get there?" This planning session took us all the way to 4:30 a.m. and the output was a plan with seven clear strategic objectives that we wanted to accomplish by the end of 1994. We would sit back again in a year's time, and have a look at how far we had gone in the accomplishment of these objectives. Then we would revise the objectives and work through them again for one year. This process was meant to be a revolving process that would last us for the rest of our lives. For the purpose of this narrative, I will document only the components of the discussion that concern me. I will leave the details of the other six strategic objectives for the family archives.

The analysis of "where am I coming from" took more than 2 hours and was alternately punctuated with laughter and tears. The response to the question, "where am I now", formed the backbone for determining the next steps in my life. In simple terms, at that time in 1988, I was a chemistry graduate with a professional qualification in education and therefore a professional chemistry teacher. However, the reality was that I had not taught anyone chemistry for seven years. Professionally, I was also a development worker who had been on the field facilitating development in several communities in northern Ghana and supporting my colleagues in other parts of the country. However, the only training I had received was a six-week course in Kenya on project management with a certificate that I could not really locate in the house. This analysis forced me to decide either to go back and teach chemistry where I had a professional qualification or seek a professional qualification in development.

The next question was "where do I want to go and how do I get there", specifically, what should I pursue in the next two to six years. We agreed that going back to teach chemistry was out of the question and that left the obvious choice - seek a professional qualification in development.

This strategic objective of acquiring an academic qualification in development required a number of activities. These included getting admission into a university that provided courses in development studies, getting a scholarship to acquire the postgraduate qualification, getting a study leave and spending time to pursue and acquire the postgraduate academic qualification in development.

The year 1989, therefore, started with clear activities to acquire a postgraduate academic qualification in development. I would describe the years 1989 to 1991 as the years of turbulence during which I searched and fought and worked hard to accomplish the strategic objectives that my wife and I had set ourselves in December 1988. For the singular objective of pursuing a postgraduate academic course in development I went into action searching for an academic institution that offered this. In those days there was no internet and the best place to look was in the libraries. I searched the Balme library in the University of Ghana, and the British Council and United States Embassy libraries. I took my time to write the names of the universities that offered courses in development studies. I found universities in the United Kingdom, USA, Canada, the Netherlands, India, Cameroon and others. I wrote to those universities and asked for brochures on the development courses they offered. It must have taken nearly a whole year to get all this information in combination with my regular work in the office. In the absence of computers and email, all the letters I wrote were handwritten or typed with a manual typewriter and posted to the various addresses. This meant that it took at least six to eight weeks to get a response to each letter. I finally settled on two universities with academic course and admission requirements that best suited my situation. These were the University of Bradford and the University of Birmingham both in the United Kingdom.

Meanwhile, life became tougher in Accra. My landlord harassed me to leave the house we were renting with the explanation that a nephew was coming back from Germany and he needed that accommodation. After leaving the house I noticed that for over six years nobody actually occupied it. I guess the nephew from Germany changed his mind and did not come home or there was never any nephew. While searching for the opportunity to study abroad, I figured out that the ability to use a computer would be paramount in the future. I therefore took on the extra task of getting to the office one hour before working hours and teaching myself to type. I bought a book on typing called "Typing Manual" and started this task. I remember asking Rev. Samuel Tigah to help me to learn how to use the manual typewriter without looking at the keyboard. I began to regret not paying attention during the typing lessons in Ghana College where we both had equal opportunities to learn typing.

By April 1990 I had been offered a place in the University of Bradford in the UK to pursue a Postgraduate Diploma in Development Studies. Then the search for a scholarship started. I got the names and addresses of scholarship awarding institutions across the world and sent letters to each of them. A few of them replied, regretting their inability to offer me any scholarships. The majority did not even bother to reply. It is often said that silence means consent. In this particular case, silence meant a resounding "No".

In the first quarter of 1991, the Ghana Association of Private Voluntary Organisations in Development (GAPVOD) nominated World Vision International as a beneficiary of one of its scholarships offered by the British council. The Head of Operations at the time, G S K Adzokpa, nominated me to benefit from this scholarship. I finally breathed a sigh of relief, relaxed and started thinking of going to the University of Bradford to study for a Postgraduate Diploma in Development Studies.

The biggest lessons I have drawn from this experience are the following. It takes individual initiative and courage to depart from existing activities in one's environment. It took courage and initiative not to attend the normal New Year's Eve church services and focus instead on our family strategic plan. Secondly, many of us learn effective principles and procedures from work but we never think of implementing them in our personal and family lives. Strategic planning is employed by a lot of people in their jobs but it is rarely applied with their own families. Finally, when one has planned and made objectives it takes persistence and determination to follow them through to the end. We took a decision on the 31st of December 1988 and it took us until the third quarter of 1991, more than two and a half years later, for us to begin to see progress in what we had planned. It may take a long time but with planning, persistence, prayer and reflection, it will come to pass. I believe that for the Christian individual, family or community, the process of Bible-based reflection, prayer for wisdom and vision and carefully worked-out planning is a cyclic process that should be employed periodically to ensure progressive living.

CHAPTER 22

EN ROUTE TO THE COMMONWEALTH GAMES

The dates 24th January to the 3rd of February 1990 will remain in my memory as the period when I was part of the Commonwealth Games held in Auckland, New Zealand. This was amazing because I have never done any serious sporting activity in my life. In fact, when I told a colleague that I had a commonwealth games medal he asked whether it was in a Bow and Arrow competition (Traditional Archery). Those who know me well know that the only game I play is Scrabble.

The circumstances leading to my being part of this sports festival in New Zealand are very intriguing. In January 1989, the Ghana Office of World Vision International received an invitation from the New Zealand office of the organisation to be part of an innovative fundraising programme. The Commonwealth Games that brought together athletes and sportsmen and women from former colonies of the British Empire to compete was going to be held in Auckland, New Zealand in January 1990. World Vision New Zealand wanted to bring together young people from around the world to perform in the opening and closing ceremonies of the games. They would also hold concerts around the country with the aim of raising funds for immunisation against the six killer diseases in developing countries.

I must say that this is one of the most novel fundraising strategies and plans I have seen in my development career. Sources of funding for projects and operations of Non-Governmental Organisations (NGOs) include major development partners such as The Bretton Woods Institutions (The World Bank and International Monetary Fund), the UN body, Bilateral Development Partners and other foundations and individuals. For funding from individuals, several NGOs use an approach called Child Sponsorship. With this approach, donors are enlisted with the organisation and promise to give a certain amount of money to the organisation every month over a period of time, say 5 to 10 years. The amount could just be $20 every month. In exchange, the donor is given the photograph and background information of a child from a developing country. The donor is given to understand that the money is directed towards the development of the community in which the child lives. This was the model of child sponsorship in operation when I worked for World Vision International, Ghana between 1981 and 1994.

It is possible that this model has changed over time. The important part of the model is that a donor gives a comparatively small amount of money on a regular basis to develop the community of a child and has constant updates on the welfare of the child. The donor or sponsor receives at least three forms of communication each year including a Christmas letter, an Easter letter and an annual report. Several sponsors communicate once a while with their children but I have seen a few sponsors who write a letter to their sponsored child almost every month.

The arrangement by World Vision New Zealand to participate in the opening and closing ceremonies of the Commonwealth Games in Auckland was very well thought through. It was also very strategic thinking to find out how to take advantage of a big global festival. The Ghana office of World Vision, therefore, had a task to select six young people and a chaperone and take them to New Zealand to be part of this programme. I was privileged to be given the task of implementing this programme. It involved finding and preparing six young people between the ages of 12 and 16 with skills in dancing and drumming. I accepted the task and waited for detailed instructions from New Zealand.

I wrote out a detailed work plan on what to do from day one until the end of the games and the return to Ghana. This was a real test of operational planning. I took several days to outline all the activities and sub-activities that had to be done from the planning stage, participation in the programme and return to Ghana including follow-up activities afterwards. It was outlined in a spreadsheet with five columns. The first column had the activities and sub-activities in chronological order. The second column had detailed timelines and the third and fourth columns had the exact completion date and comments. I got this detailed plan reviewed by my boss and approved for action. It was also shared with the New Zealand Office. This Operational Work Plan was going to be the main document for my monthly reports throughout the period of the programme.

The first step was to ensure that this programme was known by the Ministry of Education and the Ghana Teaching Service because children of school age were involved. The ministry kindly gave us a letter of introduction to any school we wanted to engage. This was easier said than done and the back-and-forth visits to collect the letter of introduction took a whole month. I anticipated this delay and it did not distort the timelines in my work plan.

Since we did not have in-house expertise in dancing and drumming, the next task was to find out where we could outsource the training of the young people. Naturally, we went to the Performing Arts Faculty of the University of Ghana. With my boss, Edward Opare Saforo, we met Professor Nketiah, who kindly agreed took ask his senior staff to assist us in the project. We were assisted from the University of Ghana by Nii Yartey and his assistant Mr. Amu.

Next was the identification of young people in the age bracket specified with skills in dancing and drumming who were in schools within Accra. With the very long timeframe for required training, it only made sense to select participants from within the city of Accra. In fact the travel & communication difficulties of bringing together participants from other parts of the country ruled out any other options. We noticed that we had taken the right step in seeking external assistance because these experts were deeply involved in the selection of the participants. We carried out auditions in the Presbyterian Junior Secondary school in Osu, Accra Academy and Bawaleshi Junior Secondary School near Legon. After a long and successful series of auditions, we ended up with seven participants made up of four boys and three girls. We thought it wise to have one extra performer as a backup until two months to departure from Ghana.

We received a package of detailed instructions containing the music to be played during the opening and closing ceremony of the festival as well as choreography instructions on the dance moves to be performed by the children. Indeed, this was the first time I saw dance choreography written on paper. It looked completely meaningless to me and I believe it would look the same to anybody who did not have professional training in Performing Arts. I was amazed when our experts in the university read the instructions and turned what looked like unintelligible marks on paper into dance moves in step with the music on the cassette. I remember the song on the audio cassette was "Man in the Mirror" by Michael Jackson.

Parallel to the selection and training of the children I had to raise funds from both the public and private sector to pay for all the expenses involved in the preparation and travel to New Zealand. The fundraising lasted all the way to the end of the year. Obtaining passports for the participants was a major item in the activity list as this took more than a month to be completed. Air New Zealand agreed to carry the participants either from London or Johannesburg to Auckland. This was during the apartheid era in South Africa and therefore transit from Johannesburg was out of the question. There were no flights from Ghana, or the rest of Africa for that matter, into South Africa because of sanctions. This was one of the hidden impacts of the apartheid regime in South Africa on non-political events. We got support from Ghana Airways to carry the participants from Accra to London. We also received support from World Vision Great Britain to take the passports of the participants and process visas for New Zealand.

One major item in the activity plan was the acquisition of local musical instruments such as a xylophone, drums and various percussion instruments. Another item was the purchase of Ghanaian dance costumes. As part of the preparation, the children were trained to perform various traditional dances from across Ghana. The drummers also learnt the different drumming styles to match the dances. The dances learnt included Bawaaa from the Upper West region, Takai and Bamaya from the Northern Region, Booboobo and Agbadzaa from the Volta region, Adowa from the Ashanti region as well as Gawu and Kpaaloogo from the Greater Accra region. It was really impressive to see how the two drummers developed their skills in drumming for the different dances across Ghana. We had to purchase all the musical instruments and the costumes required to perform these dances.

Everything went according to plan with a few adjustments here and there. In the second week of January 1990, I found myself in the airport in Accra with four young men and two young ladies waiting to board a Ghana Airways flight from Accra to London. The departure from Kotoka International Airport in Accra was a very emotional one. Parents and relatives of the children came to the airport to see them off. They were allowing their children aged between 12 and 16 to travel abroad accompanied by one man they had only just come to know.

During the last days of the training, the trainer and I made efforts to explain to these children that the weather would be cold in Europe and in New Zealand. I have come to learn that temperature cannot be imagined. It can only be experienced. This thinking became reality during our trip.

Two of the young men were drummers and two were dancers while the two young ladies were also dancers. With a metal trunk full of dancing costumes and a wide array of drums and musical instruments we boarded Ghana Airways and started our long journey to Auckland.

We arrived in London Heathrow Airport, to be greeted unkindly by the winter cold of the UK. The temperature was in single digits. I cannot remember whether it was 4 or 6 degrees Celsius. The children turned and looked at me as if to say "Is this what you meant?" Yes. This is what single-digit temperatures feel like. One of the few habitable places in Ghana where one could experience what might locally be thought of as wintry temperatures is Abetifi, in the Kwahu Mountains, and even there it is rare for the temperature to drop below 20°C.

The first drama started in London. A World Vision UK staff member called Claire cheerfully met us at Heathrow airport. Her cheerfulness was great but I am not sure it had any impact on the winter temperature and my group of children who were shivering all over. We got into the London Underground expecting to make the necessary connections to our hotel in Central London. We agreed that our host should be at the front of the party while I remained behind to ensure that we kept the children together. At the first attempt to change in an underground station our host got out of the train followed by four of the young people and the door of the train closed, leaving me in it with two of them. The train was gone in a flash. I had experience of the London and Paris underground systems in 1980, so I had a bit of a clue as to what to do next. We got out of the train at the next stop. I simply took out the reception package I was given and located the hotel we were supposed to go to and the nearest tube station to the hotel. With this information in hand, I made my way with the two children to the hotel. In panic mode, our host telephoned the World Vision office in London to report that she had lost me and two of the children. She was told that I had some experience of the London Underground system so she should head back to the hotel and wait for me. By the time she got to the hotel, I was there with the two other children. Trying to figure out what to do in difficult circumstances during my childhood days definitely came handy on this occasion.

We had two days of rest in London before starting the long flight to Auckland. We had four rooms in the hotel. The six children were to pair up in three rooms and I had a room to myself. In reality, all of them crowded into my room and the heating was turned up to create a room temperature that was almost equivalent to the temperature of Accra. These were Ghanaian children, who had lived in Accra all their lives, in the middle of London for the first time. They were understandably in a state of bewilderment and panic. The World Vision Office in the United Kingdom made an effort to entertain the team with a visit to Madame Tussauds Wax Museum in London and Buckingham Palace to see the changing of the guards. This gave the children a lot of exposure.

The day of the travel from London to Auckland arrived. These children had never travelled by air before and now after a six-hour flight from Accra, they were going to get on a 25-hour flight from London Gatwick Airport to Auckland with a two-hour stopover in Los Angeles. The Air New Zealand Boeing 747 aircraft lifted off from Gatwick with nearly 500 passengers on board. Onboard the same flight was the Scotland and England Commonwealth Games teams who started the journey quietly but increased their noise levels all the way to Los Angeles.

The 2-hour stop in Los Angeles was my first time of setting foot on the soil of the United States of America and it quickly told me one big difference between the USA and the rest of the world. At the airport, there was a cafe with the sign "We serve a bottomless cup of coffee". There I discovered that a medium-sized mug in the USA is equivalent to the large-sized mug in the UK. Everything was just bigger in comparison to what I knew. A waiter made sure I never saw the bottom of my mug when I ordered and sat down to drink a cup of coffee. The cup was indeed bottomless.

After the two-hour stopover, we had the next leg of our journey - a 13 hours and 10 minutes flight from Los Angeles to Auckland. Two or three of the athletes were celebrating their birthdays and they made sure that they enjoyed it to the fullest, assisted by the Air New Zealand Crew. Flying over the International Date Line was very confusing. I tried as hard as I could to explain this to the children during the stopover in Los Angeles. I am not sure I was successful and I wish I had listened more carefully to my geography teacher in Ghana College. We flew out of London on a Friday evening and into the night. We arrived in Auckland on Sunday morning having passed only one night during the flight. Saturday had simply disappeared into oblivion.

The arrival in Auckland presented the second dramatic moment. Skin and wood products are not normally allowed into Auckland but one cannot talk about Ghanaian music and dances without skins and wood products. My drummers were not prepared to let go of their instruments and the New Zealand immigration was not prepared to let them into the country. The letter of introduction from World Vision New Zealand helped a lot and we came to a compromise that the skin and wood products would be quarantined in the airport for 3 days and fumigated before being released to us. The drummers reluctantly agreed to this but after three days in Auckland, they were reunited with their beloved instruments.

Participation in the opening and closing ceremony of the Commonwealth Games and in concerts across the country was a whole new experience with expert organisation by the World Vision New Zealand staff.

CHAPTER 23

PERFORMING TO SAVE LIVES

I had arrived in New Zealand with two drummers, Premier Kumedzro and Kwasi Futukpor, and four dancers, Joseph Mireku, Seth Asomanin, Ritna Otoo and Akweley.

If I thought that preparing to bring these six young people from Ghana to New Zealand was a great accomplishment, I was wrong. After seeing what the organising team in New Zealand accomplished, I realised that what I did was nowhere near their organisation of the programme.

The lady at the head of the organising team was Bronwyn McConchie. Throughout the nearly one year of preparation, she responded to all messages I sent to her within 12 hours. I now realised that she and her team were doing the same amount of communication with 21 other countries. Then the logistics of arrival in Auckland, New Zealand meant that she had to organise airport transfers for about 154 people from 22 countries. Beyond that was the question of hosting the participants.

It would have been quite easy if all the participants were sent to a hotel. The reality was that the participants were hosted with over 60 families across the city. Then there was a comprehensive programme of rehearsals before the opening ceremony of the games, with the host families responsible for transporting their guests to and from the rehearsal points. The organisers, through careful planning, turned what could have been a logistic nightmare into lessons on operational planning and execution.

The children and chaperones who participated in this programme came from several countries including Scotland, Canada, the United States of America, Australia, New Zealand, Vanuatu, Solomon Islands, Western Samoa, Papua New Guinea, Fiji, India, Singapore, Hong Kong, Kenya, Tanzania, Uganda, and Zimbabwe.

The first event that impressed me the most was the bringing together of the children from 23 different countries to perform the choreographed dance moves they had learnt in their separate countries. They had rehearsed these dance moves several times and the choreography notes were the same for all the countries, so when they came together it looked as if they had been rehearsing together for months.

The experience taught me one basic lesson. That there is a universal language for choreography that can be understood across the world independent of nationality. When communication is clear and understood across multiple languages and cultures, a lot of great cooperation and coordination can take place between people.

The next big event was the sequencing of traditional dances from all these countries with each given only 3 minutes to come on stage to perform and get off the stage. This sequencing was rehearsed several times before the actual concert started. The Ghanaian group limited themselves to the performance of one of three northern Ghanaian dances. The three dances were Bawa from the Upper East Region, and Takai and Bamaya from the Northern Region. The children argued that these were very fast dances that could be performed in less than 2½ minutes and would have the necessary impact on the audience. Interestingly none of these children was from the northern regions of Ghana. The communications department of World Vision New Zealand quickly noticed that they could use Ghanaian dancers for advertisement on television and the young people enjoyed doing this to the fullest.

The opening ceremony of the games on the 24th of January 1990 was the biggest live spectacle I had ever witnessed in my life. This ceremony was held in the Mount Smart Stadium in Auckland with a capacity of 45,000. The ceremony started with performances from a large number of actors from New Zealand backed by the New Zealand choir with about 160 members. The performers re-enacted what they believed to be the creation of the Pacific Ocean and the creation of the island of New Zealand. They then followed up with the arrival of the Maoris who came to the island using huge wooden canoes. Then they portrayed the arrival of the Europeans from several countries in Europe and then the arrival of the Indians. This performance was definitely well choreographed with different colours of clothes used to depict the sky, the ocean and the arrival of the different people.

Then it was time to welcome Prince Edward who came to represent Queen Elizabeth II in the opening ceremony. The Prince proceeded to the arena and then Maori warriors came out to welcome him. It is difficult to interpret the performance of the Maori warriors as a welcoming party. The voice of their leader, which was basically a deep baritone, boomed over the loudspeaker system as the warriors sang Maori songs with menacing faces and warlike positions, holding spears that literally appeared to threaten the prince. Anybody who has seen the performance of the *Haka* by New Zealand rugby players, the All Blacks, before rugby matches will understand what I am talking about. The warriors finally sent one of their members to place an object in front of the Prince. If the prince picked up the object it meant he was coming in peace; if he did not it meant he was here for war. Representatives of the Prince picked up the object to signify a peaceful visit. The leader of the Maoris addressed the Prince, still in the Maori language with interpretation. Finally, the Prince had the opportunity to address the opening ceremony. The message from the Queen for the opening ceremony was delivered to the prince and he read this to the audience.

Athletes from 55 commonwealth countries participated in the games. This was nine more than the previous highest number of countries participating. The prince stood on the dais, waving at the athletes from all 55 countries. Most of the countries were led by a previous Olympic games medalist. The Ghanaian contingent was led by Ritna Otu, one of the girls I chaperoned from Ghana. She proudly carried the Ghana flag in front of the Ghanaian athletes. She was dressed in traditional Ghanaian kente cloth which was part of our costume that we had brought from Accra.

The Commonwealth Games flame then arrived in the stadium carried by Sebastian Coe, a former Commonwealth Games gold medalist. The flame had been carried from Buckingham palace through several countries to New Zealand and then by a relay of runners through the North and South Islands, finally arriving on the games scene just at the right time. The photography of the events was very impressively done with cameramen on the rooftops of the stadium, some on the ground to catch close-ups of athletes and other performers and two spectacular photographers in two helicopters that hovered above the stadium to provide a complete panoramic view of the stadium.

The arrangement of loudspeakers around the stadium was also unique. The microphone systems must have been unobtrusively placed on the bodies of the actors and every sound they made boomed through the speakers. From the stadium, it was sometimes better to watch on the giant screen installed there. The children who were brought by World Vision did a spectacular performance on the arena accompanied by the booming sound of the music that played in the background. I told myself that finally, this was the day for which I had been preparing, for nearly one year.

There were over 130 children from all 23 countries spread across the Central Arena of the Commonwealth Games stadium and they moved and performed choreographed dance movements as if they had been training together for months. This lasted for nearly 20 minutes and was a really captivating sight to behold. The message that ran across the screens was that while these games were going on the world should be aware that several children every day in the developing world died from childhood killer diseases that could have been prevented by simple immunisations. This message would reach millions of people who were watching the games on television all around the world, challenging them to do something to prevent such needless deaths.

At the end of the opening ceremony of the Games, the children who were brought to New Zealand by World Vision proceeded on a tour of the North and South islands of the country. I remember we held concerts in Hamilton, Rotorua, Willington, Dunedin, and Christchurch. In all these cities the children and their chaperones were hosted by families. This actually enabled us to see the reality of the lives of sponsors who contributed to World Vision programmes around the world. The sponsors were ordinary people. One of the sponsors I lived with during the tour was actually a single parent. It made me very aware that development work in developing countries was being carried out with contributions by people who were not necessarily wealthy. This was indeed a sobering experience.

During each concert, children from each country came on stage and performed a traditional dance from that country, and then left the stage within the time frame of 3 minutes. In all the concerts, every single seat was booked and the crowd applauded as different groups came on stage to perform. The team from Ghana performed one of three northern dances throughout the concerts. It was amazing to see children from the southern part of Ghana, play wonderfully on the xylophone, sing in Dagaare and Dagbani while dancing to the tunes like natives. This made me believe that tribal divisions may just be artificial divisions which can be overcome. My music experience came in handy as I played the flute sound of the keyboard from backstage to mimic the sound of Dagomba wind instruments and accompanied the Takai and Bamaya performances.

All the concerts were climaxed by a message about immunisation in the developing world. I was one of the presenters who had two minutes to communicate a strong message to the audience to contribute to immunisation in the developing world. I had a very simple message. My mother had 10 pregnancies and 9 live births. Of the nine births, only four of us survived beyond the age of 5 years. The rest of my siblings died from simple diseases that could have been prevented by immunisation. My story is not uncommon in the developing world and some families have suffered far worse. At the time of our presentation, we needed about 5 US dollars to immunise a child against the six killer diseases. The situation at the time I was born had not changed significantly by 1990. World Vision had projects in developing countries and all that they needed was donations from the audience to be able to respond to and immunise children below the age of five so that they would have an opportunity to live beyond that age. Other members of the team made similar appeals during concerts. The response to our funding appeal was overwhelming and it enabled World Vision New Zealand to raise a significant amount of money for immunisation in developing countries. For me, it was a huge accomplishment to be part of this fundraising innovation. The children from Ghana also held street performances of drumming and dancing that were filmed and used as adverts on TV New Zealand.

Travelling through the North and South Islands of New Zealand provided an interesting tourism opportunity. Rotorua was the most interesting city to visit. Entering the city, one noticed the foul smell that resembled that of rotten eggs. Indeed, this was actually the smell of compounds of sulphur in the air. The city was full of hot water springs scattered everywhere. There was actually a hot water geyser that threw up hot water into the air every 55 minutes. It brought the theoretical geography I had learnt in Ghana College to life. Apart from the geographical features of Rotorua we were able to visit farmers in other cities where the rearing of sheep and cattle was common.

Nearly four weeks of travelling and performing dances together created a strong bond between the children in each country and between children from different countries. At the end of this magnificent programme, we had to return to Ghana through Los Angeles and London once again. The interesting part of the return journey is the fact that we flew out of Auckland, New Zealand on a Tuesday night, flew into Monday and arrived in Los Angeles on Tuesday morning. This was literally like having two Tuesdays. The one day we lost on our way into New Zealand was regained on our way back to the UK and to Ghana. Back in Ghana, it was evident that we had given these children a hugely memorable experience. I was sure that it would influence them for the rest of their lives.

CHAPTER 24

IN THE MIDST OF THE POLICY-REALITY DEBATE

It must have been in the second quarter of 1991. Three powerful personalities from the international office of World Vision in the USA arrived at the Ghana office in Accra. In my village, there is a saying that "the calibre of the visitor can change the quality of the soup". These three were definitely soup-changing visitors. They included a Senior Human Resource (HR) executive, a highly placed Legal Advisor, and the Sub-Regional Director for West Africa. Their arrival created tremors in the office with the grapevine experiencing a lot of the shocks and aftershocks that ran from the roots to the leaves. Some of the news was blemished with exaggerations and some fell short of the reality. Apparently, something had gone terribly wrong in the Ghana office of World Vision International, and this delegation was here to put things right.

I sat down with hands between my thighs as one of the members of the team formed to meet the high calibre delegation from the international office. I have been constantly reminded recently that I was the leader of the team during that meeting. I have no idea how this came about. Many people have quoted what I said on that day back to me but I know that I did not prepare a speech. It must have been a divine thought that led me into the speech that I made on that day.

The legal expert from the International Office held a document in his hand and told us that claims for End-Of-Service Benefits based on that document could not be respected because the document itself was illegal. I recognised the document; it was the HR manual of the organisation in Ghana. I raised my hand and said that I had worked for World Vision International since 1981. I was recruited into the organisation based on the contents of the policy document being held up by the legal expert. When I joined, I had been obliged to sign that I had read and understood the contents of the document. I had come to work at 8:00 am in the morning and closed at 5:00 pm based on the contents of the policy document. All other staff members of the organisation had done exactly the same as me. World Vision International had registered as an NGO based on that document. To say that the document was illegal meant that the organisation had been operating in Ghana illegally for more than 10 years and all the employees had been working illegally throughout the lifespan of their work with the organisation. Members of the delegation took a deep breath, and as one of my colleagues put it, they were immediately deflated and had to come down to reality.

If my intervention in the meeting was divinely inspired, the next part of my presentation was divinely arranged. I said that the international office of World Vision and the staff of World Vision Ghana had now found ourselves in a conflict situation. We could easily take positions and argue our cases for a long period of time and come to no conclusion. On the other hand, it would be better to abandon entrenched positions that placed us on opposite sides of the table and rather isolate the problem by placing ourselves on the same side.

We should concentrate on our interests instead of our positions, and in our discussions, if we focused on satisfying the interests of both parties, we would come to a solution that would be win-win for both of us and not a win-loss situation. At this point, the senior HR executive got off his seat to come and shake my hand and said that he thought we had been reading the same book. Indeed, this was not simple wisdom from Samuel Braimah. Three months before this incident, I had strayed into Challenge Bookshop and bought a book entitled "Getting to Yes" written by Roger Fisher and William Yuri. It was about the art of negotiation. I had read this book diligently without knowing that I would have to apply it anytime in my life. My suggestion for the way forward to the team of experts was basically what I had learnt from the book.

The genesis of this episode goes back all the way to 1979/1980 when World Vision International started work in Ghana. In order to register as an organisation, there was a need to present some basic documentation and the HR manual was one of the requirements, so World Vision Ghana presented the document which was now in dispute. I am not sure whether it was called a Human Resource Manual or a Personnel manual. This manual, like every normal HR manual, referred to World Vision Ghana as the employer and staff as the employees. The manual detailed everything about Human Resource Management from recruitment, remuneration, different types of leave, promotion, discipline, exit from the organisation, etc. There was also a clause in the manual concerning retirement. According to this clause, any member of staff retiring would have End-Of-Service Benefits equivalent to three months' salary multiplied by the number of years of service. All staff, at the time of their recruitment, were obliged to sign that they had read and understood the contents of the HR manual. This looks simple enough. The magnitude of this policy was never in dispute until a senior management staff member who had been with the organisation for 10 years or more was about to retire. The retirement of this individual would require a payment of more than 30 months salary to be made. I remember one of the members of the international office delegation saying that if this policy was really correct, he would prefer to come and take a job in the Ghana office and retire from here. The big mistake the Ghana office made was that this policy document was never taken through the approval process for deliberation and signing by the right authorities. This meant that the Ghana office of World Vision was working and holding onto a policy document that was not approved until the reality dawned on everybody.

In an effort to identify the root causes of this problem, one can easily see a number of ways by which this scenario of policy hiatus could have been avoided. In the first place, the leadership of the organisation could have followed up on the approval process for the HR policy document, all the way to the top hierarchy in the international office and got it approved and signed. This could have led to a renegotiation of the draft and arrival at a mutually acceptable policy document, that would benefit staff, and at the same time not bring the international office into a confrontation with them. Secondly, a periodic policy review process, that is put in place to review all national office policies, say every two or three years, would have revealed this lacuna and responded to it appropriately. Obviously, this did not happen for more than 10 years. Sadly, there was no clear understanding of purchasing power parity on the side of the international office. While a month's salary for a worker in the US sounds like a lot of money, the same for a worker in Ghana at that time was not as big as they imagined. International organisations need to contextualize what they mean by the figures they mention in policy documents. Obviously, the international staff who joked about taking a job in Ghana and retiring on generous terms would not have accepted what a Ghanaian staff member, with qualifications and experience equivalent to his, was paid.

I cannot remember the details of the negotiations after this initial explosive meeting. But I know that the negotiations went on in a way to ensure that the staff interest was taken care of without breaking down the finances of the organisation. Policy and reality can be very different things. I found myself sitting in the midst of the two, and by divine intervention successfully led the process to a fruitful end.

Learning from this experience, when I found myself in a leadership position as a Country Director of an NGO in another country, I made sure of three things. Firstly, a lawyer recruited as HR Manager received further training in Human Resource management. Secondly, an external lawyer was engaged on a retainer and I made sure that he had a legal opinion on every HR document and meticulously read every letter coming out of the HR department. He also represented my organisation in every legal case. I took the time to familiarise myself with the common international HR policies of the organisation and the labour laws of the country in which I was working. Finally, periodic reviews of policy documents ensured that we stayed in step with evolving HR policy issues in the organisation and labour law changes in the country.

Labour issues in Africa are very dynamic and anybody who wants to play a leadership role in development work must keep their eyes on policy documents to ensure that they stay abreast of changing trends.

CHAPTER 25

ON THE HIGH TIDES IN SWANSEA

My nomination by the Head of Operations to be awarded a scholarship to pursue a postgraduate diploma in development studies in the University of Bradford under-1991/92 academic year was a straightforward route to the accomplishment of my strategic plan. However, the route did not turn out to be as straightforward as it looked in the beginning.

After my nomination, I collected the relevant forms which I completed and submitted to the offices of the Ministry of Foreign Affairs that was responsible for managing scholarships. That was when things got started. By the end of July 1991, I was beginning to get a bit anxious. There was absolutely no news from the ministry and I did not know where to go to ask for more information about the progress of my application. What happened next can only be described as a miracle and a defining turning point in this account.

I was invited to provide photographic coverage for a wedding in Nima, a suburb in Accra. During this wedding, I met a former Minister of State whom I had met only once in1988. During our first meeting, he recognised me as a member of staff of World Vision who had done some work in his hometown. I, however, did not recognise him and after a short exchange, he directed me to where he worked and said if I ever needed any help, I could call on him. So, at the wedding, I went to greet him and he remarked that he had not heard from me in three years. I apologised for not ever calling on him but told him I had a problem now. After describing my dilemma to him, he promised to go with me to the offices of the Ministry of Foreign Affairs to help find out what had gone wrong with my application. At the offices of the ministry, we discovered that the application forms had simply disappeared. I was made to complete fresh application forms and the process started all over again. And then another period of waiting started.

It was in September 1991 that things really started moving, and moving very fast. I was called to the British Council where I was told that my scholarship application had been considered and the British Council wanted to offer me a scholarship to study in the University of Swansea for a Master's degree in Economic and Social Development. I had planned to go to the University of Bradford to pursue a diploma course in development studies and now I was being given a scholarship to go to the University of Swansea to pursue a masters degree in social and economic development. I was getting a better deal than I had imagined. I was given the application forms for the program in Swansea as well as United Kingdom student visa application forms. I completed all the necessary forms and submitted them and then started another round of waiting. But these were definite signs that I was making headway. Three days after this I was called back to the British Council. My passport was taken from me and I was given an admission letter from the University of Swansea. I was given the scholarship letter from the British Council covering my tuition and boarding in the UK for one year, and I was told to call at the British High commission at 2:15 p.m where I was given back my passport with the visa.

So now, I had the scholarship to study in the UK, admission into the University of Swansea, a visa covering a one-year period as a student in the UK and an air ticket to fly out of Accra that very night. Things were moving just too fast for my understanding. In the attempt to get back home, pack and go to the airport, I had to drive by the old Post Office building in Jamestown. I was driving behind a commercial passenger minibus known as a 'trotro' when all of a sudden it stopped and the driver jumped out, came to bang on my car and told me not to move. People seemed to be running all over the place. I had no clue what was happening and was honestly a little frightened. Then somebody opened my passenger door and put my small bag onto my lap and shouted "please take good care of your money".

What? How did my bag get out of the car? This bag had all my money, my passport, air ticket, scholarship letter, admission letter and basically all the important documents I needed to travel. A thief had stolen the bag from the backseat of the car while I was stationary because of the traffic jam on the road. He had been seen by the trotro driver and other pedestrians and the commotion happening was because they were chasing down the thief. I was shocked to the bone.

But for the timely intervention of those good Samaritans who saw what happened and intervened, the dream of flying out of Ghana that night to the UK would have ended in the hands of a thief in Accra. I managed to get my composure and get back home without incident. I packed up whatever I could into a suitcase and arrived at the airport by 8:00 p.m.

The check-in to board the British Airways flight to London was quite smooth and I said a big goodbye to my family and friends and headed for the boarding gate. We got into the aircraft and after sitting in there for nearly half an hour, all passengers were told to disembark. What was it this time, I wondered! First, my forms had disappeared in the Ministry of Foreign Affairs and that got corrected. Secondly, my passport, ticket, money and everything had got hijacked by a thief and that was dramatically resolved with the help of some smart keen observers. And when I thought we would be airborne in a few minutes we were told to disembark. We were taken to the departure lounge and every passenger was given an individual letter before a public announcement that due to circumstances beyond the control of the airline, the flight had been postponed. Apparently, one of the tyres of the undercarriage of the aircraft needed to be replaced, and the only machine that could hold the aircraft up while the tyre was being replaced, was not in Ghana. Passengers who had personal telephone numbers were requested to give their numbers to the airline and go home and await further instructions. Passengers who did not have any personal telephone numbers were to proceed to a bus waiting outside and be taken to a hotel for the night. We were assured that we would not be leaving Accra before 10:00 a.m.

I was definitely among the passengers who did not have a personal telephone number and so I was taken to a hotel where another round of waiting started. The following day, in the late afternoon, I got a call from the hotel reception to make my way to a bus that would take us back to the airport. Finally, we flew out of Accra and I breathed a big sigh of relief. This was the beginning of my journey to Swansea for a fresh start.

Arriving in London at the official invitation of the British government is the best thing that can ever happen to anybody. Passing through immigration was the smoothest I had ever had. When I walked out of arrivals, there was a British Council staff member holding a placard with my name waiting for me. I was warmly welcomed into a warm London which was actually very cold by Manga standards. And then to a nearby coffee shop where my host spent some time giving me the necessary documentation and instructions on how to get to Swansea. She also handed me a one-way ticket to Swansea and my stipend for the first month as well as the necessary arrival allowances.

Using the UK's railway system, I went through a number of complicated transfers that took me from the British Railway (BR) system to the London Underground System and back to the BR system going westward to Swansea.

Then the next mistake arrived. I checked in to a bed and breakfast opposite the house where I was supposed to go. I ended up paying £10 for sleeping at the wrong place. I realised my mistake when I went to the university campus the following day.

The student orientation took one week. Within that week, I found out how to locate the library, the lecture halls, the bookshop, the computer rooms as well as how to get from my house to the university on foot. I also got to know my housemates. The course started in earnest in week two. I walked into the lecture rooms with my colleagues and sat at the back and listened to lecture after lecture for five days.

The first thing I noticed was that this was a diverse and multinational group of students. There were students from Latin America, the Caribbean, Europe, Africa, Asia and the Middle East.

The lecturers tried to give a summary of the different courses that would be taught during the one-year time we would be there. They called off the names of authors of sociology, economics and development studies literature as if these were their mother's children (as we would say in Manga). Everybody else seemed to know what they were talking about; I did not know what they were talking about. This looked like Ghana College week one revisited. By the end of day five, it was clear that I was understanding very little of what the lecturers talked about. That weekend was hell for me. Was this a mistake? I decided that I would tackle this problem on the following Monday. On that historic Monday, I got hold of my tutor, Dr David Marsden, who had been introduced to me during the orientation.

I told him that I was not following the academic discourse. He appeared to understand me and asked when I left university. I told him that I left university in 1980. He said this was actually a long time ago and asked whether my first degree was in economics or sociology. I told him I had a first degree in Chemistry and there was immediately a shocked expression on his face. He called the department secretary, Mrs. Slater and asked for my file. When the file came, he looked quickly through the documentation, looked at me and asked how I got here. Anytime I pass through a miraculous experience I get the same question. I stared back at him. After a long pause and recovering from his surprise he told me that students in this master's program are supposed to have a first degree in economics or sociology. So, my lack of first-degree knowledge of economics and sociology was the main reason that I was not following the lectures. He said that I was already here and we would have to find a way to get around the problem. He suggested that I needed to study some first-degree economics and sociology on my own. Dr Marsden believed that I had enough field experience in development work in Africa and only needed some academic literature that would help to get my practical knowledge rooted in theory. He then pulled out an A4 sheet of paper and wrote the titles of four sociology and economics textbooks. He recommended these books for me to buy and he volunteered to help me catch-up with the basics of first-degree economics and sociology while trying to understand the master's program. I left Dr Marsden's office dazed and wondering what to do next. My immediate action was to buy the four textbooks recommended and do the assignments my tutor had given me. I was supposed to read the first three chapters of one of the books and answer a question he had given.

That night was a very long night for me. I was in the middle of Wales trying to pursue a course for which I had no foundation. Now I was being faced with the task of building the foundation while building the superstructure at the same time. Once again, I spent a whole night reflecting about my future. Those were the days when there were no mobile phones. I could not call back home to tell my family about my predicament. So, I just sat alone, reflected, prayed and planned. Then I remembered one of my favourite quotations from Shakespeare's Julius Caesar. This is part of the speech Brutus gave to his troops before they went out to battle:

"There is a tide in the affairs of men.
Which, taken at the flood, leads on to fortune;
Omitted, all the voyage of their life
Is bound in shallows and in miseries.
On such a full sea are we now afloat,
And we must take the current when it serves,
Or lose our ventures."

I told myself that I was right on top of the high tides in Swansea and I must take the tide or lose all my fortunes. This was a battle I was not going to lose, as in the case of Brutus, with the help of God Almighty and with some hard work.

I tackled my first assignment with zeal and a lot of energy. By the end of chapter three, I had forgotten the whole of chapter one - and about half of chapter two. I went back to read chapter one.

On Wednesday afternoon, I submitted my first assignment to Dr Marsden. He gave me another reading assignment and I was supposed to come back on the Friday for a discussion on my first assignment. The discussion on Friday turned out to be a complete disaster. I had written the essay like a science student where hydrochloric acid plus sodium hydroxide gives sodium chloride and water. As a matter of fact, it looked like I was back to where I started. I had to learn how to write as a social science student, debating proponents of different concepts without any of them as scientific fact.

The sessions with Dr Marsden continued throughout the month of October, November and December. I had to do this to catch up with first-degree economics and sociology while attending lectures to follow the master's course. The consistent coaching managed to help me catch up with the other students by the end of December 1991. At this point, I could safely say I was on the high tide in Swansea and was not ready to lose my fortunes.

The master's program itself introduced me to some of the most significant authors of development literature such as Michael P. Todaro, the author of "Economic Development In The Third World", John Toye, the author of "Dilemma of Development", Aaron Wildavsky, the author of "Speaking Truth To Power", Dennis Rondinelli, the author of "Development Projects As Policy Experiments", Robert Chambers, who authored many development books including "Putting The Last First". It was here that I learnt the economic concepts of Adam Smith and John Keynes as well as the stages of development conceptualised by W. W. Rostow. These books became the foundation for my library on integrated development.

I got myself a 1986 model Toshiba T1100 laptop computer. I then bought the necessary literature needed to master the use of the computer. These included "Teach Yourself Word Perfect version 5.1" and "Teach Yourself Lotus 1-2-3". These were big books of nearly 700 pages each but I spent night after night going through all of them from the first to the last page and by the middle of the second term, I had educated myself enough in the use of Word Processors and Spreadsheets. This initial knowledge and foundation has been a major help in the development of my word processing and spreadsheet skills that has impacted my work in the development community. One major component of the course was the group work. The group work enabled me to share different experiences from the students that came from different parts of the world. It clearly showed the similarities and problems across the world as well as the differences in approach depending on which part of the world the development worker is coming from.

Being on the high tides of Swansea taught me several lessons. It taught me the great lesson that "the seemingly impossible becomes actually possible" if one puts his mind to it. It gave me a bigger global perspective of poverty and development. It exposed me to a large amount of academic literature on sociology, economics and development. It enabled me to apply the lessons I had learnt in my childhood at a different level. Finally, it built my confidence as a development worker with practical fieldwork rooted in academic literature.

I submitted my dissertation and returned to Ghana in November 1992 and was subsequently awarded a Masters in Economic and Social Development by the University of Swansea. This was the fortune I obtained from taking the tide at the flood in Swansea. Since the 1990s, adverts for senior staff in the development field always required a master's degree in social sciences. One lesson I have learnt is that with a focused objective and faith in God together with perseverance one can always achieve a well-defined target.

CHAPTER 26

BEYOND THE LECTURE HALLS

During most university studies, a lot more happens outside the lecture hall than in it. While thinking of the academic issues in Swansea, I was also conscious of the social and economic aspects of my life.

My first social integration task was to identify a Bible-believing church where I could worship throughout my stay in the city. With the African Christian community around me, this was very easy to find. I found a church in the city that looked very interdenominational and with a Pentecostal worship style. My first visit to the church really impressed me. Church members were eager to invite visiting students to come to their homes and share a meal with them. One particular member took an interest in me as a Ghanaian and took me to his house for lunch. I had the most pleasant surprise of my life when I entered his living room. Hidden in a small village near Swansea, this man had a life-sized photograph of Azumah Nelson, the famous Ghanaian WBC World Featherweight and Super Featherweight Champion boxer. All over the room, there were photographs of the Ghanaian boxer. I could not believe this. During the lunch, he actually demonstrated that he knew more about Ghanaian boxers than I did. As the year progressed, I visited London during most weekends to keep in touch with friends I had in the UK, so I was not able to attend the church so frequently, and my contact with this friend was reduced. However, we got in touch from time to time particularly on the phone to talk about the career of Azumah Nelson. That initial meeting with him made a strong impression, that someone who did not know Ghana at all could be so interested in a Ghanaian boxer.

I managed to establish and keep a network of friends in the postgraduate student community and maintained friendships with the broad spectrum of nationalities in the course. This enabled me to share their development experiences and understand the manifestation of poverty across the world. It also enabled me to enrich my own knowledge and to bring this into my writing. Most of these people were far more experienced in the development world than I was and I learnt a lot from them.

My interaction with students from different parts of the world varied according to the interests common in those countries. With my Brazilian, English and German friends, we talked football all the time. The Brazilians were particularly talking about how the Ghana under-17 football team beat their team in Italy in 1991. My colleagues from the Caribbean did all that they could to help me understand cricket, but in the end, I was as ignorant about cricket as I was in the beginning. With the Kenyans, we talked about athletics, knowing that Kenyan long-distance runners are a dominant force in world athletics.

Cooking with my East African friends as a group was a bit difficult. They had to learn how to eat very spicy Ghanaian food when I was doing the cooking. On the other hand, I had to make use of a bottle of pepper sauce known as *shito* to increase the level of spices in my food when I was not cooking. My jollof rice was their favourite food.

My network of friends around the United Kingdom provided tremendous support during my study in Swansea. These are people I knew from various aspects of my student, work and family life back in Ghana. They included Gladys Asumda in Reading, Issaka Ndekugri in Wolverhampton, James Tiigah and Hawa Yakubu in London, Neil and Dorothy Cameron in Hull. I will forever be grateful to these people for the support they gave me during my tough times studying in the UK. Peter and Claire Glauser in Switzerland also formed part of the social network in Europe that provided tremendous support. Back in Ghana, my family was significantly supported by the staff of World Vision International and family friends.

One of the tough things about finding your way around London in those days was learning how to use a map book called 'London A to Z'. I was recently reminded of a time that two friends, Azumah Amidini and Colin Macdonald, and I got lost. We had spent some time with Hawa Yakubu reminiscing about old times. At the end of the night, Azumah could not identify his house since we were coming from a side of town he did not know. It was a very dramatic night but we finally found the house.

Communication with my family back at home was one of the most stressful situations outside the lecture room. In the absence of a telephone line at home, I had to make arrangements for my wife to go to wherever she could get a telephone at a given time and I would go into a public telephone booth and call her. This was very difficult given that such an arrangement was made either by letter or during the last telephone call. On one such occasion, my wife went to the house of a high-level government official to wait for my call. I was on a train from Swansea to London and I expected to make the call to her ten minutes after the arrival of the train in London Paddington station. Just before the city of Reading, there was a problem on the line that caused a one-hour delay. By the time I got off the train at Paddington station in London, my wife had waited for nearly an hour without hearing from me. I rushed out of the train to the nearest telephone booth and made my call to Ghana. I was told that she had waited in vain and had just left the house. I later heard that when she was leaving the house, she was bitten by a dog and she had to go through the whole process of the administration of post-exposure prophylaxis which meant a series of anti-rabies injections. While this account may look like a fairy tale in the 21st century, in the year 1991/1992, access to a telephone in Ghana to make an international call seemed as difficult as finding water in a desert.

In terms of my personal economic issues, I tried to find out how to minimise expenditure where possible. At the same time, the Manga in me kicked in and I looked around for where I could make some money.

One meal at a restaurant and two take-away meals from a fast-food joint made me realise that these would be the most uneconomical ways of spending money. I therefore decided to purchase the necessary kitchen utensils, plates and cutlery as well as buying food ingredients in bulk to engage in my own personal catering. It is amazing how this saved me a significant amount of money.

My expenditure reduction strategy got a further boost when I agreed with my two housemates Donald and Ally from Kenya and Tanzania respectively, to cook and eat together. Cooking one meal for three people was definitely cheaper and easier than three of us cooking three different meals. However, the biggest boost came between the months of June and November 1992 when I went to live with Neil and Dorothy Cameron in Keyingham near Hull. This completely cut off my weekly accommodation bill for that period. This was another huge saving for me. Neil Cameron had taught me Chemistry in the sixth form between 1973 and 1975. Needless to say, the combined cooking with Donald and Ally gave me a huge opportunity to learn a lot more about Kenya and Tanzania. While I told my housemates about villages in northern Ghana I learnt more about the cities of Iringa in Tanzania and Nyeri in Kenya.

Clothes in retail stores could sell as high as six to ten times more than for the same type of clothes in charity shops. These sold mostly second-hand clothing although sometimes you could come across some brand-new items so I stuck to charity shops for my clothes. I also found out that the end-of-season clearances resulted in heavily reduced prices. For example, there is always a summer clothes clearance just before the winter and a winter clothes clearance, just before the spring.

Coming from Ghana, I found the electronic shops amazing. That is why I avoided them throughout my stay in the UK. I simply got myself a small radio alarm clock and a second-hand Yamaha electronic keyboard (piano) and said goodbye to electronic shops until I was about to leave and go back to Ghana.

Despite all these expenditure reduction strategies my revenue was basically my monthly stipend from the British council. The need to increase revenue with a Manga-minded background kicked in. One of my closest friends from secondary school, James Tiigah, worked for the Ghana Embassy in London and I spent most of my weekends at his house in North London. I used these weekends to concentrate on any reading and writing assignments I had. I also searched through 'Loot' - a famous newspaper that was published for free every week - for electronic items I could purchase in London and retail in Swansea. I made maximum use of this paper. I searched and found computers for sale, bought them and carried them back to Swansea where I sold them to other students for a marginal profit. At the time, second-hand goods advertised on Loot could be as good as brand new. Loot is now online.

I did not forget about my photography. I attended student parties, took photographs and printed them in the colour laboratories in Swansea to sell. The biggest income earner came when I lived with the Camerons. I got a casual job to work at a greenhouse for 8 hours a day and 6 days a week picking tomatoes. The greenhouse occupied about six acres. It was an enclosed glass shed inside which tomatoes were grown. A series of metal pipelines enabled the circulation of warm water throughout the farm, twenty-four hours a day. Each tomato plant was watered through a computer-controlled drip irrigation system. The pipelines carrying the warm water doubled as rails for the trolleys on which we the workers sat and rolled along while picking the tomatoes. Every seven minutes, we had to fill two crates and transfer the tomatoes into a waiting tractor.

I remember that on the third day after starting this job I woke up at 5:30 a.m. and when I sat up on my bed, every muscle in my body ached. I was wondering whether to roll back in bed and sleep some more or get ready and go to the greenhouse. Then I remembered all the difficult things I did in Manga to earn money, such as weeding in leech-infested swampy rice farms. I quickly jumped out of bed, got ready and headed back to the greenhouse. It was a tough job for very little money but any little money in my hands at the time was very significant. I arrived at home every afternoon covered with a green substance that I had picked up from the tomato leaves. The Camerons left their personal bedroom door wide open for me to get to a shower and wash off the green stuff. I made sure that they did not know just how much of that stuff came off my body by carefully scrubbing off the dirt from the shower tray.

I combined this 8 hour a day work with the writing of my master's dissertation. In reality, I had less than 4 hours of sleep a day for nearly five months. Despite the expert cooking of Dorothy Cameron who tried to stuff as much as possible into my body, I ended up losing so much weight that I came home in November 1992 looking like someone who had been on a hunger strike.

The biggest break I ever had during this period came when the Camerons took me out of the UK for a vacation in Germany and France. I got a two-week leave from my job in the greenhouse and we travelled from Hull to London where we passed the night with the family of John and Emma Turl. John taught Physics and Emma taught English in Navrongo Secondary School when I was in the sixth form. It was very interesting to find that they were still driving a Land-Rover that they had in Navrongo in the 1970s. It was a relaxing evening as we caught up with stories from Ghana. The next day was a very long drive from London to Ramsgate Harbour and then across the English Channel by ferry to Dunkirk in France. This was followed by a very long drive into Belgium. Driving from France into Belgium without being stopped by anybody but just waved on by border security made me wonder how long it will take us in Africa to get to this point of having a seamless border crossing between countries. This was in 1992. As at 2013, it took me at least an hour to cross the border between

Niger and Burkina Faso and the same length of time to do the same between Burkina Faso and Ghana.

It took us a whole day to drive across Belgium into Germany and arrive in the Black Forest area at almost midnight. Continuous rains during our time in Germany prevented full enjoyment of the vacation. My only joy was that I was not working and I was not studying. The weather in France was better and I had the opportunity to do some swimming in a holiday resort. It was another long ride back to Dunkirk and to Ramsgate and all the way back to Hull. This was a big rest but I soon had to put that behind me and get back to the greenhouse and the writing of my dissertation.

Life outside the lecture halls was interesting and challenging but significantly complemented my time of studying in the UK and I will always be grateful to the friends and colleagues who made this possible.

CHAPTER 27

THE OTHER SIDE OF THE GARDEN

This narrative starts in the first week of March 1994. I was sitting in the chair of the National Director for World Vision International, Ghana, with my back to the door and the time was a few minutes to 10:00 p.m. I was startled by the baritone voice of Dr. Joseph Riverson, the National Director. Apparently, he had opened the door quietly and had been standing in the doorway for several minutes. He asked what I was doing in the office at this time of the night. I reminded him that it was my last day with the organisation and I was in his office putting various documents in identifiable folders to ensure that in my absence he could find whatever document he wanted. However I left the clear message that I was available to help with anything that needed to be done. We walked out of the office together as I locked it up and handed him his keys. That was my last activity in the Ghana office of World Vision. I had submitted my resignation letter earlier and on this night I said farewell to the organisation. That also meant that I was stepping into a new job.

My new job was with a local Non-Governmental Organisation (NGO) called African Centre for Human Development (ACHD) and I was taking up the position of a Deputy Director to the organisation. Being in an international NGO, I thought that becoming a Deputy Director in a Ghanaian NGO offered me a better opportunity to contribute to strategic planning, policy development and grassroots development implementation in Ghanaian rural communities. This thought reminds me of the lyrics of the song by reggae artiste, Lucky Dube, that says "the grass is greener at the other side till you get there and see it for yourself".

I consider NGOs to be in two categories: international and local or national NGOs (sometimes referred to as Civil Society Organisations – CSOs). Local NGOs can further be categorised into those who are dependent on grants from international NGOs and the international donor community and those locally constituted groups receiving a particular development agenda. For example, I have worked with groups constituted to carry out food processing across Ghana and the African continent to make a living and who depend on grants. The characterisation of CSOs is beyond the scope of this narrative.

My career from 1981 to 1994 was with the international NGO, World Vision International. My departure from this organisation was a step into the world of the local NGO world. This move gave me an opportunity to see the operations of such an NGO. Although this looks like a study of one local NGO I have learnt over 25 years and in three different African countries that the pattern is the same across the continent.

In the middle of March 1994, I started my new job as the Deputy Director of ACHD. I believed that this was going to be an exciting job. It turned out that this was not going to be exactly the case although I learnt a lot in my new job. I believe that my rural upbringing and early education, as well as my Christian faith, helped me to develop the values that enhanced my commitment to development work. The 13 years in World Vision International established the roots and initial growth in my development thinking and practice. I expected the step out into the local NGO community to build on this foundation.

I quickly learnt that ACHD was led by an exceptionally brilliant hard-working and self-driven individual. He needed only two hours to write winning project proposals that clearly articulated the problems he wanted to respond to, with clear objectives and expected outputs and outcomes. The leader was very visionary and could see ahead of time what others did not see. His diplomatic skills were exceptional and as I attended meetings with him with bilateral and multilateral donor community members this diplomacy came in handy.

I remember an occasion when he was expected to contribute to a document I was writing. I needed the document by the end of the day but it was not ready. This meant that I had to have it first thing the following day. He assured me that I would get what I wanted. The following day I walked into his office to tell him that I really needed that document within the first one hour of the morning. He handed me 12 pages of handwritten work on foolscap sheets. I asked when he was able to do this and he told me he had come to the office at 5:30 a.m. This was a demonstration of focused hard work.

It must be said that anybody who has the courage and determination to start a local NGO in Africa (and for that matter any business venture) is most likely to have most of the qualities outlined above. However, these qualities could be undermined by inappropriate Leadership, Organisational Development and Management practices, that could arise out of ignorance or a willing compromise of integrity with the excuse that everybody is doing the same thing.

One of the key elements of capacity that are necessary for the successful functioning of an NGO is a Strategic Plan. This provides the organisation with a medium-term view of what they want to do. It also enables the donor community to see whether the strategic plan of the local NGO is consistent with their own long-term plans. Indeed in recent years, development partners are beginning to ask whether strategic plans of NGOs are consistent with the Sustainable Development Goals (SDGs) and Bilateral/Multilateral alignment with the SDGs. Local NGOs should seek to respond to the overall development needs of the country in which they operate. This may or may not be consistent with the development aspirations of the ruling government of that country.

ACHD cleverly avoided medium-term strategic planning and coined the term 'process approach' which really meant that "we will build the ship as we sail". It enabled just writing proposals to fit into any donor proposal criteria. One of the very strong attributes I found in the leader of the ACHD was his ability to identify and recruit human resources with the knowledge, experience, skills and competencies to implement programmes. Several of those recruited have gone on to work for the World Bank, the UN, Bilateral Organisations and International NGOs. I have learnt that a talented human resource base needs very strong policies and systems to enable them to perform their duties based on policies clearly defined in policy documents and not on sentiments, subjective ideas and other persuasions.

Ten years after I started work as the Country Director for ActionAid, Burundi in December 2004, I was approached by the director of a local NGO to sign a Memorandum Of Understanding and establish a partnership that would enable them to access funds from ActionAid. I requested to see a Strategic Plan for the local NGO highlighting their Vision, Mission and Strategic Objectives to enable me to make an informed decision. I was in Burundi for six and a half years and that strategic plan never arrived. The most disturbing part of this encounter was that the director of the local NGO was European. I asked myself whether the Europeans were beginning to learn the tricks of weak local NGOs in Africa.

Another key element of an organisation to operate effectively is a functioning Board of Directors. While working for ActionAid in Burundi, I was assigned to the national council for the fight against HIV/AIDS. I was sitting in a committee to assess proposals from local NGOs seeking funding to implement projects to fight against the disease and observed very interesting antiques by local NGOs. One of the criteria for assessing a project was a functioning Board of Directors. One local NGO presented us with a list of at least 7 people as their Board of Directors. It turned out that five of the people on the list presented by one NGO could not be contacted because they were either deceased or were out of Burundi. One of the two remaining members of the Board was related to the leader. I scratched my head and remembered that in my attempt to work with a local NGO in Ghana the organisation did not have a well-constituted Board of Directors known by the staff. This is a common occurrence across several countries in Africa. A young man working for a local NGO in Accra found out that the director simply picked up the phone and called people he knew and told them that they were members of his board and they should agree to say so if auditors came to ask them.

Every NGO should be able to identify and solicit support from individuals with in-depth knowledge of development to be members of their Board. The presence of a functional Board of Directors is one of the basic requirements for a good governance structure that will facilitate the efficient and effective functioning of an NGO.

Policy Documents are another important element of a properly functioning NGO. The most important documents include a Human Resource policy and a Financial Management policy. Basic HR policies should normally include recruitment procedures and processes, working hours, salary and rewards administration, promotions, and sanctions and exits of staff. Many organisations tend to use a Finance and Administration person who is not necessarily an expert in any of the two areas in order to avoid the high salaries of such expertise. However, a way out is to outsource this expertise to support the multiple tasking of a finance and administration person.

Other policy documents include a gender policy and an HIV policy. These could be organisational policies or included in the Human Resource policy. There could also be thematic policies such as a climate change policy that would form the basis for seeking funding for the implementation of programmes in these thematic areas. Other organisational policies could also include Partnership, Fundraising, and Program Initiation and Exit. The presence of such policy documents would avoid ambiguity and help define organisational practices.

Working with ACHD over the years I noticed that many NGOs did not have a salary structure administration policy; that should be in either the Human Resource policy or the Financial Management policy or both. This has resulted in many of them running the organisation without a salary scale and paying cash to staff. In the organisation that I joined in 1994, staff salaries were always paid in cash and never by cheque thus compromising the existence of a paper trail of expenditure that would facilitate efficient auditing. This is common not only in the NGO world but is also widespread among private businesses. One young man has told me that in this day and age in the year 2020 his landlord will not accept advance rent payments through the bank or the mobile money transfer system. He would rather have the cash counted and given to him. In this way, the employer can escape tax payments for his staff as well as social security contributions to the right authorities.

I have learnt that several directors in the NGO world are not able to separate funds that belong to the organisation from their personal resources. Some do not actually pay themselves but rather dip and take funds from the organisational resources as and when they need it. The absence of a salary scale is another big issue. Some local NGO directors pay their staff based on the staff's ability to negotiate. I saw this in the new NGO I joined. One could see two or three staff doing the same job receiving different salaries that were not related to their job descriptions.

One more fundamental document necessary for the operation of an organisation is a document that contains the Core Values of the organisation. Core Values should be defined by and emerge from the deep convictions and philosophical thought of the leadership of the organisation. The words that are contained in the Core Values must be consistent with the practices of the organisation for success. For example, if the Core Values of an organisation contain words such as integrity, transparency, equity and honesty and the organisation's leadership practise the opposite then there is a problem. If such an organisation does not have a salary scale and the leaders get engaged in underhand dealings and turn around to ask their staff to cover up for them the Core Values become meaningless. In carrying out strategic planning for state and private organisations I have always insisted that the words contained in Core Values must be clearly defined to avoid ambiguity and individual interpretation.

I have seen many organisations that just copy the Core Values of another organisation and display it as their own without conviction and commitment. If Core Values are well articulated, it will help incoming new staff to understand the philosophy of the organisation and align their thinking to the same.

ACHD implemented very important projects for several development partners. Such projects included an integrated project in the Kadjebi district, a capacity-building project in the Ashanti Region and a water and sanitation project in the Western Region of Ghana. I also carried out the first medium-term development plan for the Kadjebi District. The research to develop this plan lasted between 6 and 8 weeks. Although I completed and submitted this plan before my departure from the organisation, all evidence that I did this was suppressed in the final report. By July 1995, I had found out that the 'greener grass' that I thought was on the other side had quickly turned brown. I felt that I was sitting on a tree with a group of knowledgeable, skilled and competent individuals and that the roots of the tree were being undermined. I became aware that the tree would fall sooner or later. I therefore decided to get off. Whenever one finds himself or herself in an organisation that has an inappropriate organisational culture, there are usually three options of action. Option one is to join the inappropriate culture and do exactly what everybody else is doing. Option two is to stay in the culture but refuse to be part of it. In this case, one is actually an accomplice to the wrongdoing. Option three is to quit regardless of any loss. At this point I recognised that I could not change anything about the organisational culture in this job. Therefore at the end of July 1995, I resigned from the organisation. Twenty-five years after my departure from ACHD, it does not exist anymore. I went to work for the US Peace Corps, albeit with a lower compensation package, as an Associate Peace Corps Director (APCD) in charge of Small Enterprise Development (SED).

In my opinion, the inability of the founder and Director of the African Centre for Human Development to complement his superior and innovative development ideas with financial discipline and adherence to development partner funding and reporting guidelines could be responsible for the collapse of the organisation.

It is important to state that there has been very strong leadership and organisational development successes in the local NGO community. Some of these are ISODEC (Integrated Social Development Centre), Third World Network, Centre for Democratic Development (CDD), SEND Ghana, IMANI Africa and others. ISODEC and Third World Network were started in the late 1980s and early 1990s and are still operational and successfully implementing programmes with their founders no longer involved in their day-to-day running. These organisations definitely had succession planning and strong policies that have facilitated their operation for up to 30 years. The reason for this success lies in the ability of the founders of these local NGOs to strive to establish fundamental capacity requirements despite difficulties. They are able to look beyond personal gain and focus on institutional stability. They quickly think of succession planning that will enable the organisation to grow beyond the individuals. Above all this, the founders see the organisations as a step in their career development and aim for higher goals.

The critical issues I have raised above, including the questions of a Board of Directors, a strategic plan, policy documents and core values, also apply to business ventures. Any business enterprise that wants to succeed beyond the founder must be rooted in these principles.

When one looks at big businesses such as Microsoft, Apple, the Hilton chain of hotels, etc., one will realise that the founders looked beyond themselves and the organisations lived beyond them. Major international NGOs that have been successful include Save the Children Fund, Oxfam, Christian Aid, World Vision International, and ActionAid.

The organisational culture of international NGOs tends to be influenced by the culture of the countries from which they originate. This usually facilitates their existence. Laws from these home countries tend to facilitate the existence and successful operation of the NGO. Despite legislation that provides for the existence and operation of local NGOs, African governments tend to engage local NGOs in a way that stifles their work.

Until Ghanaian and indeed African local NGOs are formed not for the purpose of immediate financial gains for the founders, Africa will continue to look more to international NGOs, and local NGOs will continue to die young.

CHAPTER 28

INTO THE GHANAIAN HINTERLAND

The drummers were about six in number playing drums of different shapes and sizes but well organised in a way to produce the sounds and rhythms that compelled anyone listening to tap their feet, nod their heads, shake the body, or actually get up and dance. The dancers arranged themselves in lines and each dancer had a white handkerchief in each hand. I was one of the dancers. We bent forward moved our feet and shook our bodies according to the rhythm of the drums. The singers stood behind the drummers singing in different harmonies. Any music-loving person would have realised that they sang their parts of the song with perfection. Added to this was the brass band. They had trumpets, saxophones, trombones and all types of wind instruments. They also played their part so that the brass band music blended with the singing and drumming to create a perfect cultural display. As we moved and danced to this perfect harmony, the brass band would, once in a while, play a series of notes and then the drummers, singers, dancers and those watching would shout a big "Hey!". The brass band played another series of notes and everybody shouted again, but this time it was so loud that it woke me up from my sleep.

It was all a dream. In reality, I was in my bed. The only part of the above narrative that was true was that there was actual drumming, brass band music and singing that I could hear from the window of the room where I slept. This was in Tsrukpe in the Volta region of Ghana. I had spent the past few days with my colleague, Gershon Adzokpa, in the community facilitating a workshop for project workers. I enjoyed this cultural display earlier in the evening before retiring to bed at about midnight. I then dreamt that I was back with everybody else and was one of the dancers. This was part of the hinterland of Ghana that became part of my normal life as a development worker. Indeed, every development worker should be prepared to become part of the normal life of people in the hinterland. Most of the people who need development support are not in the cities.

These people have their traditions and cultural performances that can be very rich. Many development workers tend to dissociate themselves from these cultural amusements and entertainment and rather focus on their task of providing development assistance. It is important for development workers to do whatever they can to integrate and be part of the entertainment and cultural activities of the people they seek to help. This helps them to bond further with the community and appreciate better their way of life. Failure in this area can make proposed development assistance very artificial and far removed from reality.

*****

In 1988, I left the town of Bawku through the east with Sanatu Nantogma, the public health nurse for the then Tamale sub-office of World Vision International, and her baby after visiting school construction projects in the Missiga area. I drove through Garu, on the Bawku-Nakpanduri road, and into the valley at the foot of the Gambaga Scarp. The climb to Nakpanduri at the top of the scarp was a very slow one. The road was full of steep climbs and sharp turns. It twisted and turned sharply here and there as we went up the mountain. Indeed, this is one of the most dangerous roads in Ghana. It had signs of possible falling rocks from the high escarpment on the right. Then a market truck appeared in front of us. There were two young men with wooden blocks in their hands walking behind the truck. This meant that the truck was moving up the mountain at walking pace. The young men were ready to use the wooden blocks to chock the tyres of the truck in case the engine failed. I followed them carefully for about half a kilometre. When I got the opportunity, I stepped hard on the accelerator of my car and we went past them and breathed a sigh of relief.

We drove to Nakpanduri at the top of the scarp and went down a gentle slope to the Jilig community, which is to the south-east of Nakpanduri, where we had a meeting with the community members. The meeting lasted from 7:00 pm until about 9:00 p.m. We then had to drive back to Nakpanduri and southward towards Tamale, trying to get to our destination before daybreak. The road between Nakpanduri and Jilig was not as smooth as the earlier road we had taken from Bawku. This time there were gulleys caused by constant erosion of the road surface. I had to manoeuvre the Peugeot 504 in such a way that the tyres would be on the ridges on either side of the gulleys to avoid seriously damaging the car.

From Nakpanduri we drove southwards through forests that were known to harbour all types of wildlife. The lights of the car cut through the night darkness as tall grass bending from both sides of the road brushed against the car. The drive to Tamale, through Gusheigu, finally ended at about 4:30 a.m. Sanatu and I had just come from a part of the Ghanaian hinterland.

The challenge of travelling through difficult terrain and landscapes in order to get to remote communities and back is a normal part of development work in Ghana and indeed, the rest of Africa. Anybody who wants to do development work in Africa should be prepared to confront the different difficult landscapes and terrain that need to be overcome to get to the communities that need support.

*****

I drove the Nissan Patrol four-wheel drive out of the Cantonments offices of World Vision International followed closely by a similar car driven by Robert Djangmah and headed for the Accra-Kumasi road. Both cars carried World Vision's development workers. We drove all the way to Nkawkaw and turned right and climbed the Kwahu mountains. This is one of the scariest mountains to climb in Ghana. As one drives up the mountain, there is a steep cliff on both sides of the road, with a seemingly bottomless gulley from which one could only see mist or clouds. One of my colleagues in the car said he kept his eyes tightly closed. We got to the top and started the fast descent to the other side of the mountain. We then drove to the Volta River where we waited for a pontoon into which we drove the cars and were carried to the other side of the river. At this point, we were in the famous Afram plains of Ghana.

The drive to Donkorkrom took about an hour. We were received by an enthusiastic host of development workers and shown our rooms. As we settled into our rooms, mosquitoes hovered around hungrily and most likely aware that we were fresh food for the night. We were there to facilitate a development workshop for leaders of communities where World Vision had projects. The generator that provided electricity for the centre where the workshop was organised would be switched off at 8:00 p.m. to save fuel. Any planned activities, therefore, had to be finished before sunset.

Thinking and planning for the provision of social amenities such as schools, health facilities, water sources and other social infrastructure to communities that need them is part of the development process. However, it is important to note that these communities may be very difficult to reach. This underscores the need for the procurement of appropriate vehicles for these trips. Even after getting to them, we may be confronted with challenges that are very different from those in the city. It is the ability to cope with these difficulties that makes for successful community engagement.

*****

Four Nissan Patrol 4WD vehicles turned off the Accra-Aflao road towards Big Ada. As we entered the town, we were directed by the leading car to park our cars off the road. We then walked in between houses to the Volta River where big motorised canoes were waiting for us. We proceeded to board them. We were all staff of World Vision International. The staff who could not swim expressed concerns about the impending journey on the river especially since no life-vests were given to us. But their fears were allayed by a confident young man who would be piloting the canoes. With hindsight, life-vests should always be used in these situations in case of any accidents during the trip. The journey on the river must have taken about 20-30 minutes and then we were on the island of Pediatokope. This is one of the several islands in the Volta estuary that can only be accessed by motorised canoes. We had gone for the opening of a school building constructed with the support of World Vision International.

If development is limited to places that can be only accessed by roads, communities such as Pediatokope will struggle to benefit from any external assistance. Meanwhile, I have heard of teachers who risk their lives daily on canoes to go to such islands to provide their services to pupils in the communities.

*****

I sat on the bench in front of Naaba Abraham L. Bayelim Kanbe, the traditional ruler in the Duusi community in the Upper East Region. We were discussing priority development projects for the community. The chief and his people spoke Talni and I spoke Kusaal but we understood each other perfectly well. Out of this discussion, emerged the construction of the Duusi Primary School with support from World Vision International.

I have sat down with similar traditional rulers from various places such as Jukwa in the Central Region, Moglaa in the Northern Region, Kpasenkpe in the North East Region, and Ahamansu in the Oti Region.

While doing development work in Ghana, it is imperative to have a good working relationship with traditional rulers. They are the custodians of the land and the culture of the people. Nothing gets done in their traditional jurisdiction without their blessing and they must be treated with the utmost respect.

*****

I sat in the passenger seat of the Nissan patrol vehicle with a CD (Diplomatic Corps) registration plate belonging to the US Peace Corps. The car was driven by John Mason, a Canadian wildlife expert. We were cruising at about 100 km per hour between Techiman and Kintampo in the then Brong-Ahafo region. We branched off on our right and drove eastward for nearly 12 km. Then the purpose of our visit to this community started to manifest itself. Monkeys swung between branches, some of them crossing the road without caring about the approaching vehicle. We entered the community of Boabeng-Fiema. We sat down and had a long discussion with the chief and community members and witnessed how the community members lived in close proximity with monkeys from the nearby forest. From the forest, monkeys came along into the community, looking into pots to see what leftover food they could get to eat. They had no fear of the community members. This was a monkey sanctuary that could be developed into a tourist site and that was the purpose of our visit. I had never seen so many monkeys interacting fearlessly with humans anywhere in my life. It taught me that no matter how Ghana has been urbanized there will still be patches of communities where interaction between humans and wildlife will remain untouched. The Mole National Park in the Savannah region is another place with an abundance of wildlife and little interaction with the human population.

The Ghanaian hinterland is full of intriguing scenarios but this is not peculiar to Ghana. Every development worker in Africa should be prepared for similar experiences.

CHAPTER 29

BEYOND THE FRONTIERS OF GHANA

The Ghana Airways DC-9 Aircraft lifted off the tarmac at Kotoka International Airport in Accra, flew over the coastline and the Atlantic Ocean and turned right. I've never stopped admiring the landscape of Accra from the air and I did just that. It was an early morning in January 1996. This flight was commonly called the "West Coast flight". The cabin crew welcomed the passengers on board and announced that the flight was en route to Dakar with stopovers in Abidjan, Monrovia, Freetown, Conakry, Banjul. It was literally a passenger bus that stopped over in every village on its way to the final destination. The difference was that this was by air and we hopped from country to country.

In an hour the aircraft landed in Abidjan and I got off. I had a whole day to wait in Abidjan airport. The wait was long and boring. I went through the duty-free shops four maybe five times. I finally got a chair and took a seat in front of the electronic flight announcement board. The flight was for 9:00 p.m. so I had about 11 hours to wait. I took a power nap that lasted about 30 minutes and woke up to continue the waiting. I had checked my baggage through to Niamey in Niger so all that I had with me was a briefcase. In those days, briefcases were the order of the day. The flight to Niamey finally got called and I followed the passengers into the DC-10 Aircraft of Air Afrique (defunct since 2002) en route to Paris via Niamey. About an hour after liftoff, we landed in the capital of Niger.

I was greeted by the cold dry harmattan air of the Sahel Region. As I claimed my baggage and walked out of arrivals there was a young man with a placard bearing my name. The young man Gilbert Kofie led me into a waiting Land Rover Defender. I found out that he was a Ghanaian national. He drove me to Hotel Terminus where I passed the night under a thick blanket, trying to keep the dry cold at bay. Before going to bed I was told to prepare for a long journey the following day that would start at 5:30 a.m. At 5:15 a.m. I met the National Director of World Vision International in Niger, Ken Singleton. He quickly outlined the agenda for my visit. This visit was supposed to be for an interview. He would conduct the interview in the car during the long drive to Zinder, on the eastern part of Niger, where I was supposed to be posted. At the same time, I would get an opportunity to see the city that would become my home and workplace for the next two years. Thirdly he would get an opportunity to see me interact with the people in Hausa, the language of the area, and finally introduce me to important personalities.

The drive was a long one. We ate breakfast in a town called Madaoua. Breakfast was made up of a glass bowl of coffee and a sandwich; in this case an omelette in a long French bread called a baguette. My earlier frequent visits to Ougadougou had made me accustomed to this kind of breakfast. Then we continued our journey eastward to Zinder. The cold dry Harmattan winds beat relentlessly on the Land Rover Defender. As the sun went up the cold reduced rapidly to be replaced by head-splitting heat. The air conditioning in the Land Rover seemed to help but after 11:00 a.m it was not enough. We took lunch at a city called Birni-N'Konni. I was surprised to find out that the local restaurant surrounded by grass mats was managed by a Senegalese. What on earth was a Senegalese doing here? I asked myself. Later on, I regularly frequented this restaurant where lunch was usually a type of jollof rice called Riz Gras which had pieces of beef in it and a separate bowl of salad as a side dish. We always managed to combine this meal with grilled chicken or guinea fowl that was prepared nearby. My children have fond memories of this eating spot and can talk about it for hours.

Finally, we arrived in Zinder at 7:30 p.m after 935 km of travel. During that journey, Ken Singleton conducted the interview. I doubt whether he would have ever have had that amount of time to interview anybody else looking for a job. We checked into a hotel and I got under the thick blanket provided, went to sleep and tried to get enough rest before the following day. The next day we did all that we could do and by the end of that day, I had communicated in Hausa enough to convince Ken that I was fluent in the language. The city was not that big and one could drive from one end to the other in less than 20 minutes. The weather was harsh but I had some experience growing up in Manga under similar conditions.

The return journey was uneventful until we got back to Birni-N'Konni. To make some payments to me, Ken gave me a cheque to cash in the bank. I submitted my passport to the bank teller, collected my money and dashed out back into the Land Rover and headed west for Niamey. Ten minutes after leaving the bank I instinctively felt that something was wrong. The alarm bells in my brain were ringing relentlessly. I checked my pocket for my passport and it was not there. I opened my briefcase to cross-check for the passport and it was not there either. Panic! panic!

When you're travelling at a speed of 140 km per hour, 10 minutes can make a lot of difference. Ken wanted to know what the problem was and I told him I could not find my passport. We stopped briefly for about two minutes to check under the seat but there was still no passport to be found. Going back to the bank to check was out of the question. So we decided to drive on to Niamey and call the bank the following morning to check whether the passport was there.

The continuing drive back to Niamey could best be described as full of anxiety. Gilbert stepped on the accelerator and kept his foot down as we sped towards the elusive horizon as if we wanted to get there before the sun, which was descending fast in the same direction.

Back in the city, the battle between anxiety and fatigue raged on in my body. I had skipped out of Ghana for this interview and I wanted to get back to Accra before my boss started asking me questions. I woke up in the morning to find that fatigue had won the battle allowing sleep to reign throughout the rest of the night. I got out of bed, washed, took my breakfast, checked out of the hotel and was ready to go to the office by 7:30 a.m. The wait for Gilbert took forever but he finally came and I was in the office of World Vision by 9:30 a.m. When we finally called the bank and described the scenario of the day before, they confirmed that they had my passport with them. They were going to send it by a courier, so I should expect to receive it within 24 to 36 hours. There was no way I was going to sit there for 24 hours waiting for a passport. So we devised a new strategy. I went to report my lost passport to the Nigerian police. I took the police report and proceeded to the immigration and requested for a travel certificate that would enable me to travel back to Ghana. Luckily I had a photocopy of the passport; and my driving licence as well as my air ticket.

With the police report and a travel certificate in hand, Gilbert drove me over the bridge on the Niger River, out of the city, across the border into Burkina Faso where I waited by the roadside to get any means of transport to Ouagadougou. By some miracle of God, I found an NGO car heading for Ouagadougou and the driver kindly agreed to give me a lift. I jumped into the front seat by him, got my seatbelt on and went to sleep. He was driving like a maniac but who was I to dictate the speed at which somebody else should drive. In Ouagadougou, I checked into the Hotel OK Inn. The following morning, I had to wait once again for work to begin at 9:00 a.m. before getting into action. I called the reservations office of Air Afrique and explained my problem to them. I wanted them to reroute my ticket from Ouagadougou to Accra via Abidjan. I was told to come to the offices of the airline which I gladly did. My ticket was cancelled and a new ticket issued for me for Ouagadougou to Accra via Abidjan. The lady at the desk said they had to give me a refund but the money would not be ready until the following day. I was in a crisis mode and the refund was the last thing on my mind. I called my boss to explain to her that I was caught up in Burkina Faso without giving any details. In the afternoon, I got on Air Afrique to Abidjan and then back home to Accra. Wow! What a dramatic way to initiate my work beyond the frontiers of Ghana. My passport finally arrived in Niamey and was sent to me in Ghana by courier.

The actual process of my career move beyond the shores of Ghana started when I got an offer and contract to join the staff of World Vision Niger. It was very painful to leave my job with the US Peace Corps. I remember writing my resignation letter and walking over to the office of the US Peace Corps Director Harriet Lancaster at the time. She was surprised and disappointed that I was resigning from a job that I had been doing for less than one year. With tears running down my cheeks I told her that I had a wife and four children and my current salary was not enough to take care of them. I showed her my offer letter and the remuneration package contained in the contract. I told her that I did not know the Republic of Niger and I could not speak French so I was walking into unknown territory. If she could pay me half of what I was offered I would not leave the Peace Corps. She asked me to put this in writing which I did. She went ahead and minuted a note on my letter which she faxed to the US Peace Corps headquarters in Washington DC asking for approval to pay me my request. This was declined and I had no option but to leave the shores of Ghana. Harriet Lancaster is one of the most dynamic and efficient leaders and managers I have ever worked with in my development career and it was painful leaving her. We have remained in touch for over 20 years. The narrative of my two instances of change of job in detail is to highlight the fact that financial remuneration is not necessarily the primary motivation for changing jobs.

On the 15th of March, I joined World Vision International in Niger as the Area Development Programme Manager for the Region of Zinder. Once again it was Gilbert who drove me all the way to my new station accompanied by Ken Singleton. The two of them went back after a day and I was left alone to start pioneering work in the eastern part of Niger. The experiences of the pioneering work in Tamale became my reference point as I tackled my new job. It took me one week living in a hotel room to identify a house that I could use us my living accommodation. With the experience from Tamale, I knew that I had to start looking for office accommodation immediately. My first night in my new living accommodation was scary. Throughout my life, this was the first time I was going to live alone in a big house with a security guard in front of the house.

The most pleasant thing about living in Niger was the way their telephones worked. First thing I did was to pick the phone and call my wife at home and assure her that I was safely in a rented house and also enquire about the welfare of the rest of the family. Every telephone in Niger, in those days, was such that one could make international calls. The situation was different in Ghana. The only way one could make international calls from a landline was to apply for what was called International Direct Dialling (IDD). This was very expensive and so people preferred to go to what was known then as Communication Centres or 'Comm Centres'. From the Comm Centre, one could book a call and wait for one's turn for a long time while several people ahead in the queue made their calls. I found out that it was cheaper and faster to call somebody in Dakar in Senegal from my house than to call a subscriber in northern Nigeria. A call to Nigeria would normally be connected from Niger through Paris, London and Lagos - really ridiculous.

The headquarters in Niamey quickly purchased and sent a Toyota four-wheel-drive Land Cruiser to me to facilitate my transportation for work.

I worked in the Republic of Niger from April 1996 to the end of October 1998. My family joined me in 1997. Indeed, this was the most difficult time for me in terms of managing my family. My eldest daughter was in High School in Ghana and only travelled to join me during school vacations. I had to get an English-speaking boarding school for my two boys aged 10 and 13 in northern Nigeria. Then I lived in Niger with my wife and 3-year-old daughter.

During this time of my life in Niger, I had to learn and get used to working in the Sahel climatic zone and in the Sahara Desert. My childhood and working life had been in the Savannah Climatic zone as well as in the Forest and Coastal belts of Ghana. The Sahel region was a completely new experience for me. The landscape, the vegetation and the weather were completely different from what I knew. With the vegetation, the familiar trees I knew such as the Dawadawa tree, the Shea nut tree, etc. were missing. All that I saw around were shrubs and thorny trees. This meant that when one was out in the field the option of getting shade where one could park and rest was out of the question. Apart from the tarred roads that linked cities and major towns, all other roads were very sandy and needed skills of driving that I had to learn. I also had to carry rectangular planks of wood measuring about 20 by 40 cm in my car all the time. One of these would be placed under the car to support a car jack anytime I had a flat tyre. In the absence of this plank of wood, any effort to jack up the car would result in the jack sinking into the sand. In my bid to recruit a driver, part of the interview included a practical session to test the driver's ability to drive in sand and to get out of the sand without the vehicle digging in.

My introduction to the Sahara Desert was a completely new experience. I had to learn how to put on the turban used by the Tuaregs in the desert. I never mastered this skill and always needed somebody to put the turban on for me. It had to be put on in such a way that it covered the head as well as the nose and the mouth. This is because the air is full of sand and dust, so one had to breathe through the cloth that created a barrier to filter out the sand. Then the very sight of the sandy desert was very agoraphobic. It reminded me of my days of sailing off the west coast of Scotland. The difference is that in one case you were surrounded by only water while in the other you were surrounded by sand. Like the waves in the sea, the dunes of sand in the desert keep moving. What could be a dune could suddenly become a trough in less than five minutes. The absence of major landmarks such as trees and hills made it almost impossible to determine direction. If the sun was not visible it was difficult to tell the cardinal points. One had to have a compass in the car all the time to determine one's orientation. I am told that the Tuaregs prefer the night to find their way as they can use the location of stars in the sky to determine their direction and orientation.

The temperatures were unbelievable. It sometimes dropped as low as single digits during the night and then rose rapidly up to about 50 degrees Celsius in the daytime.

I remember sitting on the veranda of my house with my wife one evening at about 4 p.m. when a lizard fell off the tree on its back and died - killed by the heat. There were several trees in my house and my domestic worker had to water them every day despite the fact that they were adult trees. Then there were instances of sandstorms. One could see a reddish-brown cloud approaching, and then as the storm arrived and passed one would realise that it did not carry a single drop of rain but rather a huge mass of sand moving across the country. It left behind thick layers of sand everywhere. No matter how you closed up the house, the sand managed to get everywhere.

The reality of the intensity of the Sahelian heat dawned on me in May 1996 when I was driving alone from Niamey to Zinder. The right back tyre of the Toyota Land Cruiser I was driving burst while I was driving at a speed of over 120 km per hour. This started a sudden anti-clockwise spinning of the car. I quickly reacted by holding firmly on the steering wheel and shifting the gears from fifth to third, and then to second and first. This action resulted in the car being stopped by the engine and the car drifting to the left-hand side of the road. I was at this point nearly 500 km from my destination. I got out of the car and removed my spare wheel to make the necessary replacement and continue my journey. It was then that I realised that my hydraulic jack was not functional. I was stranded in the middle of nowhere.

There was no shady tree anywhere nearby. The scorching heat of the sun beat down mercilessly on me as I stood outside the car. There was no vehicle to be seen in either direction. Standing and walking up and down on the road produced droplets of sweat all over me. Sitting in the car with the engine running to keep the air conditioning working was out of the question because I did not know how long it would take to get the next help and I wanted to conserve my fuel.

After nearly 20 minutes of standing in the sun I saw an articulated truck approaching and going in my direction. I stood on the left-hand side of the road and tried frantically to flag down the oncoming truck. When it slowed down I realised that it had a Ghanaian registration number. I shouted in Twi, one of the common Ghanaian languages that most drivers are likely to know, that I needed help. The truck pulled up and the driver parked it on the same side as my broken down vehicle. Yes! They were Ghanaians and within 5 minutes my car was fixed. The empty truck was on its way to Lake Chad to collect saltpetre, commonly called *kawu* in Ghana. From then on as I did not have another spare wheel I had to drive cautiously at a low speed all the way to my destination. The incident taught me two important lessons. When embarking on a long drive in the Sahel it is best to ensure that your tyre pressure is below the recommended value. This will ensure that as the air in the tyre expands due to the excessive heat and the pressure increases, it will not burst. The second lesson is always to ensure that the jack in the car is working.

During the time of my work in the Republic of Niger I observed an economic and administrative context that facilitated development work. The CFA franc, was the common currency used throughout francophone West and Central Africa. This currency was tied to the French franc at the time and is currently tied to the Euro and supported by France. This meant that the local currency went up and down depending on the international currency market value of the French franc and subsequently the euro. The arrangement ensured a certain level of stability in the value of the local currency in the international currency market. This stability enabled the NGO and international development partners to operate budgets that were relatively stable in comparison to those in other countries where exchange rate fluctuations seriously influenced development budgeting and implementation. This was a huge advantage.

The other significant challenge I faced in Niger was the language challenge. Although I could communicate quite effectively in Hausa, I quickly found out that the language was loaded with French words. This was understandable because there are no local equivalents for development terminology such as Infant Mortality Rate or Maternal Mortality Rate. This could only be described. Words such as 'Annual Leave' or 'files' and 'folders' did not exist in the local language. I was in this place to do development and I needed loads of documentation which were only available in French. I therefore had to tackle and learn the French language and use it to work. The details and intriguing experiences of how I overcame the language barrier will be contained in my next chapter, "Scaling the language barrier".

After 3 months in my new job in the Republic of Niger, I recruited a driver, Laouali, a field assistant, Oumara, and an office administrator,

Habila. Lessons from Tamale were not lost on me. These three people were very critical and indeed pivotal in my accomplishments for two and a half years in Niger. I will forever be grateful for these three people who gave me maximum support and helped me to succeed in my new job. Unfortunately, I had to leave that country under very unpleasant circumstances. But before I left I had successfully engaged several communities in the Damagaram Takaya area and successfully carried out a detailed Base Line Survey that would form the foundation for future developments in that area.

In carrying out the baseline survey I employed standard professional statistical methodologies to collect data and do an analysis, and finally produced basic information such as the total population of the area, average family size, infant mortality rate, maternal mortality rate, population distribution, common childhood diseases, vaccination coverage, etc. This information would provide the foundation for future planning and execution of projects. I successfully completed primary school blocks to enhance education in three communities. Although I did not stay in Niger long enough to follow up and measure the impact of these projects I am convinced that it increased access to schools and that some of the children who had this access increased their opportunities for securing competitive jobs in their lifetime.

My two-year contract ended in March 1998. The National Director for World Vision International had a meeting with me and informed me that he would not renew my contract for another two years. He was looking for somebody to replace me. He therefore renewed my contract for three months in anticipation of recruiting my replacement within the three months. At the end of June 1998, nobody had been found to replace me so my contract was renewed for another 3 months. In a meeting with him in Niamey with my wife, it was she who asked him why he was making this decision.

Ken responded that my family situation was very complicated. I had a daughter in high school in Ghana, two sons in a boarding primary school in Nigeria, and my wife and I and my last daughter were in Niger. We reminded him that before I signed the contract for this job, I had declared details of my family status and indeed we had invited him to our home in Accra and he had met all our children. So we did not just arrive in Niger and surprise him with our family status. At the end of September 1998, I signed yet another three-month contract to last till the end of December. I then submitted my resignation, two days after the contract was signed.

Ken wanted to know whether I had a new job. I told him that I didn't but what was happening to me felt humiliating. I was basically a "squatter" in somebody's job waiting for a replacement to be found. Would I then be expected to jump out of the job and celebrate? No sir! My wife and children returned to Ghana in July 1998. I packed and sent my belongings to Accra by road in August 1998 before the signing of the final three-month contract. The most uncomfortable thing was that my wife had resigned her job to join me in Niger and now the two of us were back in Ghana without jobs.

It was during this period that I was diagnosed with Cervical Spondylosis - the effect of discs in my neck pressing on the spinal cord and reducing the sensitivity of my fingers. I went to the UK in August 1997 for the first surgery on my spine. However, because I was on medical insurance this surgery did not have any financial implications on the organisation. The surgery luckily did not impede my work as an Area Development Program Manager.

Reflecting on the circumstances leading to my departure compels me to make a profound statement. The future of man is ultimately in the hands of God. Unfortunately, some people think they can set up their own future and sometimes trample on the future of others in the process. After my departure from Niger, Ken Singleton proceeded to the UK for a Post-Graduate course. There is a perception that the termination of my contract was part of the strategy to ensure his easy return to Niger as National Director. An Australian was brought in to act as National Director while he was away in the UK. Ken returned to Niger in 1999 but was never able to regain his position as National Director. There was an effort by the African Regional authorities of World Vision International to get me to comment on my departure from Niger. I referred the authorities to the notes contained in my exit interview. The lesson from this experience is that it is the Lord God who determines our future. When people in power make decisions, they should think beyond their interests and consider the interests and future of the staff affected.

Back in Ghana at the end of October 1998, I lived for six days without a job. I finally got a job with the US Peace Corps again and this time as a Training Manager. The French language competence I acquired in Niger came in handy. It enabled me to collaborate with my US Peace Corps colleagues in Burkina Faso, Benin and Ivory coast to design a new

Pre-Service Training (PST) methodology for the US Peace Corps in Ghana. I successfully accomplished this within the period of my one-year contract and moved on further beyond the frontiers of Ghana.

CHAPTER 30

SCALING THE LANGUAGE BARRIER

The enthusiasm with which I arrived in the Republic of Niger to do development work for World Vision International could easily be likened to that of a 100-metre athlete at the beginning of the race; ready for a record-breaking sprint. However, my first meeting with NGO Partners, Government Officials and International Development Partners was a complete disaster. A sheet of paper was passed around with the heading "Ordre du Jour". I stared blankly at the heading since it meant nothing to me. Panic! Panic!

I soon learnt that the heading meant 'Agenda'. The meeting went on for about an hour and I could just understand a few words here and there which put together meant nothing. Documents were distributed and I opened and flipped through them without understanding one full sentence. I could not contribute to the meeting. Even when some people spoke Hausa, the number of French words and phrases included in the Hausa made understanding very difficult. What on earth was I doing here?

I was here to carry out development work to help alleviate poverty and promote the process to bring many people out of poverty and put them on track for a better future. Unfortunately, I was confronted immediately by a language barrier that I had to scale. The Hausa language that I thought I could speak very well was loaded with French words. The few words I knew in French such as the prices and the names of vehicle spare parts that I picked up while making several visits to Ouagadougou were inadequate for development work. I needed to polish my Hausa by understanding the French words blended into the language and I needed to learn how to speak, read and write French.

Development work is a career that requires engagement with the actors with whom one is dealing. The main actors are the government of the country in which one is working, partner Non-Governmental Organisations, Development Partners from the Bilateral and Multilateral community and community members in the areas where development work would be carried out. Language is the main vehicle for these engagements and one must identify, speak, read and write the languages of all these actors. I therefore tackled this language problem with zeal and with all my strength.

Step one in my bid to scale the language barrier was to engage a French teacher. Through the few friends I made, I found a gentleman called Mack Abubakar Danbargi. He agreed to have a one-hour French class with me at my house on Mondays, Wednesdays and Fridays. On day one he assessed the level of French I knew already. He found that the French I knew was woefully inadequate and did not qualify as a working knowledge of the language. In an attempt to conjugate the French equivalent of the verb 'to have', I started correctly and ended up by conjugating the verb 'to go' as well. I scratched my head and regretted not paying attention during Mr D.N. Loriba's French classes in Ghana College. The battle to learn French was on and I was determined to win.

Step two in my language learning battle was to purchase as many books as possible that would help me. With the recommendation of my French teacher, I headed for 'Librarie Labo' (Labo's Bookshop) the only bookshop in Zinder at the time. I bought books on French grammar, rules on the conjugation of French verbs, rules on French spelling and a big French-English/English-French dictionary. Yes! I had ammunition to enter the battle.

Working with the Peace Corps and teaching young Peace Corps volunteers to learn Ghanaian languages taught me a lot. The Pre-Service Training (PST) for US Peace Corps volunteers usually lasted 12 weeks and during that time, many young American volunteers became functionally literate in some Ghanaian languages. Some were able even to give their speeches at the end of the period in a local language with the right accent. What I learnt from these language classes was transferred to my language learning in Niger. I split the language into different competencies. The ability to hear and understand was competence number one. The ability to see the words on paper and recognise them and read them correctly was competence number two. The ability to write the language correctly was competence number three and the ability to speak the language confidently without looking into any paper was competence number four. By dividing the language this way one could use different methodologies for learning each competency.

For the ability to hear and understand the language the best methodology is usually to be in an environment where the language is spoken constantly until one begins to understand. For this, my teacher helped me employ four different techniques. Anytime I was at home, I tuned my radio to Radio France International and just listened to it until some words began to make sense. For example, on the anniversary of the Fall of the Berlin Wall, the word 'chute' came on the radio over and over again until I looked it up in the dictionary to find out that it meant 'drop' or 'fall suddenly'. Another technique was to find a group where people spoke French all the time. I found a musical band in the French Cultural Centre led by a gentleman from Benin, consisting of nationals from other countries and supervised by a French man. The multinational nature of the group compelled them to speak French as their main language.

The keyboard skill I had acquired in Tamale came in very handy. When I introduced myself and told them I could play the keyboard it was good news for them and indeed better news for me. I could sit there listening to all the chatter in French and ask for explanations of the things I did not understand.

I went to the French Cultural Centre to watch French movies in French although I understood less than 5% of the dialogue. I just watched the images and tried to make up what the actors were saying. Sometimes I laughed and clapped when everybody around me laughed and clapped although I did not understand anything. It reminded me of my Form One days in Ghana College, Tamale. Interestingly there were subtitles in French which I tried to read but as anybody will know, reading the subtitles, which I could not read very well, and trying to follow the action while listening to the dialogue was just too much for one person. One thing that I did was to try and remember at least three words in French and then look for their meaning after each movie. On one particular night, I was driving home after a movie when I remembered the words '*Bien sûr*'. I quickly pulled up by a street light and pulled out my English-French dictionary. As I flipped through the pages I heard a knock on the side window of the car. There were two policemen asking me to roll down the window and I complied. They asked me what I was doing and I told them I was looking for the meaning of the French words '*Bien sûr*'. The words meant 'of course'. They burst into laughter and said goodnight to me. The following day the Regional Commander of the Police whom I got to know within the first week of my stay saw me in town and stopped me. He was laughing very hard and I wanted to know why. He told me that his officers on night patrol found me under a street light looking for the meaning of a French word at 12:30 am. I corrected him, saying that it was actually 12:15 a.m. and that caused even more laughter. This shows the ridiculous extent I went to in learning French. I also went to restaurants with my French teacher, where I would place our order and have any other conversations with the waiter in French, while my teacher stood by to check what I was saying. The waiter sometimes brought the wrong order deliberately to force me to repeat my order and insist on what we wanted.

In order to read French correctly, I used the Bible as my text because I had a thorough understanding of the English version. I read the Bible aloud to my teacher for 20 minutes three times a week for 6 months. This enabled me to learn to pronounce French words correctly. I had to work very hard on the conjugation of French verbs and writing French words correctly while applying French grammar and spelling rules. It was an uphill task and I was making very little progress. My teacher was getting discouraged and I was beginning to panic. It reminded me of the preamble for a question in a Physics exam about a worm trying to climb out of a well. The worm moved 15 inches upwards during the day and slipped back 10 inches during the night.

By my third month, I had made very little progress in my efforts to study French. Then one day I was driving into town when I saw a signboard with the US Peace Corps logo for the first time. I went in the direction indicated by the arrow on the sign and got to the Peace Corps office which was also a home for one of the volunteers. A young lady came out to meet me and was relieved when she realised that my preferred language of communication was English. We laughed and I told her I used to be an Associate Peace Corps Director (APCD) in Ghana. She asked me whether I was making any progress in learning the French language. The answer was an emphatic "No". She then brought out a book called "501 French verbs" by Christopher Kendris. She told me that this could help me. I took the book home and read the first 28 pages. By the following morning, I saw the key to learning the French language.

It seems that many people in the anglophone world speak English sometimes correctly, sometimes wrongly without understanding the basic grammatical rules that underpin the language. The following week I was back in Accra on vacation and I decided that I was going to look for the textbooks that were used to teach English when I was in Secondary School. The books were "Practical English", books 1, 2, 3. These books were written by P. Tregidgo and P.A. Ogundipe.

I dedicated a full day to my search. I found myself walking through a section of Central Accra known as Tema Station. In this area, one can find a number of people selling second-hand books spread out over a polythene sheet that is spread on the ground. I approached one of them and asked for the three books. He looked at my face with amusement and disbelief. Why would somebody be looking for textbooks that were used in the 1960s and 1970s in 1996? He then told me he did not have them but I should come back in three days' time and he would see what he could do. I came back in 3 days and he had been able to find books 2 and 3. He asked for a fortune for the books but at that moment I was more interested in the contents of the book than how much they cost.

And with my 'new' old books, I went back to learn basic English grammar. To my amazement, I found out that I did not really understand the grammatical foundations for the English language I was speaking. For example, in both English and French, each verb can be conjugated in 14 different ways; I did not know that. Also, in English and French, when two verbs are used one after the other, the first verb is conjugated and the second verb is left in the infinitive - for example, in the sentence 'I am coming to eat'. The verb 'to come' is conjugated and the verb 'to eat' is left in the infinitive. A greater understanding of the English language gave me a stronger foundation to learn and understand French.

I went back to Niger better prepared to scale the language barrier. My French teacher came back and after one class and giving me an assignment as usual the outcome was completely different. Earlier in my work with him, the best I ever had in an exercise was 4 out of 10. I now scored 10 out of 10 in the first assignment he gave me. The following day he was back in my house in a flash staring at me and he asked what had really changed. I showed him the book that was given to me by the US Peace Corps volunteer and the English grammar books I brought back from Ghana. Since then my competence in spoken, written and the ability to read French and English has improved tremendously.

Two other factors that had a tremendous impact on my French were the people around me in my office and out of my office as well as the courage to say what I wanted to say without the fear of making mistakes. The staff in my office were just fantastic. They always took the time to tell me that what I was saying was wrong and showed me how to say it right. Interestingly my three-year-old daughter came to Niger in 1997 and started going to the nursery school. I learnt so many vocabularies from her nursery rhymes. For example, I learnt the French words for 'rabbit', 'ears' and 'my back' from her rhymes.

One major aspect of language learning is the concept of contextual language. Every context has its own language. There is a kitchen language, a market language, a travel language, a medical language, a development language, etc. For me, the most important contexts I needed to focus on included the economic and social development languages and the work environment language, as well as the language to use in interaction with NGOs, the Government, and Development Partners. My French teacher made sure that we used development literature in French to increase my competencies in reading, writing and engaging in dialogue in these language contexts.

One big aspect of the French language is the gender of nouns. Unlike English every noun in French must have a gender and the speaker must understand this as the gender and number of a noun affects adjectives used to describe the noun. This was a big struggle in the beginning but as the time went by they became natural to me.

When I thought that I was making significant progress in learning the French language, the false association of similar looking French and English words commonly called '*faux amis*' came out of the blue to give me a new challenge. The term actually means 'false friends' and describes words in French that look and sound very much like words in English but that mean completely different things. A few examples will demonstrate this. The French word '*librarie*' means 'bookshop' and not 'library' as it appears to suggest. The French word for 'library' is '***bibliothèque***'. The word '***medicin***' means 'doctor' and not 'medicine'. The French word for 'medicine' is '***medicament***'. '*Actuellement*' means 'at present' and not 'actually'. 'Actually' in English translates to '*en fait*' in French. Any English speaker seeking to learn French needs to take these false friends very seriously in order to understand correctly the people they are listening to and the documents they read and more importantly to avoid embarrassment in using the wrong terminology. I took natural pineapple juice from Ghana to Niger. On the package was written 'no preservatives added'. An American lady colleague of mine misinterpreted 'preservatives' in English for '*preservatifs*' in French and caused an uproar of laughter during the workshop she was facilitating. In fact '*preservatifs*' in French means 'condoms' - very embarrassing indeed. She was so embarrassed about her predicament that she stopped speaking French for almost a whole day.

By December 1996, I had acquired sufficient competence in the French and Hausa languages to be able to function officially and unofficially in the Republic of Niger. I was able to give radio and television interviews, make presentations in forums with other development workers and generally engage efficiently with anybody. This new language skill also significantly enhanced my career and enabled me to work in francophone countries across the African continent.

A member of lessons can be learnt from my experience in scaling the language barrier. Any organisation that wants to recruit and send a senior officer to a country where the language is different from the language spoken by the officer should invest in sending the person to a country where the new language is spoken for a three month immersion experience. The organisation could have sent me to a francophone country such as Benin, the Ivory Coast or Senegal where I do not understand any local language for a period of three months. This would have been a very useful investment and would have saved me a lot of time struggling to learn French. It must be said that the time I spent trying to learn French compromised the time I could have spent in field work. The second lesson is that with determination one can always accomplish what seems impossible. I also learnt that in language learning one can always learn from all the possibilities around, even including children.

I will forever be grateful to the different people who contributed to my learning and use of the Hausa and French languages.

CHAPTER 31

EXPLORING WITH THE BRAVE AND THE FEARLESS

The US Peace Corps was started by President John F. Kennedy in 1961 with the objective of supporting the human resource needs of developing countries, helping people in these countries to understand America better and also helping Americans to understand other cultures. It is interesting to note that the first 52 volunteers who left the USA came to Ghana and arrived on the 30th of August 1961. They were met at the airport by the first president of Ghana, Osagyefo Dr Kwame Nkrumah. Since then the US Peace Corps has always had an office in Ghana with volunteers of all backgrounds and ages coming to the country to provide services in a wide variety of sectors. I had the privilege of working for this interesting service of the American government from August 1995 to March 1996 as the Associate Peace Corps Director (APCD) in charge of the Small Enterprise Development (SED) project and from November 1998 to July 1999 as the Training Manager. My experience while working for this well organised institution taught me many lessons that have remained with me over the years and significantly influenced my career.

My orientation and integration into the US Peace Corps in Ghana was rapid, efficient and very well planned. I was introduced to all the staff members I was supposed to know and interact with in my work and settled into my office with a computer already set up with access to internal and external communication. By the end of the second day I had gone through the process of acquiring an official identification card from the embassy that enabled me to access US Embassy installations as a member of staff and was equipped with a high frequency radio communication set which enabled me to remain in touch with all my colleagues for twenty-four hours a day. This experience has significantly influenced my reception of new staff into the organisation I have led.

The Peace Corps has a slogan that describes the volunteer service as "The toughest job you will ever enjoy" and the determination and courage of the volunteers I encountered seemed to affirm this. The first volunteers

I received flew in from Washington DC on a KLM flight via Amsterdam, arriving in Accra at about 9:00 p.m. Working with a well-coordinated set of arrangements, different components of the reception team ensured a smooth transit through the immigration, customs and other arrival processes in the airport. The volunteers were quickly transferred to an accommodation facility quite close to the offices of the Peace Corps. The morning of the following day witnessed the official welcome of the volunteers to Ghana followed by what we called the first shock treatment. Working in groups of two, the volunteers were given a map of Accra, some small amount of money and a task to find a landmark in the city and come back with evidence that they had found that landmark. For example, one group was given the task of finding the Ussher Fort Prison in Jamestown and coming back with evidence that they had found it. The money they were given was not enough to take a taxi so they had to rely on the public minibus system in the city. Confronting this task less than twenty-four hours after arriving in Ghana, in my opinion, was really herculean. Interestingly, the volunteers had the courage and determination to accomplish the task. These young people must have gone through rigorous selection and the appropriate orientation in Washington DC.

My task was to prepare and receive volunteers and assign them to SED projects. The two main areas of focus included work with artisans who produced Ghanaian-made products and in areas with potential for the development of community tourism as a means of earning money.

In my first assignment as the APCD in charge of the SED project, I worked to promote businesses of small artisans and local community tourism. I was introduced to this job and greatly assisted by John Mason, a Canadian consultant on forestry and wildlife. Working with local artisans, a volunteer who was already in place before my arrival worked with basket weavers in Bolgatanga to assist them to improve the standardisation of Bolga baskets and linked them with the international market particularly in the US. I look at the current ease with which one can search for "Bolga basket" on the internet and get quick results, and remember the struggles in the mid 1990s when the Peace Corps volunteers worked hard to make this product known beyond Ghana.

In the area of tourism, I remember four communities with potentials for tourism that we tried to develop into viable businesses. The Laribanga community was strategically placed to develop the tourism business where tourists could visit the Mole Game Reserve to watch the large variety of wild animals and also visit the ancient mosque in that community. The Boabeng-Fiema community has developed close relationships with monkeys that come into the community and are given food. This offered an opportunity for tourists who want to observe monkeys at a very close range without posing a threat to the animals. I started to explore a potential for developing this community into a viable tourist destination.

I sent a volunteer to the communities around Shai Hills near Accra to develop a walking trail that would attract tourists who were interested in walking and mountain climbing. My days in the UK with my former Headmaster Colin Macdonald climbing Ben Nevis in Scotland greatly influenced my decision to pursue this community tourism for hikers. Then I got a volunteer to develop a tourism site at the estuary of the Volta River at Ada Foah that could give tourists an opportunity to reside by the seashore and enjoy the interaction between the Volta River and the Atlantic Ocean.

I stayed in the Peace Corps for only 8 months and was not able to see how far these initiatives went and the benefits to the communities. My departure was purely to look for better conditions of service and I must say that it was the most painful departure from a job I enjoyed so much and from a Country Director, Harriet Lancaster, who demonstrated a near-perfect example of good leadership and management. I will never forget her saying that "when I look at the budget, the figures talk to me".

In November 1998, I returned from my job in Niger to take up a one-year contract with the Peace Corps again, this time, as a Training Manager. I was required to design a new training programme that would replace the one that brought volunteers together at a training centre in Saltpond in the Central Region for the training sessions. Four different types of training sessions were organised in this centre made up of Pre-Service Training (PST), In-Service Training (IST), Mid-Service Training (MST) and Close of Service Training (CST). PST was a 12-week training session during which arriving volunteers were trained to understand the Ghanaian culture, the sectors they were going to work in, and to learn and be able to communicate in one Ghanaian language. The IST brought volunteers back to the training site to share experiences after 3 months of work , to get off their chests some of the problems they had confronted on the ground , and also to seek advice on how to go back and tackle those problems. MST was done when a volunteer was halfway through his or her service and helped to orientate the volunteers for the rest of their stay in the country. The CST was more or less a debriefing session during which time volunteers shared important experiences that could be incorporated into future PST sessions. It also gave an opportunity for equipping the volunteers with some basic skills in job searches as they prepared to go back to the USA.

I tried to explore an alternative for training volunteers to fit into their new assignments in Ghana without keeping them in a camp for twelve weeks. In order to study the different options and variations of training volunteers, and supported by a number of colleagues involved in the training sessions, we spent up to two weeks in Peace Corps offices and programmes in the Republic of Benin and also in Burkina Faso to see how they conducted similar training sessions. I then led a process to come up with the Community Based Training (CBT) model with a lot of learning from these countries and inputs from every stakeholder in the Peace Corps volunteer training process. The key features of the CBT model included the selection of a community for the training, the hosting of volunteers in Ghanaian families and identification of a common meeting place in the community for the volunteers to come together two to three times a week for lessons that involved all of them. Families who were selected to host volunteers were supported with some resources to enable them perform their role as hosts to the satisfaction of both volunteers and the Peace Corps. This model has a number of advantages. In the first place, hosting the volunteers in families promoted the principle of immersion that significantly enhanced a fast way of learning about the Ghanaian culture. Secondly, the immersion promoted a better approach to the learning of a Ghanaian language as the volunteers heard the local language spoken around them throughout the day and consciously or unconsciously assimilated the words they heard. The approach was cheaper and resources saved as a result could be used to respond to other needs of volunteers. The centre-based approach made the volunteers feel as if they were in an institution while the CBT model gave a more dignified picture of being part of a family and a community.

It was during this period that Harriet Lancaster, the Country Director, left Ghana and was replaced by Leonard Floyd, another person who displayed a very high and professional standard of leadership and management with a deep human touch. I can never forget the day I was taken to hospital when a fish bone got stuck in my throat during lunch. Leonard arranged to get my children from school and send them home and to get my wife informed about my condition. He then came to the hospital after work and sat by my bed all evening until he was sure that I was going to be safe, by which time it was nearly midnight. Leonard's basic knowledge of the Mooré language and advanced communication in French created an extra space for us for communication in a different language other than English.

During these two periods when I was in the US Peace Corps, the service had programmes in science and maths teaching, forestry, water and sanitation and small enterprise development. These have definitely changed over the years to give way to programmes that respond to evolving development issues. I was excited and pleasantly surprised to find out in June 2021 that the organisation in Ghana still uses the community-based training model for the training of volunteers. I feel a sense of pride that the little seed I planted in 1999 has been watered and nurtured by several volunteers and staff to grow and remain standing in 2021. This has been made possible by the efforts of the courageous and fearless volunteers and staff who are never afraid to try anything new. Long live the Peace Corps!

CHAPTER 32

FACILITATING DEVELOPMENT IN THE MIDST OF CONFLICT

The date was 13th August 1999. I sat on one of the left-hand window seats of the Ethiopian Airlines Boeing 757 aircraft waiting to fly from Accra to Addis Ababa. The cabin crew went through the usual formalities as the aircraft taxied to the northern end of the runway. They welcomed passengers on board, told us how long the flight would be, demonstrated the use of oxygen masks and the life vest. At the end of all this, the aircraft sped off smoothly from the end of the runway and we were off and airborne in a few seconds. This was indeed a memorable flight because it was taking me out of Ghana and for about 13 years, a situation I never imagined would happen. I was on my way to work for ActionAid in Burundi as the Program Support Manager for the organisation in that country.

Reflecting on how I got to this point, I remember a friend calling me two months earlier and asking me to look at an advertisement in the Daily Graphic (A Ghanaian state-owned daily newspaper). There was a job opportunity in Burundi and my knowledge of French could qualify me for the job. I applied for the job, went through the first interview in Accra and had the second interview in Bujumbura, Burundi. I signed the contract to start work on the 15th of August 1999 and I was now on my way to start work.

I settled in my seat, finished the dinner that was served on board and went to sleep. The flight to Addis was uneventful and so was the connecting flight to Bujumbura. I was met at the airport and taken to the ActionAid Guest House where I met Tijan Williams, a member of staff of ActionAid in The Gambia, who was on secondment to support the Financial Department of ActionAid Burundi. I settled into the guest house and got ready to have dinner with the Country Director, John Abuya. He heartily welcomed me to Bujumbura and we had a pleasant dinner.

After dinner, Tijan and I returned to the Guest House. On that night of the 14th of August 1999, I had my first 'baptism' of what working in conflict really means. The time was 9:00 pm when all of a sudden I heard rapid gunfire coming from the mountains to the east of the city.

Tijan and I looked at each other and he told me that this was a normal occurrence. We sat down, very concerned about what to do. In fact, we could not do anything about what was happening. We could only hope that the gunfire would stop or remain in the mountains. I was to continue my life in Bujumbura with the understanding that gunfire from the mountains was a normal occurrence. Indeed, it became known as 'the music'. This was the beginning of my work of facilitating development amid conflict.

The country Burundi is bordered by Lake Tanganyika to the west, the Democratic Republic of Congo to the northwest, Rwanda to the North and Tanzania to the east and the south. Bujumbura, the capital city, is a beautiful well laid-out city, sitting between mountains on its eastern and southern sides, Lake Tanganyika on the Western side, with plains and flat ground on the northern side. From the city, one can get to the Democratic Republic of Congo (DRC) in half an hour. Indeed, the city of Uvira in the DRC is located on the western side of Lake Tanganyika. The country has a population density of about 449 persons per square kilometre as at the year 2019 making it the country with the second-highest population density in Africa, second only to Rwanda, which has a density of about 524 persons per square kilometre. Compare this with Nigeria that has less than 250 persons per square kilometre or Ghana with 134 persons per square kilometre or even the Republic of Niger with 18 persons per square kilometre and one will understand how populous the country is. Conflict analysts have always established a link between conflict and high population density as well as competition for natural resources. I wonder whether this analysis could be applied to Burundi and Rwanda.

Burundi is one of the most beautiful countries in Africa. It is made up of rolling mountains and hills that run all over the country and embellished with coffee and tea plantations rolling down the valleys and up the hills. Administratively, the country is divided into provinces, the provinces are divided into communes, the communes into collines and the collines into sub-collines. The word 'colline' is actually the French word for hill. In other words, beyond the commune, communities reside on hills.

The rainfall pattern in Burundi is one of the heaviest I have seen anywhere in Africa. The first rainy season begins in the middle of February every year and finishes at the end of June. The first dry season lasts for about one and a half months starting from the beginning of July and ending in the middle of August. The second rainy season then starts in the middle of August and goes all the way to the end of December. This means the country has about nine months of rainfall. Flying over the country from one province to another, every observer will see an undulating countryside covered with a green carpet of banana, tea and coffee plantations.

The history and ethnic backgrounds of Burundi are important for a meaningful understanding of the conflict context in which I found myself in August 1999. Burundi, a former colony of Belgium, gained independence from her colonial masters on the 1st of July 1962. The country is made up of three ethnic groups namely the Hutu (about 84%), the Tutsi (about 14%), and the Twa (about 1%). Ethnicity in Burundi and Rwanda is completely different from ethnicity as understood in most of the rest of Africa. In Ghana and in most West African countries, an ethnic group has at least three characteristics. An ethnic group normally occupies a specific geographical area, they speak a language particular to the ethnic group and have cultural practices that are unique to them. In Burundi, all three ethnic groups speak the same language, Kirundi, and are scattered all over the country without reference to a geographical area belonging to one ethnic group. The cultural practices, particularly festivals and dances, are different from one region to the other and not related to any particular ethnic group. The above description of ethnicity in Burundi automatically brings up the question of how these ethnic groups are identified.

Generally, the ethnic groups are identified by physical features but this method of identification is collapsing due to intermarriages between the ethnic groups. Tutsis are generally perceived to be tall and slim with aquiline noses and a fair skin complexion. Hutus are perceived to be shorter than their Tutsi counterparts and with flat noses and darker in complexion. The Batwa are generally very short in stature with an accent different from that of the two ethnic groups. With intermarriages between the Tutsi and Hutu and a patrilineal inheritance system, one could find a person with the physical features of one ethnic group and belonging to the other ethnic group. This makes the ethnic identification quite complicated.

In July1993, Burundi held parliamentary and presidential elections and for the first time, a candidate from the Hutu ethnic group, Melchior Ndadaye, was elected as president. In the third week of October 1993, the newly elected president was assassinated in a coup d'état led by a Tutsi military officer, Major Pierre Buyoya. There were spontaneous reprisals and Tutsis in the rural communities were killed in retaliation by an angry Hutu populace. The army that was mainly controlled by the Tutsi ethnic group responded by trying to get to rural communities to save Tutsis who were there. There were reports of reprisal killings of Hutus by the Tutsi-led army. These tit-for-tat killings between Hutus and Tutsis started in October 1993 and lasted all the way until the year 2005 when a final peace agreement was implemented and elections held in that year. It is in the middle of this conflict that I arrived in Burundi in 1999 to facilitate development work.

In the last quarter of 1999 I was on my way from the province of Ruyigi to the capital city, Bujumbura. I sat in the front passenger seat of the Toyota Land Cruiser that was parked by the roadside, listening in disbelief and watching the monument while the driver, Chrysanthe, narrated one of the gruesome stories of events that happened at the beginning of the crisis in 1993. It was about the massacre of 52 children from a primary school. The Hutu teacher simply selected these children from the school and marched them to a gas filling station in a community called Kwibubu, about one kilometre away, where they were sent into a room. The doors of the room were locked and all the windows closed, petrol was poured over the room and the children set on fire. Two or three of the children managed to break through a window and attempted to escape. One of these children succeeded and has told his story to the British Broadcasting Corporation (BBC). A second child, a girl, fell into a dry well, where she survived for three days until the Tutsi soldiers arrived and rescued her. A third child climbed a tree and remained on the tree for three days until he was rescued. It was the boy on the tree who told the soldiers about the girl who fell into the dry well. A monument has been built on the site of this massacre on the road to Gitega from Bujumbura with the inscription in French and the local Kirundi language that translates to "Never Again". The teacher who committed this heinous crime was traced, found and sentenced to death and executed by hanging.

I arrived in Burundi to work as the Program Support Manager providing support to the Country Director, John Abuya. I was soon to find out that John was one of the most meticulous and efficient managers with whom I had ever worked. He made every effort to ensure that I understood everything I needed to know in order to provide support for him and the field staff. I helped to produce project reports and project proposals as well as other project documentation in English from documents that were available in French. In order to do all this, I had to be constantly in the field.

Workers of ActionAid, Burundi, from both the Hutu and Tutsi ethnic groups became victims at the early stages of the conflict with staff members being dragged out and killed by either Hutu rebels or Tutsi soldiers. It became very difficult for the office to operate but by the time I arrived the staff had signed a code of conduct and promised to abide by the terms contained in that code. Four of the main terms of the code of conduct were:

To forgive each other and stick together as development workers and work together without ethnic considerations.

To go to communities and facilitate development work without considering the ethnicity of the beneficiaries in the communities.

To seek the development and reconstruction of communities that were affected by the conflict without reference to ethnicity.

To avoid discussions related to ethnicity and the conflict in the office.

The programme in Burundi had six components, namely Reconstruction and Rehabilitation, Adult Literacy using the REFLECT (Regenerated Freirean Literacy Through Empowering Community Techniques) approach, Construction of Education Infrastructure, Water and Sanitation, Income Generation and Agriculture and Food Production. The six different components of the Country Programme were carried out using a process to facilitate peace and reconciliation. In other words, no matter which component of the programme one was working on, the work should be done in such a way as to facilitate peace and reconciliation between the ethnic groups. For example, in the Reconstruction programme, ActionAid provided support for the reconstruction of communities where people's houses had been destroyed during the conflict. Building materials would normally be provided by ActionAid. The construction of the building was usually done by the community members themselves.

In the discussions to identify beneficiaries, the question of peacebuilding was brought up and the different ethnic groups had dialogues in a way that promoted peace. In the actual work of construction, people came together to construct houses for each other without reference to ethnicity. I remember a report of a woman whose husband and male children were killed by members of the other ethnic group. In discussions during these reconstruction projects, she could identify those who killed her family members. They came forward, literally on their knees, to apologise for what had happened, although an apology could not bring the dead back. They actually worked hard in the reconstruction of the woman's house. For ActionAid as an NGO, the community dialogue that took place before the implementation of projects and which we referred to as the 'software' component of the project was leading on to build relationships that would keep the communities together and avoid future conflict. The same principle was used in all the other programmes.

The toughest part of working in conflict is the requirement for neutrality in every sense of the word. I remember on one occasion when the President of the Republic was going to visit a community in a province where we had a large office. The military authorities in that province requested to use an ActionAid truck that was normally used for carrying supplies to projects to carry soldiers to the community where the president was going to visit. This was to provide security for the President. The office declined the request and insisted that the only way was to get approval from the Country Director. The Country Director was on leave in Kenya and I was acting for him. I received this request by telephone and instructed that the request be declined. The military authorities said if we would not give them the truck willingly they would forcefully take it. I instructed the field officer to request that the threat by the military should be put on paper, signed, and faxed to me. That fax never came and the truck was not taken.

One needed courage and conviction to survive in this environment.

For the Country Director and me, the only expatriate staff of the organisation, success hinged on a number of issues. In the first place, we worked as a team professionally with transparency and trust in each other. Secondly, the national staff of the organisation provided us with maximum support and protection. We also adhered strictly to the policies of the organisation as well as national labour policies. Finally, we belonged to a network of International NGOs who met weekly to carry out an analysis of the conflict situation and advise members.

When travelling from the national headquarters to any programme office in one of the provinces, there was always radio communication between the travelling vehicle, the headquarters and the field office. The travelling vehicle was called on a radio set every 15 minutes to communicate its location on the road. Each radio communication lasted less than 10 seconds. By applying this to all my field trips, the field office and the headquarters made sure that if we got into difficulties it would not take more than 15 minutes for them to know that we had a problem.

I had to learn basic security practices and procedures which became habits in order to guarantee my survival. For example, I learnt to park the organisational car that I drove in such a way as to facilitate quick departure. The 20 to 40 seconds required to back out and drive could be the difference between life and death. I learnt to avoid routine behaviour such as leaving the house or the office at the same time every day. If it was possible one had to vary the route to the office and back home. I became security conscious and looked into my rear-view mirror while driving from time to time to ensure that there was not one particular car following me. I left the house with the understanding that I may not be able to come back again. This was the reality of working in a country in conflict.

From statistics of attacks on travelling vehicles, we established that they occurred before 8:00 a.m. and after 4:00 p.m. We therefore made a policy that all travel by road should take place after 8 a.m. and all vehicles should be back in the office before 4:00 p.m. By putting these measures in place we minimised the risk of being attacked or falling into an ambush. Another major support we received was from the United Nations. They provided air transport to some provinces and we took advantage of this to fly from the capital city to the provinces we wanted to visit. These flights were free of charge. The ability to remain neutral in a conflict situation, although difficult, guaranteed our safety with both the government forces and forces of the rebellion. I remember having a chat with a senior military officer who asked how I felt being an expatriate in the middle of this conflict. I expressed my fears and concerns. He however assured me that the government knew exactly what we were doing and he believed the rebels were also aware of our work in the communities and so both parties did not have any interest in harming any of us.

The interesting thing about the conflict in Burundi was the careful and deliberate manner in which confrontations were held. The three big industries in the country included two big breweries that produced beer and soft drinks, a big sugar production factory, and factories that produced coffee. Interestingly, none of these factories was ever hit during the conflict. As narrated earlier, gunfire around Bujumbura became a normal activity. Sometimes when the gunfire came very close to the residential areas, I would set up a small mattress in the corridor on which I would go to sleep. This guaranteed that a shell would have to pass through at least two walls before I could be hit. I sometimes wonder whether this was really so or just provided a false sense of security.

Despite this, the high-risk nature of working in a country in conflict cannot be overemphasised. In October 1999 shortly after my arrival in the country, there was an incident in the province of Rutana that resulted in the killing of 2 international staff members and 7 Burundian citizens. The UN staff had organised a visit to the province to observe relief assistance to displaced people. During the visit, rebels invaded the place, forced the visitors to sit on the ground, gave a short political speech and started shooting them one after the other. One of the UN staff had a firearm concealed and was able to pull this out and return fire, upon which the rebels fled. This assassination struck fear in the hearts of all of us who were expatriate workers in the country.

In November 2001 we got courageous enough and my wife came from Ghana for a visit. In the middle of the night, the gunfire from the mountains started and she woke me up to listen to the gunfire. I listened for a few minutes and told her where I thought it was coming from and the type of weapons that were used. She asked what we should do and I said we should just pull the bed covers over ourselves and go to sleep. She was definitely upset. The following day we had dinner with the Country Director and she asked what he did when he heard gunfire in the middle of the night. He told her that normally, he would pick up the phone and call me and ask where the gunfire was coming from. When he heard the answer, he would pull his bed covers over his face and go to sleep. My wife was not really amused by this answer but it made her understand the similar answer I gave from the night before.

On the last Sunday before my wife's departure, I was invited to a sending-off cocktail party for one of the UN staff. I attended this party with my wife and we met the UN World Health Organisation (WHO) Representative for Burundi, Dr Kassy Manlan. When I introduced my wife to him, he said she must be a very brave woman to come to visit in the middle of this conflict. Knowing that he was an Ivorian and therefore next-door neighbour back at home made our interaction very interesting. The following day I got a call at 10:00 a.m. that the WHO representative had not reported to the office. I got updates from the UN office every hour from then. At 1:00 p.m. I got the message that he had been killed and his body was found in Lake Tanganyika. This indeed was very scary.

According to an Integrated Regional Information Network report of 5th May 2005, four senior army and police officers were sentenced to death in May 2005 for the murder of the WHO representative. Unsubstantiated rumours have it that the execution was ordered by the former president of Burundi, Pierre Buyoya, and this was because the WHO representative refused to allow the importation of unapproved medicines worth about 10 million dollars. My wife flew out of the country a few days later but this incident demonstrated the risks of working and facilitating development in conflict.

During this time, I had one telephone call during which the caller threatened my life. In a strategic planning process, a decision was taken to reshuffle staff. One staff member who was in the headquarters was relocated to a province. The next morning, I received a phone call at 5:56 a.m. The caller told me that he was aware of the reshuffle and the movement of that staff member from the headquarters to the field. He then went ahead to tell me to reverse that staff member's relocation or I would regret it. I told him I was not a Director and he said he was aware that I could influence the decision of the Country Director. I told the caller that the worst thing he could do to me was to take my life and that death is the only certainty for him and for me. If he took my life, he would not be able to add anything to his own life so he should go ahead and do what he wanted to do. After the telephone conversation I called somebody I knew in the Telecommunications Department and gave him the time of the call and my number. The call was traced to a telephone booth in the centre of town therefore making it impossible to find out who actually made the call. This was the type of risky life I lived in Burundi from August 1999 to March 2003.

The most intriguing part of my work in Burundi was in March 2003. ActionAid held a send-off get-together for me in a popular bar and restaurant called Havana. While the send-off party was ongoing, shells were being fired from the mountains into the city. A friend of ours working for a sister NGO called the Country Director and asked whether we were aware of the shells being fired into the city. The Country Director said he was aware but said that if one gets hit by a shell, it did not matter where one was at the time. Our friend simply said that we needed to be wise, because if you are killed in your house, it would be easier to identify the body than if you are killed in the town in the middle of a party. We laughed over it and continued with the party. This is the extent to which we became numb to the violence and conflict that surrounded us.

The protection we received from the communities where we worked was extraordinary. I remember being in one of the provinces for meetings and when the field staff were preparing to go out to the communities, two people arrived on bicycles at about 7:30 a.m. to warn the staff not to come out to the field because there was probably going to be an attack on the communities where they were going. The staff agreed and did not go to the field and by the end of the day, we heard that there had been an attack on the communities where our staff members were supposed to work. Very scary indeed.

The documentation of my development work in Burundi cannot be complete without the story of Margaret. Margaret was a very dynamic outgoing woman who founded an orphanage called "Maison Shalom". It was one mid-morning in the year 2001. I sat in Margaret's office with a notebook on my lap and listened to her narrate the details of two dramatic events linked to ActionAid and Maison Shalom. With her constant laughter and smiles, the narrative demonstrated Margaret's courage to stand up against the army when they were carrying out reprisal killings of people from the Hutu ethnic group and her determination to hide an ActionAid staff member in her premises for more than a week during this time. Although she was a Tutsi herself, she was able to hide the staff member and save the gentleman's life. In a similar situation when a Tutsi woman and her Hutu husband were faced with the dilemma of life and death they handed over their six-month-old baby girl called Lydia to Margaret and the two of them were executed. The girl called Lydia is still alive and doing well living out of Burundi. My checks in Burundi in December 2020 indicate that Margaret had fled the country to Rwanda. The orphanage has been taken over and given to the Catholic parish, and a major building that she rented to a bank, and used the proceeds for the care of the orphans, has also been taken over by the government. Orphanage Maison Shalom is no more.

In the early part of 2002, the rebels invaded Bujumbura, the capital city and took over two suburbs of the city. ActionAid had to advise their staff to remain at home. On the second day of the invasion, my domestic worker arrived in my house in tears. He had fled his home to an Internally Displaced Camp and his wife and children had also fled but they had found themselves in two different camps. He had no clue where his wife was. He passed the night with me and proceeded the following day to try and find his wife and children. The invasion ended when the military intervened and bombed the attackers from the air. At the end of it all, we did not lose any staff member. My domestic worker found his wife and children and got back home safely. It is frightening to be in one part of the city while gunfire and battles are going on in other parts of the city. Somehow I lived through these experiences not knowing whether I was very brave or had simply became numb to the danger all around me because of the constant gunfire and security risks. While I was in Burundi a retired Ghanaian soldier, Major (Rtd) Nathan Danquah, who worked for the UN in Rwanda called me twice a day for three months to give me security advice. I will forever be grateful to this man for his commitment to providing me with security advice that was so dear to me.

In the first quarter of 2003, when the rebels fired rockets into the city from the mountains, I almost lost my life taking the risk of driving from my house to the office. We had asked all staff to stay at home. In the afternoon, when there seemed to be some quiet and I could no longer hear the firing of rockets into the city, I decided to drive into town. For anybody who knows Bujumbura, I got on the road from Kiriri to the city centre. As I went past a popular restaurant called Chez Andre, a rocket landed barely 15 metres from the position of my car but off the road. The impact on the ground swayed my car from one side to the other. By a sheer miracle, it did not shatter any of the windows of the Toyota RAV4 I was driving. I stopped, turned around and went back home, badly shaken but alive. With hindsight, I acknowledge that attempting to drive from my house to the city centre was rather reckless on my part. My escape, I believe, was one of the divine interventions in my life.

I have always looked back and felt very pleased that the outcomes of our development interventions were actually worth the risks we took. By the end of the year 2001 the organisation had successfully provided support for the resettlement of over 3000 families. While we provided building materials such as roofing sheets and cement, members of the communities supported each other through manual labour in the construction of homes.

The REFLECT programme described above had a huge impact on the thought processes and behaviour of community members, many of whom did not have formal education. While I was talking to the Governor of the

Ruyigi Province, Isaac Bujaba, he said he could easily identify communities where ActionAid was involved in development facilitation. When having communal meetings in such communities, members of the community were actively involved in the meeting and were very organised in their thoughts and presentations, soliciting answers that would contribute to the development of the community. For me, this transformation of the communities from being passive receivers of development aid to becoming active partners in the development process was a huge accomplishment.

One of the projects in Burundi was a microcredit project that sought to give loans to individuals at zero interest. This was supposed to be a revolving fund. Instead of cash, members were given goats with the expectation that the offspring of the goats would be given to the next set of beneficiaries. In the final analysis, this project could be described as unsuccessful. The staff of the organisation who worked on the project did not have the technical skills for the management of microcredit projects. Studies across Africa have shown that microcredit projects by NGOs have largely been unsuccessful. These are but a few examples of the outcomes of my work in Burundi. Generally, the peacebuilding aspect of the programme was a huge success.

This narrative highlights a number of issues related to working or facilitating development in a conflict situation. The idea of a code of conduct that all staff will be required to sign up to and respect was key to our success in Burundi. The neutrality of the organisation enabled us to work and be understood by both parties in the conflict. Development cannot be delinked from politics but NGOs have the capacity to be non-partisan. The existence of realistic policies in NGOs and the close respect for these policies make it possible to work in the context of conflict without bias. Professionalism, transparency and courage are needed in such circumstances. Anybody who wants to work in Africa and in situations of conflict, in general, should be aware of these high risks. I thank the Almighty God that I survived in Burundi from August 1999 to March 2003. Unfortunately I have had no post-trauma counselling and I believe that the numbness that characterised my behaviour could have been due to trauma.

CHAPTER 33

JOINING PARTNERSHIPS TO FIGHT HIV/AIDS

In the early years of my career as a development worker in the 1980s, the Human Immunodeficiency Virus (HIV) pandemic that causes the Acquired Immune Deficiency Syndrome (AIDS) hit the world. The pandemic will remain one of the biggest public health challenges in modern times. Throughout my career I have come to learn that the United Nations General Assembly has become the main forum where the global Social Development Agenda is set and followed by the rest of the world. In the year 2000, the United Nations came up with the Millennium Development Goals (MDGs) with seven goals. The sixth goal was aimed at combatting the HIV/AIDS pandemic across the world.

One of the key guidelines that inform NGO development thinking is the information from the UN General Assembly. In ActionAid, the MDGs immediately became a guide across the organisation. In Burundi, we quickly began to include programmes on HIV in our already existing programmes. In the year 2000, the Department for International Development (DfID) of the British Government called for proposals for the funding of a programme called Support to the International Partnership Against AIDS in Africa (SIPAA). This was funding for work on HIV/AIDS on the African continent. ActionAid set up a team in Harare, Zimbabwe, to write a proposal to access this funding. I was privileged to be part of this team made up of ActionAid staff from across the African region. They included Joan Sawe (the Africa Regional Finance Coordinator), Colin Williams (Africa Regional Director), Ephraim Ndlebu (African regional programs coordinator), Sledge Salifu (Programs Manager for Ghana on secondment to Rwanda), Dr. Jacqueline Batarangaye (African Regional HIV/AIDS Coordinator), and Ahmed Jamal (Programs Manager for Ethiopia).

Together, we spent nearly two weeks working as a team to produce a winning proposal. The different members of the team worked on their areas of specialisation to ensure that the proposal was professionally written to cover areas such as HIV/AIDS technical information, Programming,

Human Resources, Administration and Financial Management. One person with expertise in programming worked hard to reduce the document to a Logical Framework. At the end of it all, when we submitted this proposal, the organisation won the bid with funding of £45 million to be disbursed and used for interventions over a period of three years.

There were three major components of the proposal. The first component was to provide support to HIV interventions in four countries, namely, Ethiopia, Ghana, Burundi and Rwanda. This is where the ActionAid Country Programmes that already had structures and programmes for HIV/AIDS had a comparative advantage. These countries had already engaged various local NGO partners in HIV programming. In Burundi, the partners included the National AIDS Council and local NGOs working on HIV.

The second component of the project provided funding for ActionAid as an organisation to get into countries where the organisation was not yet fully operational and use HIV as an entry point for extending interventions into other areas of development. The third component identified a research institution that was continental in outlook and provided funding for research that would feed into the rest of the programme across the continent. For this research institution, we identified the Health Economics and AIDS Research Division (HEARD) of the Faculty of Economics at the University of Kwazulu-Natal. With this setup, we provided a superior proposal to DfID.

The biggest lesson I learnt from this exercise is the need for international NGOs in their bid for funding from development partners to look at three areas that contribute to the production of a successful proposal. These are forming coalitions and partnerships for programme implementation including partnerships with government institutions, research as part of programme implementation for learning and improvement of interventions and clearly defining their own interventions in the programmes they intend to implement. The other important lesson is the ability to create a team with multidisciplinary expertise to work on project proposals. The synergy in this team was extraordinary and this could be seen in the final document.

Back in Burundi, when the project was approved and funded, the Burundi Country Programme received funding of £4.15 million for the implementation of HIV/AIDS interventions over a period of three years. Our major partner was the Burundi National AIDS Council. I had the privilege to be appointed as the Technical Advisor to the National AIDS Council. The interventions and support we gave to the National AIDS

Council included the rental of office space for the team of experts who were previously crammed into a small office.

The Executive Director of the National AIDS Council was Dr Joseph Wakana, a dermatologist and specialist in infectious diseases. I found this man to be an amazing expert with extensive knowledge and competence in dealing with the issue of the pandemic. His calm disposition and professional approach to everything enabled me, who was not an expert in that area to provide the necessary expertise in programme monitoring and evaluation as well as implementation. Apart from providing accommodation for the HIV/AIDS team, we also provided a Monitoring and Evaluation (M&E) Specialist, Social Mobilisation Specialist and a medical doctor to support the Council.

I had to work extra hard to read around the subject of HIV/AIDS to be able to provide the support I was supposed to provide. At this point, I had joined the fight against HIV/AIDS in full force.

As part of the learning process, I joined staff members of the National AIDS Council to participate in a training programme organised by HEARD in the University of Kwazulu-Natal in South Africa. The course was titled "Planning for HIV/AIDS in Sub-Saharan Africa". This was in the northern hemisphere summer of 2001. I have specified "northern hemisphere" because the same period is the winter in the southern hemisphere where South Africa is located and the weather at that time in South Africa can be very cold. On the third day of this six-week programme, one of the major events in my life occurred. Together with participants in the workshop, I sat quietly and listened to the morning presentations. In the middle of one of the presentations I was called out to go to the office of the training centre to receive a telephone call. In that office I was told to call my boss in Burundi. When I called him he told me to call my wife in Ghana. My heart raced like a high-speed train in France. My boss definitely knew something he did not want to tell me. I called my wife and the first thing she asked me was whether I was sitting or standing. That immediately spelt trouble. When I told her that I was sitting, she informed me that my mother had passed away. It was very difficult to talk. I broke down and wept uncontrollably. A multitude of ideas ran through my mind. I managed to communicate this sad news to the organisers of the workshop. A young research assistant called Gavin George was asked to take me back to the university campus and see to it that everything I wanted could be provided. This was one of the most difficult times in my life. In the university, I was taken to the office of the Director of HEARD where I had access to a telephone and I was told that I could make as many calls as I needed. South Africa has an interesting telephone billing system. The cheapest calls are calls made to telephone subscribers in South Africa. Telephone calls to the countries belonging to the Southern African Development Community (SADC) were the next highest. The third category is made up of subscribers in Europe, the USA, Canada, Australia and New Zealand. The fourth and highest category is made up of subscribers in what is described as "the rest of the world". I needed to make phone calls to Ghana and Burundi which are actually in the "rest of the world". This was definitely going to be a heavy telephone bill for the University. After nearly two hours of planning, phone calls and discussions, all the while in tears, I managed to reorganise myself to fly out of South Africa to Ghana to attend to family issues related to the passing of my mother and get back to work in Burundi.

The University allowed me to return in 2002 to go through the 6-week workshop that I was not able to complete in 2001. It was in this workshop that I got a technical and professional understanding of the subject of HIV/AIDS. I understood how epidemics in general progress, the economic and social impact of HIV/AIDS and how to plan to combat the spread of the disease and cope with its impact. I learnt to use different software to model the epidemic. This involved the use of social and economic data of a given country such as the population, the population growth rate, the mortality rate, the Gross Domestic Product (GDP), the economic growth rate and HIV prevalence over a 10-year time frame and then making projections of how the epidemic will behave over the next 10 years. The model then becomes an important tool in the hands of governments and other institutions for planning. My own understanding of the various components of development planning came to enhance my work on HIV/AIDS.

Back in Burundi, we made a deliberate effort to recruit one member of staff who was HIV positive and who had openly declared her status. This was to provide an internal opportunity for staff who needed counselling and somebody to talk to without necessarily disclosing their status to the organisation. In tackling the epidemic in the country we had a sequence of programmes. We had a programme on Counselling and Testing, Behaviour Change Communication and Support to local business ventures.

The programme on Counselling and Testing was intended to identify persons who were HIV positive and thereby generate the necessary statistics for planning and also for treatment with Antiretroviral (ARV) drugs. The Behaviour Change Communication programme was based on the fact that HIV/AIDS thrives on sexual behaviour and one way of tackling its prevention and spread is to educate the populace about how it is spread and how to prevent it. We did this massively through media (radio and television) discussions as well as discussions with focus groups. The Small Business Venture component of the programme was based on the belief that young people, particularly women, because of poverty, are driven into transactional sex, sometimes with multiple partners leading to the spread of the disease. It was assumed that if these young people got into small business ventures and earned sufficient income, they would not go into transactional sex and therefore the chances of getting the disease and spreading it would be reduced. It must be understood that these were only theories based on which we planned and executed projects.

It was interesting to discover across the African continent that poverty and the lack of income may not necessarily be the motivation for transactional sex. Similarly, our Behaviour Change Communication programme revolved around the fact that knowledge leads to behaviour change. This is not necessarily true.

I had joined the fight against HIV/AIDS and I was going to stay in the middle of this fight in different parts of the African continent for several years. The biggest lesson I learnt from this experience is that the fight against poverty in Africa is multi-dimensional both in thematic work and geographical implementation. A person may start development with the basic effort of providing educational infrastructure or rural water in one African country and end up fighting HIV/AIDS in a different part of the continent. The fight against HIV AIDS continues unabated and may continue for generations to come.

CHAPTER 34

CONTINUING THE FIGHT AGAINST HIV/AIDS IN SOUTH AFRICA

I joined the fight against HIV/AIDS as a development worker trying to implement projects to fight poverty in rural and urban communities in Burundi in particular and on the African continent as a whole. Indeed, HIV/AIDS had become a major development issue, affecting the Social and economic development of rural and urban populations. My participation in the workshop on "Planning for HIV/AIDS in Sub-Saharan Africa" organised by the Health Economics and AIDS Research Division (HEARD) of the University of KwaZulu-Natal (UKZN) in South Africa as part of my preparation to tackle this task has been described in the previous chapter.

During this workshop, HEARD advertised for the position of a Senior Researcher. This advertisement was on the noticeboard of the training centre where the workshop was being held. The directors of the workshop also made sure that the advertisement of the position was repeated to participants at the beginning of every session. I was later personally approached to consider studying the requirements for the position and applying for it if I thought I would like to take up the job. After three weeks of reflection alone in South Africa and on the phone with family members in Ghana, I finally thought that this would be an interesting position to apply for. I definitely felt that it would be difficult to get out of field work and commit to academic work in a university. However, the idea that I could come and live in South Africa with my family and a few other advantages were really very attractive and compelling. I had not lived with my family for three years and I thought that this would be a good opportunity to do so. I decided to apply for the position. The interview was conducted before the end of the workshop and I returned to Burundi. By the end of the year 2002, I had been offered the job. The news of my new job as a Senior Researcher in UKZN was received with mixed feelings. My boss was definitely unhappy that I was leaving. I gave him to understand that having my wife and children together with me in South Africa was paramount for me. I was hoping that it would be better than my survival in this conflict context where we jokingly said that the life expectancy was 24 hours.

In April 2003, I started my new job in HEARD in UKZN as a Senior Researcher. UKZN is one of the largest universities in South Africa, with four campuses, namely, Howard College, Nelson Mandela School of Medicine, Westville campus and the Pietermaritzburg campus. With a staff population of over 3,500, working here was like getting lost in a huge city, but given the professionalism of the people around me, I did not have any problem.

There were three main aspects of my family and career life that influenced this career move, and as a family, we unanimously agreed that the move would be beneficial to us. In the first place, we expected that the move would offer us the opportunity to live together as a family as stated earlier. Secondly, we were convinced that the academic and research work would contribute to my career as a development worker across the African continent. My earlier short stay in South Africa gave me the impression that the country looked very much like Europe. The third important consideration was therefore that if I worked here, the family would benefit from the European facilities that would be available to us while living and contributing to development in Africa. In reality, these three issues played out within a context of a post-apartheid country where racial segregation was a deeply rooted social construct that influenced every economic and social aspect of the country. As I started work, I became aware that this social construct could not easily be dismantled by simply abolishing apartheid and then making and implementing new state laws. The genesis of apartheid can be traced back to the arrival of Europeans in that country. Dutch immigrants arrived in South Africa in 1652 and are now called the Afrikaner whilst the English arrived in 1795. The indentured Indian community, brought by the Europeans to provide labour on sugarcane plantations, arrived in the year 1860. The details of how immigration from Europe and India to South Africa influenced the history of that country and the evolution of relationships between races is beyond the scope of this narrative.

A brief description of the reality I observed in South Africa is important for a better understanding of the circumstances in the country. The social setup, deeply rooted in apartheid, the form of government that institutionalised racial segregation, manifested itself in several ways, including human settlement, public and private employment, education and the economy.

In the area of human settlement, South African communities are distinctly divided into Suburbs, Black Townships, Indian Townships and Informal Settlements. The Suburbs used to be called White Suburbs but since the end of apartheid, these Suburbs are no longer occupied exclusively by white people as some black people now own properties and live in these areas. Such people are either South Africans who have benefited from the Black Economic Empowerment (BEE) programme that offered substantial financial assistance to potential South African black businessman or people from other parts of Africa who moved to South Africa to take up professional and skilled jobs or start private businesses. The Suburbs can further be categorised into upper-class and middle-class areas.

In Durban, the suburbs include areas such as Glenwood, Carrington Heights, Berea, Manor Gardens, Umhlanga, etc. For example, a suburb such as Umhlanga (pronounced 'Mshlanga'), where every house has a well-kept swimming pool, is considered an upper-class suburb.

The most prominent Black Townships in Durban include Umlazi and KwaMashu. The largest Black Township in South Africa is Soweto and the name Soweto is actually an acronym for South West Township as it is located in the southwest of Johannesburg. The most prominent Indian Townships in Durban include Phoenix and Chatsworth. The biggest informal settlement in Durban is Cato Manor. This segregation of human settlement made life in South Africa a bit complicated. For example, it is not advisable to go into a Black Township where one is not known as this would definitely result in being mugged or even killed. I lived in a suburb where over 90% of the residents were white South Africans.

The deeply rooted social construct created its own dynamics in employment in the public and private sectors. For example, although public and private institutions were required to have a number of black human resources in their employment, the history of the country made it difficult to get black South Africans with the required qualifications and experience to occupy positions that were available to them. Public and private institutions therefore resorted to seeking black human resources outside South Africa. The job I applied for required a person with a postgraduate degree in social and economic development as well as up to 15 years experience in senior management with a development organisation, and being bilingual in French and English. This was a very tall order for citizens of a country that had ended apartheid less than 10 years before 2003.

The impact of the history of the country on business was even more devastating. A member of my family walking through downtown Durban with a South African friend observed that all the shops in the business centre were owned by either Indians or black people from other parts of Africa such as Nigeria, the Democratic Republic of Congo, Somalia and Ghana. Consequently, discrimination had taken a new twist, with black Southwest Africans discriminating against black people from other African countries. This new version of discrimination emerged from the argument that black South Africans had fought for their independence and now that the fruits of that fight were becoming evident, black people from other African countries were coming to enjoy them.

HEARD had a very small team that was very dynamic, professional and well focused. The team enabled me to settle seamlessly in Durban, both in the professional and social environments. Professionally, I quickly buried my head into reading as many documents as I could lay my hands on in order to bring myself abreast with issues concerning research in HIV/AIDS. I wrote papers for publications in monthly and quarterly journals. I carried out desk research and wrote papers that contributed to the development of policy documents for the United Nations Commission on HIV/AIDS and Governance in Africa (UN CHAGA). This brought me into contact with United Nations Economic Commission for Africa (UNECA) in Addis Ababa with a very famous Ghanaian, K. Y. Amoako, who impressed me with his knowledge and understanding of the UN system. The biggest work I did while in South Africa was a piece of research on the impact of HIV/AIDS on the public sector in four different countries in Africa, namely, Zambia, the Democratic Republic of Congo, Kenya and Ethiopia. This work took me through the four countries, where my research work focused on specific ministries such as the Ministry of Finance and Economic Planning and the Ministry of Social Welfare. I was not able to bring the research to the final conclusion before I left South Africa and it remains a very interesting subject for further research. With the introduction and improvement in the quality of antiretroviral drugs, the relevance of this research is now quite debatable. Travelling to carry out research in these four countries highlighted the difficulties of working with Government bureaucracies across the African continent. It was very difficult to schedule meetings with government officials and for those meetings that I was able to set up punctuality at meetings was completely compromised. I remember scheduling a meeting for a technical government official to be held at 9:00 a.m. and ending up being told at 11:00 a.m. that the meeting had been cancelled.

HEARD appointed me as the Co-Director for the workshop on "Planning for HIV/AIDS in Sub-Saharan Africa" with Professor Tony Barnett who was then a social scientist with the London School of Economics. This was for the year 2003. I directed this workshop alone in 2004 before I resigned to return to ActionAid in Burundi. However, the Director of HEARD in UKZN negotiated with the Regional Director of ActionAid for me to go back to UKZN in 2005, 2006 and 2007 to play this directorship role, which involved leading the whole process of planning the workshop. This included getting in contact with participants from across Sub-Saharan Africa, organising and facilitating the movement of participants to South Africa, organising and planning the Programme and content for the workshop, ensuring that all facilitators have been contacted and will be present on time for their presentations and carrying out all other activities related to the workshop and finally writing a workshop report. I took advantage of my role as the director of the workshop to introduce and facilitate sessions on Strategic Planning and several other subjects on development including The Evolution of Development Paradigms, The Rights-Based Approach to development and The Key Elements of Democratic Governance. With participants coming from West, East, Central and Southern Africa, this workshop had a huge impact on HIV/AIDS interventions in Sub-Saharan Africa. With a dynamic team and the level of efficiency in the department, I must say that most of my work went on automatically and in a timely manner like clockwork. Once again, as the years progressed, the relevance of this workshop began to be called in question. In fact, my extensive knowledge of HIV/AIDS can be attributable largely to my work in UKZN.

Living in South Africa and working for UKZN presented several opportunities from which I benefited. Within the first three weeks of my living in that country, I quickly discovered that it was cheaper to take a loan from either the bank or a housing company that offered housing loans to buy a house and pay the monthly mortgage than to rent a house and pay a monthly rent. Indeed, South Africa had a thriving and vibrant housing market at the time we were there. Many workers who got new jobs in parts of the city located far away from their places of residence were most likely to sell their old houses and buy new ones as close to their new workplaces as possible. I started the search for a loan, assisted and supported tremendously by Gavin George, who was then an Assistant Researcher. Gavin now has a doctorate. We spent weekends looking through the property advertisement section of newspapers to identify houses that were in the market for sale within close proximity to the university. We were also exploring loan facilities in the banks and mortgage companies. Finally I bought a house in Carrington Heights from where I could drive to the university in less than 15 minutes. Indeed, by June 2003, I had taken a car loan from the bank and bought a brand-new car that could transport my family around when they came from Ghana. These two mortgage facilities would have been very difficult to obtain in Ghana. Even if one got such a loan, the balance increased while one tried to pay the loan off, due to the combined effect of the continuous depreciation of the Ghanaian cedi and inflation in the Ghanaian economy.

The other interesting part of living in South Africa was the quality of their roads and the way business worked. South Africa has one of the best road infrastructure in Africa and probably in the world. Throughout our stay in that country, it was practically impossible to see potholes on the roads, at least the roads I plied most of the time. The use of credit and debit cards for transacting business was the norm and one hardly moved around with liquid cash. The invitation by shops to buy on credit was very common. After shopping for groceries one would be asked at the payment point whether you wanted to pay for everything or for only 50% of the groceries and spread the rest over a period of time. Coming from Ghana, I had never seen anything like this. The health facilities were also very good. Then the question of health insurance also made access to health services rather easy.

I can never forget a particular situation in the Year 2006 when my wife needed surgical intervention for a life threatening condition. The surgery was done in a private hospital upon the advice and approval of our medical insurance company. Four hours after the surgery, a mistake that occurred during the surgery was detected and she had to be rushed to the intensive care unit of the hospital. I was called in and told that she had to be taken back to the operating theatre but the surgeon needed the approval of our medical insurance company. The telephone conversation with the insurance company, the completion of the approval form, sending the form by fax to the company and getting the approval faxed back to the hospital, took about 3 minutes. This was amazing speed. My wife was taken back to the theatre and she survived the procedure. Six months after this surgery, I received monthly enquiries from the insurance company, wanting to verify whether there were any unpaid bills for the surgery - really very impressive.

The biggest challenge in South Africa was the question of security. Armed robbery, sometimes in broad daylight, was very scary.

The 9th and 10th of October 2003 will remain significant dates in the memory of my family. Sitting in my office on the 9th floor of Howard College in UKZN on the 9th of October, I was very nervous throughout the day. I called wife in Ghana literally every 2 hours. This was the day that the whole family was scheduled to migrate from Ghana to South Africa. I had a list of actions I was supposed to complete before the arrival of the family. Madeline, the secretary for HEARD, came over to my office to ask whether I would need help in the airport to bring the family home. I said I would, and she promised to come to the airport with her husband who had a pick-up, called a *backie* in South Africa, to help with the transportation of the luggage. For such a major move, I was expecting that the checked-in luggage and hand baggage would be enormous. By 6:00 p.m., I was at home, going from room to room and checking to make sure that the house was ready to receive the family. I made my final call to my wife in the night after they had checked in at Kotoka International Airport to fly on South African Airways to Durban via Johannesburg. Then I went to bed and tried to get some sleep. Sleep never came because I was following the progress of their travel in my mind. If the 9th of October was troubling, the 10th of October was dramatic. I went to Durban International Airport and got to the arrival lounge nearly an hour before the arrival of the flight on which my family was coming. Madeline and her husband arrived 5 minutes before the arrival of the flight. Finally, the aircraft arrived and the 20 minute wait for the family to come out seemed like two hours. When my wife and children finally walked out of the arrival lounge, they were pushing several trolleys of luggage. Most of the luggage went into the pick-up Madeline brought. We drove back home and went through the process of getting all the luggage into the house. I thanked Madeline profusely and started the process of getting my family to settle in. It was then that I learnt about the troubles that the family went through on their way to Durban. In Johannesburg airport, the port health authorities found out that one of the children, Stephen, did not have yellow fever vaccination. They therefore took him aside and administered the vaccination. My wife waited for the vaccination to be administered while other members of the family went through immigration and customs formalities and waited at the arrival lounge. This may look very simple but it was quite stressful to a family that was arriving in South Africa for the first time. It was indeed a major migration.

From then on, South Africa became our home. We now had benefits from what we called the interesting facilities in South Africa but we also had to cope with the difficulties that came with such facilities. We were not aware of the level of crime in South Africa and then suddenly had to cope with this. We engaged a security company to install the necessary alarms in our home and we had to become very alert and conscious of our environment in order to stay safe. The reality of the security situation was strongly impressed on me at the beginning of September 2003 before my family arrived. One day, I had to work late in my office, and ended up driving home after 9:00 p.m. As I approached my house, I used the remote control for my garage door to open the garage and drive straight into it. As I came out of my car, there were two men in uniform standing outside my garage, with holstered handguns on their hips and their hands on the guns. My heart missed a beat as I anticipated trouble. The smiles on their faces were a bit reassuring. One of them asked whether I was Mr. Braimah and I responded in the affirmative. They showed me their badges at a distance and I assumed that they were genuine. Getting closer to them to verify the genuineness or otherwise of the badges was out of the question. They asked me why I was coming home at this time. I explained that I had to work late. They advised me that it was dangerous to be coming home after 7:00 p.m. Apparently they were from the company that provide the security for my house. They advised that anytime I had to leave the university campus after 6:30 p.m. I should call their number and tell them the gate from which I will be leaving the campus and then give them 10 minutes before driving through that gate. They promised to provide me with an escort from the gate to my house in such situations. I breathed a sigh of relief and got into my house and then heard them toot their horn and drive away. I stuck to this instruction and benefited countless times from the escort of the security company. This experience strongly highlighted the insecurity of the situation that existed. In comparison, Burundi suddenly appeared to me like a very safe place to live in. I did not need an alarm system in my house in Bujumbura and I could drive home at any time of the night, apart from during curfew hours, without the fear of being attacked or the need for security escort.

One challenge we did not anticipate was the fact that my wife could not work in South Africa based on my work permit, which was the normal condition in Europe. This was very frustrating.

Racial segregation seemed to penetrate every aspect of life, including sports. I attended a rugby match in the ABSA Stadium in Durban with three of my white South African friends. Looking around where we were sitting, I could not find one single black person or Indian. The spectators in rugby matches were predominantly white. My efforts to enjoy the match were frustrated by my limited understanding of the rules and terminology used in the game. At the end of the match, my friends and I quickly got out of the stadium and tried to count the number of black people who came out of one of its eight gates.

We counted only eight people. Statistically this meant that there were perhaps about sixty to seventy black people in a stadium with a capacity of about 45 thousand people. One could get similar results in the case of a football match where the majority of the spectators would be black or a cricket match where the majority would be Indian.

One of my children was attacked in high school by black boys because he could not respond to their question in Zulu. He was protected by white boys. During a presentation on the African personality that one looks up to for inspiration, my ten-year old daughter referred to Kwame Nkrumah who had been voted earlier in the year 2001 as the African personality of the 20th century. Her teacher had never heard of Kwame Nkrumah and scolded her for writing about an unknown person instead of focusing on a personality such as Nelson Mandela. I was so angry that I had to go to her school and give the teacher lessons on Ghanaian history and the history of the struggle for independence by African countries.

I was very surprised when during a meeting, very educated South Africans kept saying "when I go to Africa", as if South Africa was not part of Africa. The degree of ignorance among South Africans about the rest of Africa was shocking. I went to a restaurant with my friends, once again white South Africans, and it was interesting to find out that I was the only black person in that place. The longer we stayed in South Africa, the more it became apparent that we were not wanted.

The final straw that broke the camel's back came in 2004 when I was trying to renew my work permit. After collecting and completing the necessary forms from the Home Office, I was in a queue with my wife from 8 a.m. to 2 p.m. only to be told that we had completed the wrong forms. The officer who talked to us was a black South African woman and when she looked at what I was supposed to be doing in Durban, she asked "Don't we have senior researchers in South Africa?". She then dropped the forms on the floor and gave us new forms to complete and resubmit them on the following day. I was told that I could only be given a work permit for one year and not more. This raised alarm bells in my mind. Then the policy came up that any employer who wanted to renew the work permit of a non-South African employee had to prove that the employee could not be replaced by a South African. There is a saying in my language that "when you consult a soothsayer you should go home and consult your common sense ". As a family, we sat down and consulted our common sense and common sense told us that it was better to get out of that country. Indeed, this was more divine counsel than common sense.

Earlier that year, my former boss, John Abuya, had contacted me to ask whether I would like to come back to Burundi because the position for leadership of ActionAid in that country was available. At the time I was contacted, I had quickly declined the invitation but the evolving situation in South Africa compelled me to go back and consider that opportunity. I got hold of the telephone and call John Abuya to ask whether the deadline for application for that position had expired. I was told that the deadline would expire in 24 hours from the time I made the call. I quickly went into our study, switched on my computer and started a process of revising my CV. By 2:00 a.m. I had finished the revision, written an application letter, sent it to the right HR personnel and was ready to go to bed. This is the genesis of my return to the conflict zones of Burundi. It looked obvious that those conflict zones were safer than the deceptive comfort of South Africa.

I left South Africa at the end of November 2004 to take up the leadership for ActionAid in Burundi. My family remained in South Africa until December 2006 and then moved back to Ghana. By the middle of 2007 I had sold our house and car and paid the balances for the house mortgage and the car loan. In 2008 the xenophobia attacks started, a situation we had seen looming as early as 2004. I believe that the Almighty God granted me divine protection, guidance and wisdom in decision-making through these times out of Ghana. It reminds me of the saying that "not all that glitters is gold".

With my family, we have always asked the question whether migrating to South Africa was a mistake. The answer is an emphatic "NO!". We believe that our Almighty God took us to South Africa for a purpose and brought us out at the right time. Nothing happens to the Christian by mistake. Our paths are divinely ordained by God. I also learnt that one can contribute to development in Africa regardless of where one lives.

CHAPTER 35

DIRECTING DEVELOPMENT IN A NEW DISPENSATION IN BURUNDI

The first day in a new job can be very intimidating. One hardly knows where to start. In my case, in the first week of December 2004, the situation was different. I had spent more than three and a half years in this office, and I was now back as the head of the organisation.

Turning around in my chair, I looked at the serene atmosphere of Bujumbura through the window. I imagined that underneath that serenity were different categories of people. Angry people grieving over the loss of loved ones in the conflict. Hopeful populations, looking forward to a peaceful country after several years of peace negotiations in Arusha, Tanzania. Opportunists who might have benefited from the spoils of war, waiting to benefit from the gains of peace. I was supposed to join in this mix and facilitate development. The journey I started in August 1981, under the guidance of Kofi Hagan, Gershon Adzokpa, Emmanuel Aye and Clement Odua-Mensah, with contributions and additions from several individuals and institutions, had brought me this far. I said aloud to myself "Ebenezer! Thus far has the Lord brought me". I was back in Burundi, a country that had better support for transition from conflict to democratic governance than I had I left in March 2003.

My arrival as the Country Programme Manager for ActionAid in Burundi was part of an evolving strategic and operational arrangement that was started in the year 2002. In that year, an analysis was carried out which showed that three countries namely, Burundi, Rwanda and Eastern Democratic Republic of Congo, where ActionAid had programmes, exhibited similar climatic, ethnic, socio-cultural and development conditions. The programmes in these countries could therefore have their development activities implemented under a common management, thereby reducing cost and maximising accomplishments. This led to the development of the Great Lakes Strategy that had Country Programme Managers who would report to a Great Lakes Director. The three programmes could then share strategic logistics such as vehicles, and human resources, such as the Head of Finance, Human Resources Manager and Policy Coordinator.

At the time of my arrival in Burundi, the Headquarters of ActionAid was relocated from London in the UK to Johannesburg in South Africa. Out of the blue, the concept of the Great Lakes Programme was challenged from the International Office in Johannesburg. The Great Lakes Director was asked to produce a signed document as evidence that the concept had been approved by the International Office. He could not produce this approval document, so that brought an end to the whole concept of the Great Lakes Programme. The well thought-through and laudable ideas that resulted in the concept of the Great Lakes Region was put aside, simply because of a process failure. It made me wonder whether the process of getting the concept approved was more important than the content and substance of the concept.

Meanwhile, I brought up the issue of the difference between a Country Programme Manager and a Country Director, since the job descriptions of the two positions were exactly the same. After a long hard debate, my job title was changed from Country Programme Manager to Country Director.

As I started my new job, I believed that I had a clear understanding of the task that lay ahead of me. Burundi was at the end of a post-conflict transition period that encompassed a series of actions supported by the United Nations (UN) and the international community. These included the demobilisation of troops of the Rebellion or freedom fighters, depending on which side of the political divide one stands, disarmament of these troops, their integration into communities and their rehabilitation to fit into these communities. The country was also preparing for democratic elections at all levels that was supposed to lead to Democratic Governance. I was required to lead a team that would align development facilitation activities to these processes and ensure that all the other interventions of ActionAid progressed without interruption.

A description of the scenario in Burundi at the end of 2004 will provide a better understanding of the context. Before June 2004, the African Union (AU) deployed Peacekeeping Forces in Burundi, made up of Armed Forces from African countries, with a majority of them coming from South Africa and Mozambique. Implementing a UN Security Council resolution that was signed in May 2004, the UN facilitated the conversion of the AU Peacekeeping Forces to a UN one and opened an office called

ONUB, the acronym for "Organisations des Nations Unies au Burundi" the French translation for "United Nations Organisation in Burundi". The UN Peacekeeping Forces were made up of 5,650 military personnel, 120 civilian police, support personnel in the form of 200 military observers and 125 military staff. This was an operation resulting in 7,000 human resources being brought into Burundi. In the usual efficient functioning of the UN, prefabricated materials were brought in and a whole village constructed to accommodate the personnel as well as the supplies that came into the country. Powerful electricity generating plants where brought in and installed to ensure uninterrupted power supply. There was a massive influx of vehicles, mostly four-wheel drive cars, to provide logistics. There was the observation that out of every five cars in Bujumbura, three were UN cars, although this was not substantiated by any statistical data. The fact that this was now a UN mission meant that the forces came from all over the world, including forces from countries such as Canada, Pakistan, India, Fiji, etc. Interestingly for me, there were soldiers from Ghana, and this significantly relieved my loneliness end chronic isolation from Ghana. The 6th of March 2005 will always remain a memorable Ghana Independence Day celebration. The members of the Ghanaian contingent who were serving in the UN came together in my house and we enjoyed Ghanaian fellowship drinks.

In order to accomplish the task ahead of me, I set out to ensure that the organisation, ActionAid, had the capacity to help me do so. My understanding of capacity is the presence of qualified and experienced human resources that seek to accomplish a well-defined strategy, using clearly articulated policies and state-of-the-art systems. If these are supported by adequate infrastructure, logistics and funds, the organisation will be acknowledged as having the capacity to deliver on its mandate. In terms of human resources, very critical recruitments that were made before my arrival, provided a solid foundation from which I could stand and make progress. Where there were gaps, I made recruitments to fill those gaps and also sought support from other Country Programmes. It is said that a leader is as good as the people he leads and this was very true in my case. I believe I led a group of qualified and committed development workers who provided professional services to the organisation and whose work resulted in successes for the organisation and the country. One big lesson I learnt is that, leaders will always perform better if the people they lead are specialists and professionals in their fields to be able to provide appropriate advice. With the help of a highly motivated and qualified Human Resources Manager, we developed policies that were aligned with the policies of the organisation internationally and consistent with the national labour and other laws of the country.

The Head of Finance was seconded to us by the Ethiopian office of the organisation, but realising the competence and performance of the staff member, the secondment was renegotiated and eventually converted to a permanent employment. A key member of my team was my Personal Assistant, a young lady who was recruited in 2002 through one of the most rigorous recruitment processes I have ever seen, including the participation of the candidates in a strategic planning workshop, taking down the notes in English and submitting the final report to the interview panel. Her calm disposition, wise counsel and consistent reminders that prompted me to be on time in meetings, played a significant role in my performance.

In January 2009 I became more conscious that I had only two years left to complete my contract as country director. I realise the need to strengthen senior management so that the country programme would be stable on my departure. I therefore relocated one programme coordinator from the province to the headquarters in Bujumbura to assist the Director of Programmes. This enabled me to share more responsibility with the Director of Programmes and to prepare the staff who had just moved to the headquarters to take his responsibilities. It was this arrangement that enabled me to be absent from Burundi for six consecutive weeks made up of two weeks' vacation in Ghana, two weeks' official duty in Denmark and another two weeks' vacation in Ghana without affecting the continuous flow of work in the office.

One Sunday morning, I went to my office to catch up with work and prepare for the Monday morning. Just after 11:00 a.m., I got a call from one of the senior management members. He went straight to the point. Director of Programmes, Mamert Nshirimana, was dead. In my confusion I asked whether this was a joke and he said no. On the Monday of the previous week, Mamert had come to ask for a one week leave. He wanted to take his children to the village to visit their grandmother. He was on his way back on that Sunday when his car was involved in an accident and he died on the spot. I was hit by a very deep sense of grief. I went to the hospital where his body was brought and looked at my colleague lying lifeless. Unbelievable!! I did the official communication to all our partners in Burundi and declared three days of mourning during which the office was closed. I began to wonder whether bringing in somebody from the field to understudy him was simple forward planning or a premonition. I believe this was divine guidance. It is said that "man proposes but God disposes". I thought I had worked out the perfect plan but it turned out as something else. The fact that I was the only non-family member to be allowed to see the body of my friend and colleague before the coffin was closed and sent to the mortuary was an indication that the family understood my closeness with this man.

Before my departure in March 2003, a state-of-the-art accounting and financial management system, SUN Accounts, was engineered to fit our data requirements and installed to ensure quick and efficient access to financial information for planning, monitoring and evaluation, reporting, and all other purposes. This system continued to work efficiently for me throughout my second assignment in Burundi. Together with the team, we developed a well-articulated strategy that became the roadmap for our development interventions. With this solid foundation, the question of infrastructure, logistics and funding fell into place. Looking back, I can say that we had the capacity to deliver development in Burundi.

One of the toughest challenges in leadership and management revolves around the various initiatives the leader and manager should take to stay ahead of the team in strategic thinking and yet ensure that nobody in the team is left behind. I had to stay ahead of the team in strategic thinking and yet remain tightly attached to the same team in operational planning and execution. In December 2004, I participated in a meeting in The Gambia, organised by the Africa Regional Office of ActionAid, for their Country Directors. It was in this meeting that the regional leadership of ActionAid took time to explain the global Strategic Objectives of the organisation and link them to practical regional initiatives such as the Comprehensive Africa Agriculture Development Programme (CAADP) of the African Union under the New Economic Partnership for African Development (NEPAD). The regional team also ensured that Country Directors clearly understood and internalised the Rights-Based Approach to development, which became the dominant paradigm for the implementation of the organisation's programmes and projects on the ground.

It is important to give a brief summary of what the Rights-Based Approach (RBA) to development is all about. This quotation forms the foundation for the Rights-Based Approach to development: "When I feed the poor, they call me a Saint. When I ask why the poor are poor, they call me a communist " (Archbishop Hélder Pessoa Câmara OFS of Brazil). Development organisations base their field work on a particular development approach. Earlier approaches to development include Needs-Based Approach, the Community Development Approach and the Participatory Approach. The Needs Based Approach focuses on the basic needs of the poor such as food, clothing and shelter. The Community Development Approach focuses on developing social and economic facilities in the community such as schools, health services, etc. The Participatory Approach focuses on the participation of community members by contribution of ideas and resources to the development of the community. The RBA arrived in an effort to tackle the root causes of poverty and to increase the chances of sustainability in development interventions. In this approach, the two main actors in the development arena are the State as the Duty Bearer and the rest of the population as Rights Holders. The NGOs and Civil Society Organisations as well as the media are recognised as development facilitators. Any activities and development processes are therefore aimed at strengthening the Duty Bearer to deliver on their mandate and strengthening the Rights Holders to claim their rights while honouring their responsibilities. The provision of resources serves basically to facilitate this process.

The analysis of poverty using RBA goes beyond simple consideration of economic indicators such as GDP or inflation. While these indicators may show the economic progress of a country they does not indicate how the economy is redistributed for the benefit of the poor. It is possible that 80% of the country's income may lie in the hands of only 10% of the population. The approach tries to create a linkage between all dimensions of human development such as health, education, housing, personal safety, administration of justice, freedom of expression and political participation. Development is no longer limited to the provision of services and includes the dimensions of empowerment populations and advocacy. It gives a new meaning to the concept of democracy which must include all forms of political and public participation in decision-making.

This meeting clearly defined the starting point of my job in Burundi for me. I set out to have a series of forums that would ensure that every member of the team in Burundi had a clear understanding of the Rights-Based Approach to development and the global strategic objectives of ActionAid. These were the two basic foundations for the development and implementation of a strategic plan for the country. In order to do this, I developed my own presentation entitled "The Evolution of Development Paradigms". In preparing this presentation, I took a lot of information from the book entitled "Democratizing Development: The role of Voluntary Organisations " by John Clark. I also included the ideas and approaches posited by academics such us David Marsden, Alan Fowler, Robert Chambers and other writers on approaches to social and economic development. This presentation was repeated in several forums, until every member of ActionAid in Burundi understood the foundations for the global strategy, the linkage to initiatives in the Africa region, and the transformation into projects and programmes for implementation in the country. I revised and used this presentation for the training of Africa Regional staff of the Lutheran World Relief in a one-week workshop in Mauritania, and for workshops in Durban, South Africa.

The other levels of my engagement with the rest of the team included weekly Senior Management meetings, monthly expanded management meetings, general staff meetings that were held at least twice a year, and other informal team building activities. We referred to the weekly senior management meetings as Monday Morning Meetings (MMM) and it was a forum where the senior management members reviewed accomplishments of the past week and strategised for implementation of activities for the current week.

The monthly expanded management meetings were organised in such a way that the venue for the meetings rotated between the headquarters in Bujumbura and the three provinces where we had programmes. One full day during the monthly meetings was used to visit projects and the outcomes of our interventions on the ground in the province where the meeting was being held. This made it possible for the management members to be on the ground at least nine times a year.

General staff meetings were used to respond to staff welfare issues as well as programme implementation queries. The general meetings enabled us to dispel rumours very quickly and keep staff focused on the work at hand. On the informal opportunities I spent a significant amount of time, once a week and during field visits, to sit with staff on a one-to-one basis and chat about other things apart from work. For example, I wanted to know more about the staff and their families. This exercise drew me close to several staff members, thereby establishing the understanding that they were more than just human resources providing services to the organisation. The most interesting informal arrangement was the declaration of Friday afternoons, from 4:00 p.m. onwards, as a time for sports. On Fridays, staff members came back to the office from the afternoon break, dressed in sports gear. At 4:00 p.m. we all stopped work and went to a park where we did all types of sporting activities, including walking around the 800 metre circumference field, playing games such as volleyball, basketball, football etc. At 6:00 p.m. we would end the activities and get together at a drinking spot where we shared beverages and kebabs and used the opportunity to chat with the people with whom we had little contact in the office. As we shared drinks and jokes, we got closer to each other and the team grew stronger.

One of the most important parts of my team building efforts was to develop the capacity of team members to the point where the organisation could run on 'autopilot'. This meant I had to send as many senior staff as I could to strategic ActionAid meetings worldwide and in Africa. I sent as many staff as I could to other Country Programmes for experiences that they could not get in Burundi. In January 2021, one former staff member I sent to an African Country Programme to learn the basics of agribusiness, sent an email to tell me that he was now a Food and Agriculture Organisation (FAO) expert on agribusiness. The capacity building and frequent delegation of authority meant that I could attend two other issues while the rest of the senior management team ran the office.

With this team in place, I set out to tackle several angles of management of an organisation including efficient resource management. Three areas of resource management that significantly reduced cost were in the areas of staff transportation, staff medical care and salary administration. Because of the insecurity situation, ActionAid in Burundi used the vehicles of the organisation to go around Bujumbura and transport staff members from their homes to work. The vehicles were then used to transport the same staff members home for lunch and bring them back to work after lunch. They were finally transported to their homes after work in the evening. I need to mention here that, unlike many cities, particularly in Anglophone Africa, all workers in Bujumbura go home for lunch during the two-hour lunch break. We realised that this was a strain on the drivers and the resources of the organisation. We therefore carefully worked out transport allowances that were calculated as a percentage of staff salaries and consistent with national labour law provisions and paid this to staff. This replaced transportation of the staff using organisational vehicles. The challenge of this exercise was that, different staff members received different amounts of transport allowances depending on their salaries. However, we agreed that staff members should take personal responsibility and decide on the types of transportation they needed to use to the office. This arrangement resulted in a significant reduction in transportation cost, thus saving finances for other purposes.

With the assistance of my senior management team, we carried out an analysis of expenditure patterns and noticed that the money spent on staff medical expenses was a major drain on the finances of the organisation. At that time, all staff members sought medical assistance and bought medicines for themselves and their family members from health facilities and pharmacies of their choice. Receipts for these expenses were then presented to the organisation, and staff members were refunded the money they spent for the services and medicines. This was under the policy that the organisation would pay the medical expenses for staff members and their families. Looking more closely at the detailed implementation of this policy, we noticed loopholes and then came up with a refined process. We identified and signed a contract with one major private hospital that provided consultations and treatment in every field of medicine. All staff were required to seek medical attention in that hospital only. We then identified three pharmacies from which staff members could go for medication, if the hospital did not have that medication. The hospital and the three pharmacies then submitted bills for payment at the end of each month. Finally, staff members were assisted to provide photo identification cards for themselves and members of their families to ensure that people visiting the hospital and claiming to be family members of the staff were actually who they said they were. This arrangement took medical expenses out of the hands of staff members and reduced expenditure in this cost centre by about 45% without compromising the quality of medical care to staff members and their families. There is a very strong perception that the medical expense cost centre, particularly in the public sector as well as the NGO community, is one of the loopholes for financial leakages that can be difficult to deal with.

I must say that these cost reduction reviews were dictated by rigorous adherence to financial reporting standards required by the organisation. For example, the percentage of direct programme cost to the total expenditure was expected to be above a given figure and staff costs were to be below a given percentage. I must also add that Country Directors were motivated and inspired to meet the required standards in order to keep their jobs. Although the management team in a given country contributed to the expenditure reporting, the final responsibility lay on the lap of the Country Director. The absence of such high standards and failure to hold high office holders responsible in the public sector and civil service in many African countries accounts for the corruption and lack of financial integrity in these countries.

As I made every effort to ensure efficient and effective management and leadership, I went back to look at notes I had taken in Kenya in 1985. Time management came up as one of the biggest challenges for managers and a careful time management plan could easily result in cost-saving. In order to keep a very good paper trail of financial transactions for audit purposes, a majority of payments to staff members, suppliers and contractors were made with cheques. Because of my open door policy that allowed staff to come into my office at any time they wanted, I had staff of the finance department coming into my office several times a day to get cheques signed. With a simple unwritten policy that required me to sign cheques only at 11:00 a.m. and at 4:00 p.m., I reduced the frequency of interruptions in my work. Then came the signing of salary cheques for staff. The last week of the month was always a nightmare as I had to sit and sign the staff salary cheques, numbering up to over 50 and above. By asking staff to have bank accounts in three major banks in Bujumbura, we were able to reduce the salary payment process to the signing of only three letters to the banks, with a list of staff who have accounts in the respective banks and the amounts to be paid to those accounts.

One major lesson from these experiences is the importance of managers and leaders going beyond the routine they find in their workplaces and 'thinking out of the box' to develop new ways of doing things that will save cost and improve efficiency. The narratives above are only a few examples of several policy and process reviews, new initiatives and reforms that I superintended over a period of six and a half years.

Meanwhile, the high risk of working in conflict was not completely over. I lived in a suburb of Bujumbura called Gatoke, two houses away from the house of the Chief of Defence Staff (CDS) of the army. This was very much like a double-edged sword. While I benefited, to some extent, from the security around his house, my house could also be hit unintentionally, in case of an attack on him. On one occasion, when I came home with a different car from the one they were used to, the security guards of the CDS stopped me and advised me to be consistent with one car that they could recognise all the time. One evening, as I relaxed to catch up with news on the television, I heard loud voices in my compound. When I went out to verify what was happening, I found several soldiers outside my gate, arguing with my security guards. Upon enquiry, I was told that the guards for the CDS had security intelligence information that there could be an attack on the house on that night. They wanted permission to get into my yard and use it as a defensive stance in case of an attack. I had to refuse vehemently to allow this to happen, and after nearly 20 minutes of argument, they gave up and left. I breathed a sigh of relief. I thought that the war was all over but it looked as if this was not the case.

Parallel to the continuous team building exercises and process improvement efforts was the real programme work that was expected to support Burundian citizens in the fight against poverty. As the country was preparing for elections in 2005, facilitating the election process became our main priority. We launched a campaign with the theme "Women have the right to vote and to be voted for". This campaign was taken to all the communities in the three provinces where we had projects. The result was a massive turn-out during the elections between June and September 2005. It also ensured that we had several women from these provinces in parliament. The lessons we learnt from our engagement in the election process in 2005 as well as lessons from other election processes in Africa became a foundation for supporting the election process in 2010. In this year, ActionAid organised live radio discussions to talk about the role of civil society organisations in the upcoming election. We also organised an international conference and invited facilitators from Ghana and Kenya to share their experiences in the engagement of civil society and faith-based organisations in facilitating peaceful elections with their Burundian counterparts. One key message that came out of this conference was the fact that post-election violence only benefits the leaders of political parties who are never hurt by these occurrences. Such violence only maims and destroys the livelihoods of the most vulnerable in society while negatively affecting national and local economies because of the withdrawal of external investors.

The work of the UN Peacekeeping Forces described earlier resulted in the demobilisation and disarmament of over 21,000 'ex-combatants'. This created an opportunity for ActionAid to participate actively in the integration of the demobilised forces into their communities and their rehabilitation. It is important to note that the civil war had been going on since 1993. Some of the combatants were taken to the war when they were as young as 8 or 10 years old. A child in this age bracket would have been between 20 and 22 years old at the end of the conflict. This meant that such a child had completely missed the opportunity for the foundations of formal education. We launched into the reintegration and rehabilitation programme with all zeal. Young ex-combatants were supported to acquire skills in trades such as carpentry, masonry, welding, fitting etc. Others went into traditional occupations such as farming and animal rearing. We made funds available to all those who received support in skills development to form associations and make their new skills available to those who needed them. It was very exciting for me to see a young woman, who had mastered the art of carpentry, on top of a roof, displaying the skills in roofing a house that she had learnt in her trade.

We then carried out several research activities to develop and establish evidence that would promote development and peacebuilding in the country. This included a research on the impact of World Bank loans and grants conditionalities on basic education, the outcomes of the work of the UN peacebuilding commission, etc. I wrote two reports in 2006 and 2008 and made presentations to the United Nations configuration on Burundi in New York. These visits to the USA enabled me to make presentations to the US State Department in Washington DC and the Department for Peacekeeping Operations (DPK0) in the United Nations in New York, on the need for increased support for peacebuilding operations in Africa.

The team studied and made available the skills developed in strategic planning to the evolving democratic process in the country. We worked hard to support 7 communes in the province of Karusi to develop medium-term strategic plans. I put in place other initiatives and reforms during the six and a half years of my time as the leader of Action Aid in Burundi. Salary rationalisation leading to a new structure and improved equity was a bit rancorous but worked in the end. We agreed to sell off the organisation's trucks and other vehicles that were not required in our new development approach which required more development facilitation with partnerships within communities than service delivery. We had to reduce the number of drivers from 9 to 4. We did this using stringent human resource management policies that were consistent with state labour laws and ensured that we did not end up with court cases. We introduced life insurance coverage with an insurance company that did not cost the organisation very much but resulted in significant benefits for staff members.

The six and a half years I spent in Burundi during my second duty tour, from December 2004 to June 2011, were the most pleasant years of my development career. It was particularly a learning session as well as a time during which I could experiment on ideals and practise realities. At the end of the day, Burundi has become my most preferred destination for an interesting development facilitation career.

CHAPTER 36

FACING THE PROBITY AND ACCOUNTABILITY CHALLENGE

Many formal workers love or loath Monday mornings for different reasons. For those who love this day of the week, it is an opportunity to start the week on a strong and purposeful note. For those with different sentiments, it is an interruption of their weekend parties and celebrations. I am one of those who love Monday mornings. One such morning in April 2006, I was at my desk and ready to work at about 7:50 a.m. My normal routine at the beginning of every day included a silent moment of prayer, after which I was ready to get on with the day's work.

At about 8:00 a.m., the direct telephone line to my office rang once. I wondered who could be calling me on this line so early in the morning. My family was in South Africa, which had the same time zone as Burundi. Could it be my wife calling? The telephone rang again the second time. The fraction of a second between consecutive rings sounded like ages. The other person with my direct number was the Africa Regional Director of ActionAid based in Nairobi, Kenya. The telephone rang for the third time and I picked it up. I introduced myself and found that I was actually talking to the Regional Director. After we had exchanged the normal pleasantries that precede serious discussions, she asked whether I was aware of issues of corruption and procurement breaches in my office. She said that something had been detected and the Regional Office was sending out an auditor to help me identify and deal with the problem. I told her that I was not aware but was glad that it had been detected and would be very happy to have the help offered. She mentioned the name of the auditor who would come. I was very grateful and asked when this would take place. It was then that I got the shock of my life. The auditor was already at Bujumbura airport and all that I needed to do was to send a driver for him. In effect, the whole audit process had been planned and I was not trusted to be part of the planning process. If I had anything to hide, I had less than 30 minutes to do so. I thanked her once again and promised to be as helpful to the auditor as I could. I sent a driver to the airport and within 30 minutes the auditor was sitting in front of me.

The lesson came straight home to me. As a manager, one must be prepared at all times for all types of surprises. Never think that everybody trusts you. Always be prepared to help even when your superiors do not trust you. There is absolutely nothing wrong with such surprise forensic audits. Indeed, it is another way of finding out whether the leader or manager is on top of his or her job.

I quickly called my Senior Management Team to a meeting where I introduced the auditor, his mission and asked for maximum cooperation in the provision of documents and files that he would request. I asked the Head of Finance to make the password for our financial management system available to him in order to give him access to documents at all levels without needing permission to input data. Interestingly, he did not have any Terms of Reference for the audit but he explained that this was a forensic audit. In other words, an unexpected audit with the aim of investigating suspected fraud. This looked like it was going to be a week starting with a negative agenda. Something was going wrong in my office and I did not know. How did the Regional Office find out that something was going wrong amiss?

Then the next lesson came home strongly to me. I had put in place several policies, structures and procedures to enhance efficient and effective management of human and material resources. All these were now going to be tested.

We prepared an office for the auditor and ensured that he had access to the internet. From the morning, all the way to 3:00 p.m. he walked up and down the office, asking for files and documentation of procurement processes. He came back to my office several times to ask questions. By 3:30 p.m. the trend indicated that I was the target of the audit. At this point, I asked whether this audit was all about me. He mumbled several words, went around the point, and in the end admitted that it was about me. I leaned back in my chair and burst into laughter. He wanted to know why I was laughing. I gave him a bit of my background and told him that the last thing I would ever want to do would be to defraud anybody or any organisation. But I wished him good luck and the audit continued.

My insistence on clarity of policies and rigorous documentation of procurement processes that were meticulously adhered to by the Human Resources Manager and Head of Finance began to prove very useful. When documentation has been properly done, it takes only a few minutes to dig them up. The activities of the week had been thrown out of kilter and turned into an audit week. I encouraged the appropriate staff to search and submit the relevant documents that were requested. It was at this moment that I remembered the arrival of the words "probity and accountability" on the Ghanaian political scene in 1979 when the Armed Forces Revolutionary Council (AFRC), led by Flight Lieutenant Jerry John Rawlings, came to power in Ghana. This was my version of facing that issue.

I spent a lot of my time during the week seeking answers to several questions that crowded my mind. After carefully developing procurement processes that I thought were professional and foolproof, what did we get wrong? Who managed to find a loophole in the processes? How did the Regional Office find out that there was a problem here? Who managed to break through the procurement processes and frame me? I went to sleep each night going over these questions in my mind. My nights became full of nightmares that always related to difficult situations in my life. In one of these nightmares, I would find myself in an examination hall, and after looking through the questions, I would realise that I could not answer even one of them. Then by the time I figured out an answer for one of the questions, the invigilator would say that time was up. I would then wake up sweating profusely.

While going through this troubling time, I went through the procurement process in my mind. Every procurement process that was completed had a full dossier, well-filed in the Human Resources and Finance departments. The first document in that dossier would be the minutes of the management meeting where the decision for the procurement was made. The specific decision, including timelines and personnel responsible for the execution of the decision, would be highlighted for easy reference. The second document would be the advert to announce the procurement, specifying whether the announcement would be by radio, newspaper advert or person to person contact. All bids to compete for a procurement were required to be submitted in a sealed envelope and submitted personally by the bidder, who was expected to deposit the envelope containing the bid in a box through a small hatch on top of the box that only allowed materials to be inserted. The box was usually locked with two padlocks and the keys were kept by two different people.

The last document in the procurement dossier would be the minutes of the tender committee meeting where the selection decision was taken, giving details of the supplier or contractor who was selected and why. The decision was usually based on the best value for money, after a careful analysis of the technical and financial proposals of each bidder. The minutes were normally signed by all members of the tender committee and approved by me as the Country Director.

It was during this 'forensic audit week' that I became aware that the owner of the company that supplied stationery to the office was the landlord of the office building. The auditor drew my attention to this and invited me to a meeting with this gentleman called Jean-Marie, to be held on the Thursday of that week. The meeting was a very interesting scenario. Jean-Marie did not communicate in French or English, the two languages in which I could communicate very well. He spoke only Swahili and Kirundi, two languages I could not understand or speak. The auditor could communicate in Swahili and English and not French or Kirundi. In order to facilitate communication, Jean-Marie brought his own translator to the meeting. The translator was a Congolese who could communicate in English, French, Kirundi and Swahili. In the meeting, it became very evident that it was not possible for me to communicate with Jean-Marie in private since we would never be able to understand each other. Through the translator, the auditor established that I had never had any private meeting with the supplier without other parties since we did not have any common language for communication. I always met him in my office with at least two of my senior management team members.

The audit ended on the Friday without the usual audit exit meeting and a draft report. Two weeks after the departure of the auditor, we received the draft report with the usual provision at the end of each finding and recommendation for management responses. If you wanted a classic case of the 'criminal' being found and the detective asked to 'fit the crime' to the criminal, this was it. There was this narrative in the report that was supposed to implicate me in breaches of the procurement processing. According to the narrative, we received proposals from different competitors for the supply of stationery. One particular competitor had a lower quotation than the rest of the suppliers and he kept winning the bids to supply the stationery. According to the auditor, the other suppliers operated big enterprises, and therefore had higher overhead costs. The supplier who was winning the bids did not have such overheads and so could afford to quote lower prices. It was interesting that the auditor went as far as to find out why one supplier quoted prices lower than the rest. In our management response, we indicated that as long as the quality and quantity of goods were the same, it made sense for us to select the supplier that had the lowest price. We were not responsible for price control in Burundi. Having said that, our investigations showed that the so-called 'small supplier' was actually an importer of stationery who supplied the big stationery shops, and that was why he could quote prices equivalent to the wholesale prices that he gave to the big shops. We never got any response from the Regional Office and that forensic audit was never referred to again. Very interesting indeed.

About one month after this drama, I got an answer to one of the questions that I asked myself in the beginning, namely "How did the Regional Office know what was happening in Burundi?". Apparently, a staff member who had been dismissed for theft, got in touch with the Regional Office to report procurement process breaches in my office. The Regional Office or an interested party paid her airfare to fly to Nairobi and have a meeting with the Regional Director to tell her story. I believe that the people in the Regional Office at the time are still not yet aware that I know how they got the information from Burundi. Indeed, I had the full minutes of how the tale of procurement breaches in Burundi was told. The person who took the minutes was instructed to print and submit it to the Regional Director and delete the original document from the computer, thus suppressing all evidence that the meeting ever took place. This was indeed criminal and showed a lack of transparency to say the least. If the Regional Director had taken a neutral position there would have been an effort to keep the minutes of the meeting on the records to inform future investigations.

There are many lessons to draw from this experience and some of them have already been noted. One lesson is the importance of establishing and respecting procurement procedures that are transparent and consistent with organisational policy and state laws. If these procedures are respected for all procurement processes it will be difficult for anybody to find fault with such processes. As a leader one must learn to distance himself or herself from delegated processes and allow systems put in place to run their normal course. Another lesson is that your line manager may be part of the plot to set you up. I believe that if one remains faithful in everything one does, the Almighty God will expose those who plot and set you up to be accused.

The other difficult truth is that managers should be prepared to be confronted with reprisals anytime they take disciplinary action against a staff member who is found guilty of a crime. In my case, it was one who had been dismissed for theft who proceeded to accuse me of a non-existent crime. I remember a similar situation in the year 2002 when a driver who had been laid off in an organisational restructuring process came to the Country Director's office with a grenade. He announced that he was going to blow himself up with the Country Director. By a sheer miracle, he changed his mind and ran out of the office with the grenade. This was at a weekend and that would have ended the life of the Country Director.

Effective and efficient leadership and management practices are rooted in the principles of probity and accountability and anybody who wants to adhere to such principles should be prepared to face the challenges that go with them.

CHAPTER 37

CLIMATE CHANGE DISCOURSE & EXIT FROM ACTION AID

The end of November of the year 2010 remains a significant milestone in my life. It was the end of my second three-year contract term. The ActionAid Human Resources policy at the time was that the three-year contract of a Country Director could only be renewed once. Thereafter, one could sign a one-year contract that could also be renewed only once. So I could only renew my contract for one more year.

For logistical reasons, it was agreed with the Acting Sub-Regional Director for West and Central Africa, my line manager, that this contract should be signed in January 2011 while attending a strategic planning conference in Johannesburg, South Africa. The conversations that preceded the signing of the contract subtly pointed in one direction - he thought that it was time for me to leave the organisation. That was later made explicit through email communications, leading to a face-to-face meeting with him and the Regional Human Resources Manager in Nairobi, Kenya. How my acting boss managed to turn the conversation around to look as if I wanted to leave Burundi was beyond my imagination. However, I decided not to go against the odds. My contract as the Country Director for ActionAid in Burundi was renewed for the period from November 2010 to the end of June 2011. A new position was created out of the blue and I was given a contract from the 1st of July to the 31st of December 2011. The new position was Regional Adviser on Climate Justice or something to that effect and I was to be based in the Ghana office of ActionAid. Climate change? Who said I knew anything about climate change? A few questions about that part of development which I must have answered correctly was used as a good reason for my appointment. In the NGO system, when a decision has been made to get a staff member out of the organisation, the leaders will always find a path that will lead the person out. I am told that the position I was given disappeared with my departure. As at April 2021, there is no regional officer in ActionAid in charge of climate change.

I returned to Burundi after the meeting in Nairobi and completed my job as the Country Director before taking up my new job. The last 3 months of my service in Burundi was both challenging and exciting. Challenging because I had to ensure that whoever was coming to take over as Country Director did not have any difficulties in settling in. Exciting because I was really impressed by the commitment of the staff who wanted to ensure a smooth transition between my leadership and that of the next Country Director, although one was not appointed before my departure. The most touching moment was the send-off party that was organised for me. The ladies in the organisation came to the ceremony clothed in identical dresses that were made specially for the occasion. For me, this was deeply touching and will forever remain in my memories.

I cannot complete my narrative on my stay in Burundi without writing about my limited social life and the friends who kept me alive and sane. Two Ghanaians, Seth Awutey and Nathan Dankwa became part of my social life during this period. Seth was the financial controller of Ecobank in Bujumbura and Nathan was the Chief Security Advisor in the United Nations. We spent several hours visiting each other and catching up with news from Ghana. Seth and I particularly spent several evenings in a popular entertainment centre called Havana, watching the English Premier League because we could not afford the subscription fees required for cable television that would enable us to watch the matches from home. We discovered and enjoyed eating a variety of fish called Kuhé that could only be found in Lake Tanganyika and was served almost boneless with a special flavour difficult to find anywhere else in Africa. For Seth and I, we spent hours talking about which one of us came from a poor background. The companionship of these two fine gentlemen significantly contributed to my social life and remains a support I will never forget.

Two other important people who supported me during my stay in Burundi were Gideon and Vincent. Gideon was my domestic worker and was responsible for cleaning the house, doing my laundry, and preparing my meals. For about six and a half years, he was the first person I saw each day of the week except Sundays when he stayed away from work to go to church and rest. He came to work at 6:00 a.m. each morning. We agreed that he should knock on the door of my bedroom anytime he arrived, just to make sure that I was there and alive. This was part of my personal security arrangement. He learnt how to prepare Ghanaian dishes such as light soup, plantain and beans stew, etc. On several occasions I heard him humming Ghanaian music tunes which he heard over and over again from the stereo system I played when I was at home. His dedication was exceptional and he was part of my security and social network. Vincent was my garden worker and he trimmed the plants around the house as well as the grass in the garden. My relation with him was rather interesting as he could not speak French and I could not speak Kirundi either. I had to speak to him through Gideon. With about 9 months of rainfall a year, the garden was always green. I took my time to teach Vincent how to cultivate onions. I had learnt to cultivate onions as a child and I took the opportunity to pass the skill on to Vincent. He turned some flower beds into onion farms. By the time I was leaving Burundi in June 2011, Vincent had cultivated and harvested onions about four times. These two men were the closest to me in Burundi and I will forever remain grateful to them.

I left Burundi very satisfied with the mission I had accomplished and thankful to God for giving me this big opportunity to enhance my career as a development worker and documenting lessons for other people to learn. Life in my new assignment started in the Ghana office of ActionAid where the Country Director kindly provided office accommodation for me. Being relocated in Ghana gave me the greatest pleasure of coming home to my family at the end of every working day although this was constantly interrupted by my extensive travel across the African continent.

I had to redefine my relevance in the organisation and get busy for the last six months of 2011. I reverted to my usual way of tackling development issues about which I did not have complete mastery. I had to do extensive reading on climate change in order to understand the phenomenon and how the United Nations and the global development community were tackling it. The biggest lesson for me is that, when one is thrown into the gutter or the branches of a tree, all that one has to do is to learn more and survive in the new environment. One piece of advice from my father came back to mind. He always told me that one must learn how to do many things in order to survive in this world.

The United Nations Climate Change Conference (the 17th Conference of the Parties or COP 17) for that year was scheduled to take place in the month of November in Durban, South Africa. I therefore organised activities that focused on this conference and the participation of the organisation in other climate change forums in the Africa region.

I did three main things during this six-month period. I read intensively around the subject of climate change in order to bring myself up to date with global developments on the subject. This automatically added a new professional competence to my career. At the same time, I represented the organisation in various forums in preparation for COP 17 in South Africa. This also increased my network as I met and engaged with specialists in climate change, particularly in East and West Africa. Finally, I facilitated meetings of journalists in Burundi, Rwanda and Uganda, to increase their understanding of the climate change phenomenon and debate and also prepare them to provide journalistic coverage of the Durban conference from a position of historical, technical and development understanding.

The comprehensive timeline to indicate the progression of debates on climate change is a bit difficult to construct. However it is known that the first-ever United Nations conference on the environment took place in Stockholm, Sweden in 1972. Climate change was hardly mentioned in this conference, which concentrated on pollution of the atmosphere, the effects of atomic bombs and whaling. The conference however ended with the creation of the United Nations Environment Programme with its headquarters in Nairobi, Kenya.

In 1987 the Montreal protocol that was intended to limit the emission of gases that could destroy the ozone layer was agreed. The ozone layer is a layer of ozone gas that envelopes the earth. It provides protection to the earth by absorbing ultraviolet radiation from the Sun and trapping infrared radiation from the Earth, thus playing a part in the regulation of the Earth's temperature.

In 1992, the treaty known as the United Nations Framework Convention on Climate Change (UNFCCC) was negotiated at the United Nations Conference on Environment and Development (the 'Earth Summit'), held in Rio de Janeiro, Brazil. This treaty required developed countries to return greenhouse gas emissions in their various countries to 1990 levels.

The biggest milestone in the Climate Change debate was the signing of the Kyoto Protocol in Kyoto, Japan, in 1997, which has remained the foundation on which other Climate Change debates are developed. This timeline gave the journalists in Burundi, Rwanda and Uganda an opportunity to extrapolate and follow developments of the UNCCC all the way to 2011.

The major issues on this subject that engage development organisations include climate change mitigation, climate change adaptation and the formulation and implementation of policies on climate change. Climate change mitigation has to do with taking actions such as planting trees to slow down the phenomenon. Forests act as a carbon sink to absorb the carbon dioxide emitted by humans and other animals and also through natural processes and industrial emission. Adaptation has to do with learning how to live differently from what we are used to in an environment that is changing.

The process of leading journalists through this learning opportunity was quite tough but at the end of the day I managed to get them prepared to engage meaningfully with development workers during COP17. I took a personal interest in the subject of Carbon Sequestration, the process of fixing carbon in the soil to mitigate climate change, and prepared papers that I presented to the East Africa Climate Change Conference in Nairobi in August 2011, the ECOWAS Climate Change conference in Bamako in October 2011 and to the World Bank Climate Change meeting in Washington DC in November 2011.

I resigned from my job before the end of my contract when I was recruited by Oxfam NOVIB (the Dutch affiliate of Oxfam based in The Hague) as the country director for the organisation in the Republic of Niger. I was very glad to find myself heading back to Niger where I started my international Development The and where I learnt to work in French. One lesson I learnt from my transition from ActionAid to Oxfam is the fact that every new situation is an opportunity for learning and could be the stepping stone into the next job in one's career. My recruitment by Oxfam must have been influenced by my understanding of Climate Change and its effect on food security as well as my experience in living in the context of human insecurity as these were the major focuses of their programme in the Republic of Niger.

Working for ActionAid was a huge career building opportunity and will remain very relevant for the rest of my life.

CHAPTER 38

LEADING THE RESPONSE TO HUMAN AND FOOD INSECURITY IN NIGER

I walked from the tarmac into the airport terminal in Niamey Airport and all the memories of 1998 came flooding back. It was now the 9th of January 2012. Indeed, not much had changed since my last travel through this airport fourteen years earlier. I went through port health, customs and immigration and then walked out into the arrivals hall of the airport. A young man held up a placard with the name "Oxfam" boldly written in green and I walked over to him and introduced myself. This marked my entry into the Republic of Niger to begin a second assignment in that country, but this time, as the Country Director for Oxfam. I felt very happy and excited to be back in the country where I started my career as an international worker and had learnt to be functional in written and spoken French. The following day I received a very big welcome into the Oxfam office and was shown my office where I would be working for the following two years.

The Republic of Niger was confronted with human insecurity from the North and the south as well as food insecurity throughout the whole country. The Arab Spring that started in Tunisia in October 2010 and spread across the rest of the North African Arab countries and the overthrow of Colonel Gaddafi in Libya coupled with the arrival of Islamic fundamentalists in the Republic of Mali created a major insecurity situation in the north of Niger. There were a number of kidnappings in Niamey. Parallel to this situation was the instability in northern Nigeria caused by another Islamic fundamentalist group called Boko Haram. Meanwhile a severe drought across the Sahel region resulted in poor crop harvest at the end of the rainy season of 2011, plunging the country into severe food shortages. I was here to lead a team of dedicated aid workers to respond to the shortages while ensuring that the large expatriate staff were safe and protected from any kidnapping or bodily harm.

At the time I started my work in my new assignment, three affiliated offices of the organisation headquartered in Great Britain, Canada and The Hague worked in the Republic of Niger. One of these affiliates, Oxfam Novib, was the leader of the three and referred to as the managing affiliate. Although we had three different affiliates, my role as the Country Director covered all three. The organisation was operating a new management system called Single Management System (SMS). This was to ensure that one director represented the organisation in the country while enabling autonomous operations by each affiliate. The SMS was launched in my first week in the organisation.

In order to tackle effectively the problem of human insecurity, a security coordinator was recruited and given the task of being abreast with evolving security situations in the country and giving the necessary advice and actions to be taken. Then we came up with a well thought-through security policy written in French and English, and spent a significant amount of time explaining it to staff members and answering questions to eliminate any ambiguities. The most difficult part of the management was ensuring that the large number of expatriate staff members remained in the national capital while effectively supporting the field work. Although the security was a daily struggle, frequent and regular briefings helped us to make it work.

During my two years leadership of the organisation in Niger, Oxfam carried out a series of interventions in response to the humanitarian need and to facilitate long-term development. There was the provision of potable water to camps that accommodated populations displaced by the insecurity in the north. There was a series of tree planting projects designed to mitigate climate change and halt the fast southward expansion of the Sahara Desert. Participating in one such tree planting exercise in the department of Zinder, I helped in the transplanting of seedlings into the downstream sides of half-moon shaped troughs to ensure that the troughs held rainwater long enough to keep the trees growing during the short rainy season. The purchase and distribution of food and non-food emergency relief items was one of the major activities of the organisation. Heavy rains in the Republic of Guinea and the Republic of Mali resulted in excessive flooding of the Niger river, leading to the displacement of several households. This situation required the distribution of non-food items such as blankets, tents, cooking utensils and water containers. The floods disrupted the water supply system and we had to provide water for the victims. The distribution of relief food items was a nationwide activity because of the failure of the crop season in 2011.

Tackling the problem of food security was a bit more complicated. I had to lead the process of fundraising to purchase foodstuffs from suppliers and send these to areas where they were distributed to the population in need. Each of the three affiliates of Oxfam headquartered in Great Britain, Canada and The Hague carried out their own fundraising and relief responses and we held weekly meetings to share information about what each affiliate was doing. Although most of the food was bought in Niger, almost all of it actually came from northern Nigeria. We had a media coordinator who ensured that I had a fact sheet highlighting our total financial need, the amount we had received and the balance we needed to complete the requirement in order to respond appropriately to the emergency situation. The fact sheet was in both French and English and ensured that I could grant interviews to the international press at very short notice. I made presentations to the BBC and other radio and television stations in Canada and Belgium. These presentations were necessary for our fundraising and emergency response drive.

All throughout my work I made every effort to be part of a food distribution activity. With the associate director for Oxford Great Britain we flew to Agadez to continue by road to the Aïr Mountains in the north of Niger. As we flew over several kilometres of desert sand dunes I remembered flying over the dense forest of the Democratic Republic of Congo and the endless stretch of water between Los Angeles and Auckland in New Zealand. I scratched my head and thought to myself "What a planet!". The UN aircraft in which we were flying landed on the gravelled runway of Agadez aerodrome raising up a cloud of desert dust that chased us all the way to the end of the runway. The plane realigned to the terminal building and we walked out of the air-conditioned cabins into the energy-sapping dry heat of the desert. The drive to the hotel where we had made reservations was very short and we soon found ourselves in cool air-conditioned rooms. I was worried that the rapid changes between hot and cold temperatures could be detrimental to my health but to my relief this was not the case. The ability of the human body to adjust to sudden temperature changes is astonishing.

The following morning, we had an amazing drive to the Aïr Mountains. The journey took us through the sandy and rocky parts of the desert, meandering and ascending on narrow winding roads that passed between huge rock formations of about 20 to 30 metres high. Then all of a sudden, the climbing was over and we started descending into the valley. The community that lived here depended on cereals from the southern part of the country for their food. With the food shortages in the country, a lot of cereals were supplied by aid workers and that was the reason for my visit. It was really a fascinating and exciting experience for me. There were date palm trees with fresh fruits all over the place. The limited rainfall in that geographical area made it impossible to grow crops such as millet and sorghum, the predominant cerials in Niger. Instead, they cultivated vegetables, particularly the white variety of onions. The vegetable gardens were watered from a hand-dug well of about two metres in diameter and over 20 metres deep.

The concrete opening of the well was about 1 metre above ground level. Across this, a log had been placed lying in troughs at each end. A rope was attached to, and wound around the log and tied to a big container at the other end that could hold up to 60 litres of water. This could be lowered and raised by rotating the log, but the most ingenious part was that the log was connected to a gear arrangement mounted above it that converted horizontal rotation to a vertical one and allowed the system to be operated by a donkey walking round the well.

Meeting community members and hearing their stories was one of the most intriguing experiences of my life. In our interactions with community members, I wanted to know the number of people who had family members in the cities on the west coast of Africa such as Abidjan, Accra, Lome, Cotonou or Lagos. Nobody had a family member who had travelled to these cities. One community member wanted to know why I asked the question. I told them that I wanted to know the level of migration out of the community in search of better jobs. I had to reframe the question and ask for the number of people who had family members in Libya or Algeria. The response shocked me because almost everybody knew or had a family member who had travelled to these two countries. The reality then hit me like a thunderbolt. From the community, one could get across the border into Libya in a few hours while it would take about four days of hard-driving to get to Accra. I was nearer the Mediterranean Sea than the Gulf of Guinea. One would have expected these people, who survived the year with insufficient rainfall and who worked hard to produce vegetables that sometimes went rotten before they could be bought, to look gloomy and discontent. On the contrary they looked confident and cracked all sorts of jokes and laughed. It drove the message home that happiness and contentment has nothing to do with the magnitude of wealth.

I participated in the distribution of cereals to the people. They had organised themselves into distinct identifiable groups and this made the food distribution orderly and easy. Almost all of them had no idea what a tropical rainforest looked like. I went away from the community telling myself that the world can be tougher elsewhere and I was privileged to come from a part of Africa where people could grow food and be dependent on it without looking for outside help. On our way back to Agadez, our car went past a number of people standing by the roadside holding 2 litre bottles of water and raising the bottles up and down. After we had passed the third group of such people, I asked the driver what this meant and he replied that they were begging for water. Really? I had no idea that the bottles were empty. I was really very surprised because we had several bottles of mineral water in the car that we had not used and I thought we could have stopped and given them to the people by the roadside. The driver simply shrugged his shoulders and told me not to worry because somebody else would stop and give them water. The frequent encounter with such situations had simply made the driver numb to the reality. Unfortunately, we never saw any of them again until we arrived in Agadez. The Aïr Mountains remain in my memory as one of the toughest areas in which to live in Africa.

On another occasion, I returned from one of my field trips outside Niamey and as I relaxed in my chair to enjoy the cool air from the air-conditioner in my office, my Personal Assistant walked in to inform me that I had been summoned to the office of the Prime Minister and was required to be there at 5:00 p.m. In my development work of more than 30 years I had never been summoned to the head of government in any country but there is always a first time so I prepared my mind to go as requested. After going through the usual security checks and other formalities in the secretariat, I was ushered into the office of the Director-General of the Prime Minister. It turned out that I was not to meet the Prime Minister himself and that gave me some relief. My host gave me a warm welcome and introduced himself and I did likewise. He then proceeded to tell me that information reaching his office had brought to his notice that Oxfam was engaged in politics in Niger. He said his understanding of the mandate of NGOs in the country was that such organisation were in the country for the sole purpose of providing humanitarian assistance and development and not engaging in politics.

In my response, I explained that as an NGO fighting poverty by providing humanitarian assistance and facilitating long-term development, it was impossible for Oxfam to avoid engaging in politics. The policies that enhance development and the fight against poverty or entrench poverty are made by politicians. (Incidentally the same French word, '*politique*', is used for both 'politics' and 'policy' in English.). In my opinion therefore, I thought that the best way to fight poverty is to engage with the policies that promote or prevent it. I added that it was important to draw the line between being political and being partisan. I did, however, want to know the specific situation where our actions were interpreted as being political. Finally, I understood that he was referring to a piece of research conducted by a local civil society organisation and funded by Oxfam to determine the adherence of the humanitarian response in Niger to the ECOWAS protocol on humanitarian assistance. This research was also carried out in Mauritania, Senegal, Mali, Burkina Faso and Chad. The report on Niger was presented at a weekly meeting of donor agencies jointly chaired by the UNHCR and a representative of the Prime Minister's office. The research found out that some development partners and aid agencies were trying to influence the distribution of relief items in communities in the country.

I took the opportunity to tell my host that as an independent NGO, Oxfam would not be intimidated by any diplomatic mission. We would do all we could to respect the laws of Niger but we would also engage politically and support the government where the need arises and also raise issues with policies that fail to defend the poor. At the time of the meeting the president of Niger had put in place a community grain bank policy that encouraged community members to store their grains in community banks instead of selling them to the grain merchants. Oxfam as a development organisation applauded this policy and so we felt it our duty to support local civil society organisation to investigate and establish the adherence of the humanitarian assistance in Niger to ECOWAS protocols. At the end of this meeting we parted after a very warm handshake. I was very happy that this high-ranking person in government had a clear understanding of the policy advocacy role of Oxfam in Niger. My three associate directors were waiting for me in the office to hear the outcome of my meeting. After my narration of the encounter and its conclusions my colleagues were very happy that one of us had managed to communicate our policy and advocacy stance to the government. Although every individual project I led and facilitated in Niger was important, I consider that the one-hour meeting in the office of the Prime Minister was my biggest accomplishment in that country.

Several years of experience in leadership, management and development facilitation have resulted in the evolution of my personal philosophy in these areas. Events of the first quarter of 2013 revealed that my philosophy on development was different from that of my line manager. I sought the input of one of my associate directors in responding to a set of questions intended to be part of a planning process. In a meeting with my line manager in Dakar, I was sternly told that what I did was not acceptable. The Oxfam affiliates are supposed to be competitors and my actions demonstrated a lack of ambition to perform better than the other affiliates. My calm reaction to the outburst of my boss resulted in more scolding. He used words which I do not wish to repeat but were to the effect that he expected me to be so upset after his queries to the point of soiling myself with my own excrement. I immediately saw the differences in our philosophies. I believe that the fight against poverty could make better progress if the actors in the field of development collaborated and established strategic partnerships leading to synergy. I do not believe that the ability to instil fear and awe is a mark of good leadership. I came to the conclusion that my boss and I were in the same boat but with different understandings of how to sail through the waters.

This incident confirmed my concerns at the beginning of my contract. On my first day in office and during the launching of the SMS, I gave a speech in both French and English with a few words in Hausa. My boss called me from The Hague in the evening and one of the things he said was that he had heard about a very good speech I gave that morning. We laughed this off but I suddenly became aware that whatever I did in Niger was quickly communicated to The Hague. It brought back memories of the book titled "1984" by George Orwell which had the expression "Big Brother is watching you". So big brother was watching me from the Hague. I do not believe this is good human resource management practice. At the beginning of my work in January 2013, I became aware that my associate director from Oxfam Novib had competed with me for the job of Country Director and was not successful. While in The Hague in February 2013, I asked my boss whether this was the case and he replied in the affirmative. In human resource management it is not best practice to place two people who have competed for the same job in the same department with a direct reporting relationship when one of them has been given the job. I wondered whether I was set up to fail. This arrangement led to frequent and subtle undermining by that associate director. Everything seemed to be working against me. At the beginning of every year in the last ten years, I have always repeated the prayer of the American theologian Reinhold Niebuhr – "Lord Grant me the serenity to accept the things I cannot change, the courage to change the things I can, and the wisdom to know the difference". I did not think that I could change anything in this job and I was ready to accept that and move on. Indeed, the threat that I would have to prove within 6 months that I would perform differently in order to ensure the renewal of my contract said it all and I started planning my next move. In September 2013 I resigned from Oxfam and returned to Ghana to take up the job as the Executive Director for the African Evaluation Association.

Oxfam is one of the biggest international NGOs in the world. Working with them was such a huge advantage and I learnt a lot from the different affiliates particularly. Their contribution to my understanding of integrated development and humanitarian response in case of emergencies has been enormous and I greatly appreciate this.

CHAPTER 39

DIVERSITY OF THE AFRICAN CONTINENT

Africa is in many ways the most diverse continent in the world. A first impression of this came from my work in development in the 1980s and 1990s among the rural communities in northern Ghana and Burkina Faso, which is located across the savannah ecological zone and the Sahel region. Sometimes there seems to be no logic in the diversity, and indeed the similarities and differences can be very confusing. As an example, a lay person's observation of access to groundwater shows that it is easier to drill a borehole and get water in the upper regions of Ghana and in Burkina Faso than to do the same in the Savannah Region in Ghana even though the latter is further south and records heavier rains than the others.

While working with the US Peace Corps in November 1998, I visited a community in the Republic of Benin called Ganvie, where the people lived in bamboo houses built on bamboo stilts elevated above the water level in Lake Nokoué. According to Wikipedia, the community had a population of about 20,000 as at the year 2020. Believe it or not there was a market, a drinking bar, restaurant, a mosque, a church and other facilities that could be found in any community in Benin. Travelling from one house to another was normally done using canoes and every house had one or two canoes to facilitate movement around the community. We were taken to the restaurant where lunch was served and people ate and drank in a relaxed atmosphere, as if sitting in a restaurant build on bamboo stilts was completely normal. It was difficult for me to relax in that restaurant with the water constantly lapping below. I calmed myself down with the thought that I could swim and if anything went wrong, I would be able to stay afloat until help came. And this was part of the African continent. I have tried to explain my experience to people in different parts of Africa and have always been met with incredulity. Interestingly there is a similar community built on water called Nzulezo in Ghana. I have never been to Nzulezo but it appears to be a smaller community than Ganvié.

In the year 2001, I participated in a workshop in the city of Mutare in Zimbabwe. The journey from Harare to the city took over four hours. I relaxed on the window seat of the bus as we travelled through beautiful grassland and farmland. Memories of my rural upbringing flooded back into my mind and I imagined what kind of small animals one could find in these bushes that could be killed as game and quickly roasted on the shepherd grounds or sent home for a meal. My development training led me to think about the opportunity for rural community farmers to get in there and cultivate the land and increase crop yields to combat the perpetual food shortages in Africa. What I found amazing was that every inch of land was fenced. I kept asking why there were wire fences all over the place. I was told that it showed the demarcation of the land so that the owners could identify the boundaries of their farms. This was unbelievable for me. In my travels in West Africa, I have never seen wire fences put up to identify ownership of land in rural communities. It brought home to me once again the reality that Africa may look like one continent but the practices in different parts can be very diverse. In the year 2002, I participated in a workshop in Sodere, a town located about 125 km southeast of Addis Ababa in Ethiopia. The drive to this town was a very pleasant one, going through the countryside and I was reminded of similar scenery in West Africa. Sodere gave me a very interesting experience that I will never forget. There was a river very close to the hotel where the workshop took place and the stream came from a hot water spring. Sitting down by the banks of the stream and dipping my legs into the water felt as if my legs were in a bucket of warm water. The only place I had ever seen hot water springs was Rotorua in New Zealand and this brought back memories of my visit to that country in 1990. This was a very pleasant experience that highlighted the diversity of the African continent.

In the year 2001, while I was being driven from Bujumbura to one of the provinces in Burundi, I was admiring the beautiful hills and valleys when I saw what looked like water flowing out of the side of a hill. I asked the driver to stop and when he did, I asked a number of questions about what I saw. Indeed, it was a water spring from which freshwater gushed out of the hillside. I was later to learn that what I saw was a natural occurrence in several parts of Burundi. I later found out that ActionAid's projects that provided water to many communities did not actually involve the drilling of boreholes as was the case in Ghana. The projects involved tapping water from a spring at the side of a hill, directing it to a reservoir, treating it and then laying pipelines that took the water to standpipes for the people to fetch. Amazing! I remember that in 1986, in the Tamale area in northern Ghana, the World Vision International Rural Water team could drill up to forty metres deep in some places without getting any sign of water, and here was water springing out spontaneously from the side of a hill. I had just seen another angle of diversity.

From the front seat of the Toyota Land Cruiser, I watched the spectacle on Mount Nyiragongo with awe and fear. The car was parked just over 14 km north of Goma in the Democratic Republic of Congo and I was driven there by Edward Kakande, the Country Programme Manager for ActionAid in the DRC at the time. The mountain was shaped like a cone. From the point of view of a northern Ghanaian, it looked like a gigantic yam mound and I could see what looked like a huge fire burning at the top. I was told that this was a volcanic lava lake. It was about 7:00 p.m. and the activity on the mountain was bright red, strongly breaking through the darkness of the night. The volcano had erupted in January 2002 and lava flowed to the town of Goma, covering part of the runway of Goma International Airport. I kept asking myself whether we would be able to get out of our seemingly safe location fast enough in case another eruption happened right at the time we were there. As we turned around and drove back into the city of Goma, my fears remained with me for a very long time. That night I had a nightmare of running away from advancing red volcanic lava. While in the process of writing this chapter the volcano on Mount Nyiragongo erupted on the 21st of May 2020. I have followed the lava flow with so much emotion. Having been so near to the volcano before has made such an impact on me that hearing about the eruption felt personal. This was part of the diversity of the African continent.

In the year 2005 I was in Uganda to participate in a workshop that was held on an island called Kalangala, one of the Ssese Islands in Lake Victoria. The journey on the pontoon from Entebbe to the island took about three and a half hours after which we could say that we were surrounded by the waters of Lake Victoria, the largest lake in Africa and the second largest freshwater lake in the world. As we got off the pontoon and were driven into the town, it was difficult to imagine that this was an island. It had the normal vegetation of Uganda and for everybody, it was business as usual. We joined in the activity and conducted our workshop as normal. Every evening I went out with other workshop participants to find out what local foods we could get for dinner. There were all sorts of options of local food but the most intriguing was the grilled fish. The sizes and the quantity of the tilapia fish that were being grilled were just beyond description. Many of the people were fishermen and they simply went into the lake to catch their fish. Some of them actually constructed fish farms in the lake and harvested the fish they had fed periodically. This was just another part of Africa - the continent with a diversity that might never be fully exploited.

I responded to the call from the Jomo Kenyatta International Airport announcers in Nairobi to board the South African Airways flight that was bound for Johannesburg and took my seat near one of the left-hand side windows after putting away my hand baggage in the overhead rack. I was preparing for my usual travel sleep. Yes! I have always been teased for sleeping in any moving vehicle that travelled for more than 30 minutes. The captain's voice came over the public address system to say that the flight would be delayed for about 10 to 15 minutes because he was seeking an unusual permission from air traffic control. He said the weather was very fine, and being a mountain climber who had climbed Mount Kilimanjaro before, he wanted permission to fly in a circle around the mountain when we got there and give passengers an opportunity to see what it looked like from the top. Mount Kilimanjaro is the highest mountain in Africa located in Tanzania and near the border with Kenya with its highest peak at 5,895 metres above sea level. It takes less than 20 minutes to fly from Nairobi to Kilimanjaro. I was all agog. I had tried twice to see the top of the mountain from Kilimanjaro Airport and from Arusha and had never succeeded. The top of the mountain was always covered by clouds, hence the saying that the mountain had a 'cloud necklace'. So, this was a great opportunity to see what I had failed to see in earlier attempts. The sleep vanished and I waited in anticipation of this opportunity. In less than 10 minutes the captain was back speaking to us. Air traffic control had given him permission to do what he wanted and within 20 minutes after take-off we were flying over Mount Kilimanjaro. Luckily for me the mountain was on the left-hand side of the aircraft during this manoeuvre and the aircraft banked with the left-wing downwards to my advantage. I was looking at the top of the mountain and stared at the crater and ice cap. The captain gave a running commentary that was very helpful for passengers like me who did not know much about the mountain. The ice cap is called the Furtwangler glacier. Slightly over a year earlier, I was looking at the red-hot fire of the lava lake on Mount

Nyiragongo and now I was looking at Furtwängler glacier on the top of Mount Kilimanjaro. What a continent! The diversity of Africa goes beyond imagination.

Examples that illustrate the diversity of Africa in topography, weather and other areas are endless. The development issues faced by communities in different parts of the continent evolve from this diversity and development efforts to respond to them are equally diverse. A well thought-through strategy to respond to a particular issue in one part of the continent may be absolutely irrelevant in responding to a similar issue in another. I have learnt that as a development worker, my experience in one part of the continent may not necessarily be relevant in another.

CHAPTER 40

TRAVEL NIGHTMARES

Since my first flight out of Ghana in 1980, and joining the international development community in 1981, airports became part of my professional and private life until my retirement from active development work in 2018. Because of this intensive use of airports, I have had some experiences I call 'nightmares' that I will never forget.

My airport nightmares started in the 1980s when I was working for World Vision International in the Tamale sub-office of the organisation. The commonest problem at the time was the lack of certainty of flying with Ghana Airways to Accra even after booking and confirming a flight. A person could book and confirm a flight to travel from Tamale to Accra, get to the airport at about 8:00 a.m, be checked in to fly out of Tamale and then wait until 3:00 p.m. only to be told that the flight had been cancelled. Passengers were then advised to get back to the offices of Ghana Airways and make fresh reservations for future flights. I have no idea how many times I have suffered this travel setback. On one occasion in 1984, after three days of flight cancellations, I was compelled to drive my guests, Kofi Hagan and Akwasi Agyeman-Dua throughout the night from Tamale to Accra. With the advent of private airlines and electronic booking, this situation has significantly changed in the 21st century.

It was not much different in the 1990s when I had to go on international travels from Kotoka International Airport in Accra. Suffering the consequences of flight cancellations and rescheduling of travel plans became so much part of my life that my family would always say "if we do not see you back at home, we will know that you have travelled".

Sometime in 1998, I was on my way from Accra to Kano via Lagos. The flight from Accra to Lagos was delayed so much that I ended up arriving after 7 p.m. and it was impossible for me to get a connecting flight from Lagos to Kano. Lagos airport has two terminals, one for international flights and the other for domestic flights. I decided to find a hotel near the domestic airport terminal that would facilitate my travel the following morning. Anybody who knows Lagos International Airport knows that the international and domestic terminals are at opposite sides of the runway. I walked out of the airport with my suitcase and my laptop. A tall lady approached me and asked whether I needed help and I said yes. She got hold of my suitcase and I followed her meekly like a lamb. She opened the boot of a Peugeot 504 saloon car and placed my suitcase inside. She then opened the front passenger door for me to get into the car. At that moment I realised that the car was grey and did not have the colouring of taxis in Lagos. She got into the driver's seat and asked where I was going and I said I did not really know but I wanted to get a hotel as close to the domestic airport terminal as possible. The alarm bells started ringing in my head. Panic! Panic!

I had agreed to follow a lady I did not know. Of course, not that I would know anybody in Lagos. I noticed the car was not a taxi and yet I got in. And now I was telling the lady that I did not know exactly any specific hotel I wanted to go to. But before I could recover from my train of thoughts my 'kidnapper' was out of the parking lot and joining the Lagos night traffic. Everybody on the road seemed to be blowing their horns and the lady joined the chorus of horn-tooting Lagos drivers. After taking a few turns she entered the gate of a huge building and I saw the sign "hotel ". I breathed a sigh of relief. It looked as if my kidnapper was actually my rescuer. She parked the car and opened the boot and the 'boys' in the compound picked up my suitcase. We got to the reception and she spoke a language I did not understand to the receptionist who asked me to give him my passport. I opened the front pocket of my computer bag to pull out my passport and found that it was entangled with my vaccination card. Getting the passport out without the vaccination card took a few seconds. The receptionist handed me a form to complete but I suddenly became aware that I had not paid my rescuer. I turned to look for her and she was gone. I rushed to the door of the reception and she had gone out of the gate of the hotel. I shouted for the security to stop the car but she turned into the busy traffic and melted away into the night of the most populated city in West Africa. She was gone. I scratched my head and wondered what on earth had I just happened to me. Was this an angel sent by the Almighty God to rescue me again? Yes! I believe so.

On the subject of angels, I am aware of the different manifestations of angels as messengers sent by God to respond to the needs of men. One of the manifestations as recorded in the Bible shows angels undisguised with the form of a human and always depicted to have wings on their shoulders interacting with humans to deliver a message from God. The idea that angels have wings is an extrapolation from the description of the seraphim and cherubim. This must have been the manifestation recorded in Luke 1:26-38 when the angel Gabriel appeared and announced the birth of Jesus to Mary. The appearance of angels to the shepherds as described in Luke chapter 2 after the birth of Jesus Christ, singing to the glory of God is another example. The second type of manifestation is related to God sending angels to appear as humans and intervening in the challenges faced by a person. An example of this scenario can be found in Genesis chapter 19 when two angels presented themselves as humans and were entertained by Lot and later led Lot out of Sodom and Gomorrah. The other example of this manifestation is found in the book of Genesis chapter 32:22-32 when Jacob wrestled with a 'man of God' (an angel that appeared in the form of a human). The third situation where God uses another human to intervene in the challenges faced by a fellow human. An example of this in the Bible is described in 1 Kings 17:6-17 when the widow of Zarephath kept Elijah in her house and fed him for several days. The widow was a real human being but in this particular case I believe she was more like an angel responding to the needs of Elijah. The person being used may or may not be aware that he or she is being used by the Almighty God for the intervention. I believe in a fourth situation when the angel could intervene in the challenges faced by the human but is invisible to that person. My experience of driving from Takoradi to Cape coast and going from the west gate of the university of Cape coast, going past the central and the east gates on a continuously curving road while fast asleep as narrated in chapter 42 could only have been accomplished by an invisible hand holding the steering wheel.

The following morning I took breakfast and was at the local terminal of Lagos International Airport to fly to Kano. The scenario at the local terminal was very interesting. At this time in Nigeria, there were over 10 domestic airlines. Each of them had a ticket-selling counter and the prices of their tickets were displayed on blackboards and written in chalk. So the prices of tickets from Lagos to Kano were not necessarily the same. Once in a while, an airline would clean off the price for their tickets to a particular destination and replace it with a lower price and this action would result in people drifting from one airline to the other. It was amazing. I was not interested in different prices. I spent a lot of time looking at the faces of all tall ladies with the hope of finding the 'angel' I met the previous night but all in vain. The important issue here was to get a ticket and fly out of Lagos. I had made up my mind that the only airline I would always take between Lagos and Kano would always be Kabo Air, so I got hold of my Kabo Air ticket to Kano and waited for my flight to be called and then joined the running crowd to the aircraft. When the call to board a domestic flight in Lagos was made the passengers ran to the aircraft. We queued up in front of the aircraft, presented our boarding passes and boarded. After a few minutes the aircraft took off and we were in Kano just after an hour and a few minutes of flying. The nightmare was over but I was aware that there would be many more nightmares in the future.

In August 2006, I was invited to present a 'poster' at the International AIDS Conference in Toronto, Canada, on "Carrying out HIV Interventions in a Context of Conflict". I checked through Bujumbura airport and boarded Ethiopian airlines on my way to Toronto via Addis Ababa. The flight was uneventful and we were in Addis at the scheduled time. In Bujumbura, we had been told that the boarding passes we were given for the Addis Ababa to Toronto lap of the flight were only provisional and we would be given boarding passes for the last lap of the flight in Addis Ababa. That was where the nightmare started. The airline ground staff started calling names of the Toronto passengers and issuing boarding passes. As we stood around and watched, a pattern began to emerge. The passengers who were being called out were mainly of European origin. As the numbers grew smaller the number of Europeans also grew smaller. At some point, a Congolese woman who was a member of parliament in her country started to raise her voice and ask that the boarding passes be given according to the order of names on the manifest. Nobody took any notice of her protestations. Panic part one of my trip started. I went to the counter and called one of the airline staff aside and showed him that I had a presentation to make in Toronto and if I missed this flight, that presentation would be completely missed. He collected the provisional boarding pass I was given in Burundi and told me to stand aside and wait. After about half an hour of waiting, he came and took me by the hand to follow him and identify my luggage and it would be taken out from among the luggage that was waiting to be loaded onto the next aircraft. I identified my suitcase and I was pulled along, jogging, into a British Airways flight to London. I asked what exactly he was doing and he said, since I could not get on their flight to Toronto, he was putting me on a flight to London and there would be a connecting flight to Toronto. He had made the necessary changes and he gave me the boarding pass to London and the second boarding pass for the lap from London to Toronto. Finally, I got into the British airways flight and sat down with a sigh of relief, thinking that all was over. I was unaware that part two of the nightmare was to yet to come.

The flight arrived in London Heathrow airport at about 5:00 a.m.. As we trooped out of the aircraft, we were all directed into one section of the airport and told that all passengers from all flights were to go through immigration and get out of the airport. As I listened to conversations around, it became clear to me that there was a bomb scare in the airport. The intention of the British immigration was to get everybody out of the airport building. At immigration, I was given a 3 months visa as a visitor to the UK. With that hurry and rush, I found myself outside Heathrow airport. The electronic announcement board just showed flight after flight being cancelled, and others postponed indefinitely. I really needed to talk to somebody in the UK. I had the numbers of Ebenezer Tetteh and Neil Cameron on my cell phone but I could not use it because I was in the UK. I tried looking for a telephone booth from which I could make a call. Interestingly the number of telephone booths I saw in 1980, that is 26 years earlier, had simply diminished to single phone booths here and there. In most of those phone booths, one could only use a credit card. The airport was definitely moving with the times but I was not. A young American lady, seeing my desperation, asked me whether I wanted to use her phone and I replied in the affirmative. I made two calls, one to Ebenezer Tetteh to tell him that I was stranded in Heathrow, and the other to Neil Cameron with the same message. Neil Cameron promised to call me back at about 3:30 pm, if I were still in the airport and if the owner of the phone was still around where I was. By that time British Airways had advised all passengers to make fresh reservations and confirmation of their flights to Toronto. Neil Cameron called me at 3:30 p.m. and I told him about this development. Since he lived only 15 minutes drive by car from Heathrow airport, he asked me to wait at the passenger pickup point at the arrivals Terminal. I thanked the kind American lady profusely for being there to help me on this crucial day. In the story of my life, I believe the Almighty God sometimes provided angels to help me in times of crisis. This might have been one of those angels. In 15 minutes, I was really delighted to see Neil Cameron's car pull up and I jumped into it, exhausted and relieved. He took me home to a warm and comfortable room. It had been raining throughout the day at Heathrow and passengers huddled in small groups in areas where they could avoid getting wet. So getting into a comfortable home was the first thing I really needed. Neil and Dorothy Cameron got me some real food to eat and then I got a warm shower and proceeded to bed.

Memories of my five-month stay with the Camerons in Keyingham came back to me, and I drifted off to sleep. Neil took the responsibility of sitting by his telephone with my ticket and trying as hard as he could to get a fresh reservation and confirmation for me to travel on the earliest flight to Toronto. He persistently went on until he succeeded well after midnight, but the flight was two days away. I was stuck in London in the house of a friend with the clothes I wore from Bujumbura and my hand baggage with my laptop computer.

The following day, I had to go to a supermarket and buy new clothes and necessary attire for a presentation in Toronto in case I arrived without my baggage. Meanwhile a friend who had communicated with me on the internet was at Toronto airport at the scheduled time for the arrival of Ethiopian Airlines flight from Addis Ababa, waiting to welcome me. He was terribly disappointed when all the passengers on the flight walked out and I was not one of them. I finally got on British airways to Toronto but arrived after the time I was scheduled to make my presentation. When the checked-in baggage arrived at the baggage reclaim point, my suitcase did not arrive. I checked into my hotel with whatever I had and stayed in touch with the airline to recover my luggage. At the end of it all my luggage came and I went through the International AIDS Conference as a participant and not a presenter. This was a big nightmare for me. I learnt a number of lessons after this experience. As a traveller, one must always keep a basic change of clothes in one's hand baggage, but in every tight situation, God will always make a way out.

The attempt to get back from Toronto to Bujumbura was equally unpleasant. I ended up spending hours with a travel agent to re-route my flight from Toronto to Manchester and then to Heathrow to get on board an Ethiopian Airlines flight to Bujumbura via Addis Ababa. The flight from Toronto to Manchester was a really cheap one where passengers were asked to pay 10 US dollars for earphones for the soundtrack of the movie on the screen. I told the cabin crew that I could lip-read and did not need an earphone. The passenger sitting by me laughed her head off. When food was served on the flight, we asked whether we had to pay for that as well. We did not have to pay for our food but this inflight drama became part of my airport nightmares.

In July 2009, I was a passenger on a KLM flight from Accra to Copenhagen via Amsterdam. On the day of the flight, I got a call from the airline, advising me to be in the airport by 4:00 p.m.. I was told that the airport would be shut down from 5:00 p.m. and no passenger would be allowed in or out after that time. To go to the airport at 4:00 p.m. to check in for a flight scheduled to depart after 11:00 p.m. was not ideal. Passengers were informed that this security measure was due to the departure of President Barack Obama of the USA. Shortly after 5:00 p.m. I finished checking in and the long wait started. Apparently, all airlines were instructed to be on the ground before 5:00 p.m.. The departure of the US President from Accra had changed everything. Passengers waited and waited, and finally President Obama boarded Air Force One , the official presidential aircraft, and it lifted off with three helicopters hovering around the runway to ensure security of the plane. 'The Beast', the official presidential car, rolled into the belly of Air Force Two which also took off elegantly into the night skies of Accra. I scratched my head and wondered whether the transportation of The Beast to all places visited by the President of America was a way of ensuring his security or a statement about his insecurity. It is advisable to avoid any airport in Africa on a day when the President of America is visiting.

In October 2014, I was on my way from Accra, Ghana, to Denver in Colorado, to participate in the annual conference of the American Evaluation Association. I went on British Airways to London Heathrow and decided to break my flight for a few days to visit a family in Manchester. I rescheduled my flight to fly from Manchester Airport to Heathrow with the connection to Chicago and then to Denver in Colorado. The Manchester to London flight was early in the morning. I was taken to the airport and proceeded to the British Airways check-in desk where I presented my printed boarding pass to the desk crew, as I had already checked in online. They collected the documents and gave me actual boarding passes to proceed to the boarding gate. My checked-in luggage went through to the aircraft and when I turned to pick up my hand baggage, it was gone. Wow! I had no idea what happened but my hand luggage was simply nowhere to be found. I told the airline staff and nobody seemed to know what had happened to it.

The gentleman who had brought me to the airport and I were in panic mode. We called airport security and described the bag and they said they could not find it. We pointed out the closed-circuit TV cameras that were around and told them that they would be able to see whoever took the bag if they reviewed the video footage of the images the camera was taking. Shockingly, we were told that the cameras were not working. What?! If this were in an African country, I would have seen it to be normal that there were installations that did not work, but we were in Manchester, in the United Kingdom. This is the place that we would call a developed country back at home and the CC cameras were not working? I just found this unbelievable. Meanwhile passengers on that flight from Manchester to London were being told to get on board. Finally, I was told that I had been taken off the flight because I did not go through the final security checkpoint at the scheduled time and I needed to pay extra money to be put on the next flight to London if I wanted to go. I had to take the quick decision to proceed to fly to London and to Denver in Colorado without my hand baggage. The hand baggage had my laptop computer and 5,000 US dollars in cash that I was carrying to pay allowances to some staff of the African Evaluation Association who were heading from different parts of Africa to the same conference. After paying the extra fare, I jogged into the next aircraft, accompanied by two uniformed security officers. It looked as if I was under arrest and one of the officers actually said so and we all laughed.

The aircraft from Manchester arrived in London and as I got out and switched on my cell phone, I saw the text message. My hand luggage had been found intact with all its contents. Another passenger had inadvertently taken it and when the person got to the last security check point before boarding, he or she found out that the contents of the bag were not his own. It had been a huge nightmare but miraculously I eventually got everything back intact. Meanwhile, in Heathrow airport in London, I was told that I was the last passenger they were waiting for and so I had to run to the Chicago-bound flight. I found myself in Denver without my laptop and without the cash and had to make alternative arrangements that were indeed costly.

Anyone engaged in international development work or any form of international travel should be prepared to go through air travel nightmares across the world. The list of such incidents in the life of a development worker who is a frequent traveller can be endless.

In the year 2005, I arrived in Goma in the Eastern Democratic Republic of Congo, with a visa obtained from the Congolese embassy in

Bujumbura, only to be told that the visa was not acceptable in this part of the Congo. It took nearly an hour of my refusal to pay for another visa before I was allowed into the country. In 2004, I arrived in Kinshasa in the Democratic Republic of Congo. There were so many unauthorised people in the baggage reclaim area that one had to fight hard not to pay somebody for taking your suitcase off the conveyor belt that brought it in. At the point of departure South African Airways had to install their own metal detector on the tarmac for passengers to pass through before boarding the aircraft. In 2014, while travelling out of Cameroon from Yaoundé, I was almost at the end of the departure process before I was told that I had to pay for a departure visa. Unbelievable! I knew all about entry visas but I had never been told to pay for a departure visa. I actually had to run back to a part of the airport where I could change US dollars into central Africa CFA francs and pay for the exit visa.

My air travel nightmare stories are so many that it is impossible to narrate all of them. Airport just became a necessary evil that one had to endure in order to be part of the international development community.

CHAPTER 41

THE LAST STOP

The African Evaluation Association (AfrEA) is a non-profit umbrella organisation for African Voluntary Organisations for Professional Development (VOPEs). It serves as a leading source of evaluation knowledge for individual evaluators in countries where national evaluation associations do not exist. AfrEA was founded in 1999, in response to Africa's growing appeal for advocacy, information sharing and advanced capacity building in evaluation. The organisation's main focus was to respond to limited evaluation opportunities by building strategic bridges for African evaluators to connect, network and share experiences.

AfrEA formally established itself as a non-profit umbrella organisation registered in Accra, Ghana, as an international NGO in 2009 as a key, legitimate partner in African development, joining the efforts of governments and other international partners to develop a strong African evaluation community. Its objectives, as articulated by the founding members are:

Supporting evaluations that contribute to real and sustained development in Africa.

Promoting Africa-rooted and Africa-led evaluation through sharing African evaluation perspectives.

Encouraging the development and documentation of high quality evaluation practice and theory.

Supporting the establishment and growth of national evaluation associations and special evaluation interest groups.

Facilitating capacity building, networking and sharing of evaluation theories, techniques and tools among evaluators, policymakers, researchers and development specialists.

Its secretariat located in Accra, Ghana, was started in 2013. The organisation had seven board members made up of representatives from the five different subregions of Africa i.e. north, west, central, east and southern Africa and a treasurer from Ghana. The subregional representatives came from Algeria, Niger, Cameroon, Kenya and South Africa. The seventh board member represented one of the organisation's institutional partners, the African Development Bank. The representatives from Central and West Africa also doubled as the Acting President and General Secretary respectively.

Membership of AfrEA included individuals, VOPEs and institutional members. Institutional members included national evaluation associations and networks, multilateral and bilateral development partners, foundations such as MasterCard and the Bill and Melinda Gates Foundation, Banks, academic institutions and other institutions interested in monitoring and evaluation. These members paid annual membership fees that were renewed every year. Any individual who was a member of a national association was automatically a member of the African Evaluation Association. Individual evaluation experts who did not belong to any national associations could apply for membership and pay annual membership fees. The collection of membership fees was one of the sources of income for running the organisation.

I was recruited as the first Executive Director, starting work on 1st October 2013. The decision to take this job was influenced by the fact that the secretariat was located in Accra, Ghana, and was going to be the opportunity to return to my home country and have more time with my family while working. I found myself in an office with only two other staff members, a drastic change from my previous jobs where the number of staff members varied between 55 and 200. I was later to learn how this situation could work negatively for an individual and for an organisation.

I had to identify and do all that was needed for the building up of AfrEA as an organisation and to establish an office and also attend forums that required the official presence of the organisation. Using my criteria for determining the institutional capacity of an organisation, I considered the capacity of AfrEA to be weak. The organisation did not have the human resources with the requisite qualifications, knowledge and experiences to ensure its efficient functioning. I found myself without the necessary expertise in human resources, finance and programme management that I needed to build the capacity of the organisation. There was no clearly outlined strategic plan that could have provided the roadmap for its operation. There were no policy documents to eliminate subjectivity and ensure consistency in management decision-making. There was no system based on which the office could operate. The office was in a rented building and this could pass as adequate infrastructure. Logistics was a problem and I used my personal car to run the organisation. Funding was also a problem as only one development partner committed funding over a three-year period to support institutional capacity building. The governance structure was made up of a board of directors who were independent evaluators based in several countries across the African continent.

During the nearly two-year period that I worked for AfrEA, I tried to lay the foundation that others could build on to establish a strong organisation in the future. My first assignment was to participate in the 2013 annual conference of the American Evaluation Association (AEA) in Washington DC and take the opportunity to meet the board members of AfrEA for the first time and also engage potential development partners, including the World Bank, the International Monetary Fund, USAID and the Bill and Melinda Gates Foundation. Participating in this conference was very strategic as it enabled the board members and staff of the secretariat in Accra to meet partners who were attending the same conference and also hold meetings among ourselves to discuss strategic issues. After this conference, and supported by the Office Manager who was my single support staff member, I settled in to tackle key issues for the year 2014.

We successfully organised an international conference for the organisation in Yaoundé, Cameroon, in March 2014. The organisation of that conference was a huge fundraising and logistics challenge. The energy and commitment of the Acting President supported by the board of directors in the organisation of this conference was exceptional and provided a solid platform on which the secretariat could stand and succeed. We raised funds from multilateral development partners such as the UN institutions, bilateral partners such as the UK Department for International Development (DFID), the United States agency for International Development (USAID), the Danish International Development Agency (DANIDA), the Swiss government and from foundations such as MasterCard Foundation, the Bill and Melinda Gates Foundation, etc. The funding was required for air tickets to Yaoundé, hotel accommodation and per diems for the hundreds of professional evaluators from all over the world who were coming to present papers on field experiences in evaluation. Indeed participants and presenters at the conference came from Europe, Asia, the Americas and several African countries. During this conference, a new board of directors as well as a President, a General Secretary and a Treasurer were elected. This brought membership of the board of directors to nine. The subregions were represented by Algeria, Côte d'Ivoire, Kenya, Gabon and Zimbabwe while the President, General Secretary and

Treasurer came from Nigeria, Niger and Burundi respectively. The African Development Bank, as a strategic partner, provided the ninth board member.

I look back at the year 2014 as very successful in my career as I worked diligently to lay the foundation for an organisation with weak institutional capacity to grow into a thriving one. With the help of the Acting President at the time I was recruited, I accessed an existing draft constitution and working with a consultant and some input from the new President, produced a final draft. Then I tackled the writing of policy documents. Once again with the help of a consultant, I led the production of an operations manual that contained policies on human resource management, finance and administration, procurement, transport and logistics and communication. The finalisation of this manual also received some input from the President. The production of a strategic plan to provide the road map for five years for the organisation was the next big challenge. I did not have the luxury of involving a large number of staff members and partners as in my earlier work in the production of strategic plans, so I had to do this alone, starting with an original draft of ideas given to me by the Acting President at the time I was recruited and then got the input of the new president. Then I established a website that was tailor-made for such associations for the organisation with the latest state-of-the-art features. The site enabled online membership registration, event management, webinars, instant reminders for members who needed to renew their membership, etc.

The drive to increase membership of the Association was significantly promoted during the conference in Yaoundé, Cameroon, which was organised with intense involvement of the Acting President at the time. Much was also done in this area at the American Evaluation Association conference in Denver, Colorado, where we paid for space for the Office Manager to set up and manage a booth for people to visit, learn more about AfrEA and complete membership forms if they were interested in joining the Association. In the same meeting in Denver, the Bill and Melinda Gates Foundation organised an evening event where the President made a presentation to various development partners, highlighting the strategic directions of AfrEA. In the same conference also, there was an opportunity for a meeting of a number of practitioners in evaluation to discuss what was termed 'Made in Africa Evaluation'. This was intended to explore various means of data collection and other practical evaluation procedures in Africa that may not necessarily follow laid-down techniques that evolved from the western world. I was unable to attend the annual conference of the European Evaluation Association in Dublin, Ireland, due to visa acquisition difficulties but the Office Manager was there to set up and manage a booth that also enabled individuals and organisations to apply for membership. I maintained a strong fundraising drive particularly with USAID and the Bill and Melinda Gates Foundation. I researched and presented a paper on 'the role of evaluation in the development of Africa' to the Moroccan Observatory of Human Development in Rabat, Morocco, 2014.

I entered the Year 2015 riding on the back of these accomplishments. Little did I know that it would be the year when I would say farewell to working for local and international organisations. One of the most quoted verses from the Bible can be found in Ecclesiastes 13:1-8. Verse 1 of the chapter says "There is a time for everything and a season for every activity under the heavens". The year 1981 was the time to start working for NGOs and 2015 became the time for saying farewell to them.

The events that brought about my departure started in the second quarter of the Year 2015 when two cases of inappropriate financial management practices came up against me. In the first case, I submitted a trip report with a balance that was understated. This was a complete mistake but interestingly, instead of drawing my attention to the mistake, the Office Manager forwarded the report to the President of the Association. That is when the practice of managing only one person came back to bite me. In a big organisation with several staff in the finance department, this would never have happened. Indeed I have had understated and overstated trip report balances referred back to me for correction on several occasions throughout my development work of more than 30 years. The lesson here for any manager is that any financial report that should be submitted should be given to an accountant to cross-check and ensure that the balances are correct or draw attention to any mistakes. Unfortunately for me I did not have an accounts department and an accountant with whom I could do this. The office manager was everything.

The second case was about my use of the organisation's credit card for 'personal purchases' without authorisation. This was a legitimate case and I consider it a management mistake or poor judgement that put a dent on my integrity despite the logic and justification of those purchases. Indeed, almost all the purchases were for air tickets directly related to work and official travel and saved the organisation a significant amount of money. The lesson here is that, no matter what genuine reasons one may have, it is important for managers to seek authorisation for everything they do in order to keep their integrity above board. It takes several years to build one's integrity but a single indiscretion to destroy it. I had worked in the NGO community for nearly 34 years and this single indiscretion brought my integrity into disrepute. In addition, when managers do not stick to policy procedures and processes that entrench integrity, it becomes difficult for them to require the same measure of adherence to such procedures from the people they manage. The next problem is that such a situation creates an opportunity for the people who rely on your integrity, to extrapolate what has happened to include their wildest imaginations of what else you could have done wrong without any basis and this was exactly what happened in my case.

In May 2015, I had a meeting with the AfrEA President and the Office Manager and agreed on a schedule for me to refund all monies due to the organisation. I believed that this was the end of the matter but I was wrong. Suddenly, the President came up with a new set of instructions for the withdrawal of funds from the organisation's bank accounts that left me practically unable to transact any serious business on their behalf. The next action of the President was even more bizarre. He wrote to tell me that I "had access to the manager and the two relationships managers" of the bank where the organisation had its account and that the security of their finances had been compromised. He actually copied this message to all board members and to a development partner whom he advised to reverse funding to the organisation. He then went ahead and withdrew my signature from the bank and instructed the Office Manager to "secure all cheque books" in the secretariat. Secure cheque books? I wondered why. All of a sudden I looked like a criminal running around with the intention of stealing money from the organisation. I began to wonder what exactly had gone wrong with the President. He went ahead to institute an audit and an investigation to find out whether there was any financial misappropriation in the bank. In reality, I did not have any personal dealings with any official of the bank so the audits and investigations came to nothing. Indeed, I considered this as an insult to the Ghanaian banking system if one could believe that an individual could get into relationships with a bank and misappropriate money from an organisation's account. The email about compromising the security of the funds of the organisation in the bank made me look as if I was attacking the finances of the organisation. Everything I had done since 1981 to build my reputation in the

NGO community, working at the highest leadership and management levels with organisations such as World Vision International, the US Peace Corps, ActionAid and Oxfam as a Country Director over a period of nine years, and at the University of KwaZulu-Natal, was being destroyed by one person. I thought I had myself to blame because I opened the door for him to imagine anything he wanted. I sent a detailed message to the members of the board, describing what had happened and asking for an intervention. I only received messages of acknowledgement of receipt of my email. This was understandable as all the board members were located in eight different countries across Africa and each of them had their own official jobs to manage. Then out of the blue, on the 12th of July 2015, I received an email from the President telling me that the board had set up a four-member committee to meet me and resolve the issues between us. I noticed that the message was copied to only three board members and that prompted me to begin to ask questions. If the committee was set up by the board, why was the message not copied to all members of the board and why did it not come from the General Secretary of the Association in the first place? After back-and-forth messages of clarification, I went to the designated location to meet the committee.

All my messages in response to the original message were copied to all members of the board and this was queried by the President as my lack of respect for email protocol which required that in responding to an email, I should have copied only those persons who were copied in the original mail. This should be the case if one believes that the original email was copied to the right people, otherwise the necessary thing to do is to copy anybody else who is an interested party. It is important to understand what one is expected to do in order not to be threatened and confused with so-called laid-down protocols, particularly if one thinks that the person they are dealing with is not acting in their best interest. Interestingly, when I showed up for the meeting at the designated location, there were only two people present, namely the President himself and one board member from Zimbabwe. I smelt a rat – indeed, a very big rat. The two other members of the committee from Algeria and Burundi were absent. This explained why the original email was copied to only three members of the board. They were the three who were supposed to be at the meeting. Then I found out that the two members who were present for the meeting arrived in Accra on the 10th of July without my knowledge. They had actually spent that weekend in the office going through all sorts of documents in my office with the assistance of my Office Manager and Assistant/Cleaner. There is an Akan proverb which, when translated into English, says "If an insect will bite you, it is in your cloth". The sneaky travel into Accra without my knowledge followed by the visit to my office could not have been possible without the connivance and collusion of my two staff members. Very interesting! I refused to attend the meeting in protest, as I did not think that the President should be the judge in a case involving himself, and I did not believe that only one person would be objective in settling our dispute. An attempt to get the other two members of the committee to participate in the meeting via Skype failed, as both of them sent messages to indicate their inability to do so. The President and member of the board from Zimbabwe left Accra in exactly the same way they arrived - without the courtesy of telling me about their travel plans. It was all rather underhand for people of that calibre. At this point, the AfrEA secretariat was being run single-handedly by the President who was making payments for basic services such as water and electricity supply.

Meanwhile, I had only received three months salary out of the first seven months of the year. So here was I, working without being paid and sitting in an office run by the president of the Association who was in Abuja in Nigeria. I did not need a human resource consultant to tell me that I should move on. I submitted my resignation from the position of Executive Director of AfrEA on 1st August 2015. In September, the General Secretary of the organisation, based in Niger, sent a strong message to board members stressing that a face-to-face meeting of the board was "imperative". All the other board members responded to this message to indicate their agreement with him. The President never responded to this mail. Apparently, the board had a 24 month mandate that started in March 2014 and for the first 18 months of that time, they had not had any face-to-face meeting.

In January 2016, I took AfrEA to court to reclaim monies due to me from them. On the first hearing of the case, my lawyer and their defence lawyer agreed to have an out-of-court settlement under the Alternative Dispute Resolution (ADR) facility recognised by the courts in Ghana. The settlement was made to me in September 2016 and that ended the case.

On the 22nd of March 2016, the board of AfrEA met in Accra and took a unanimous decision to "terminate the appointment" of the President. In the layman's language, he was fired. This was their first physical meeting in 24 months, thanks to the ability of the President to prevent such a meeting from taking place earlier. The Acting President at the time that I was recruited organised several face-to-face as well as online meetings with the board and the secretariat within the six month period from October 2013 to March 2014. The reasons given for the termination of the President's appointment included his inability to organise a board meeting throughout his tenure as president, failure to represent the organisation in strategic partner meetings without apologies, single-handedly running the secretariat down to a point where electricity and internet were disconnected due to lack of payment of bills and his unwillingness to prepare the next international conference of the organisation. The image of the organisation before its partners was getting damaged. As I followed developments, I appreciated the fact that I had got out of the ship before the President had run it aground.

With the determination of the board which was made up of professional evaluators, AfrEA was revived and by May 2021, they had already organised two conferences and were in the process of organising a third one. The secretariat was reorganised and became functional.

I look back at my experiences in the organisation I call 'the last stop' and try to imagine what really went wrong. I have identified a number of learning points which could be management and leadership lessons for future generations as the principles that inform these lessons are not likely to change with technological advancement.

After my resignation and retirement, I had time to look at the advert to which I responded that led to my recruitment and found several things I had ignored after my recruitment. For example, the advert said that the Executive Director would be the Chief Executive Officer of the Association. For the two-year period I worked there was no indication of who was their Chief Executive Officer. The advert said the Executive Director would work closely with the Chief Financial Officer. I got into the job and there was no Chief Financial Officer but instead, I had an Office Manager who did everything in administration, keeping financial records, etc. If I had had a second look at the advert I would have been asking the board to explain why the reality on the ground was different from what was on the advert and I am sure we would have been able to come up with a practical solution. Anyone who takes up a job at management and leadership level should take time to review the advert after starting work in order to arrive at a workable reality. The advert for my replacement that was published in February 2017 did not have the terms "Chief Executive Officer" and "Chief Financial Officer". This is an indication of a growing organisation as the board members must have looked at the advert and revised it to correspond to reality. Indeed the person currently running the secretariat in Accra is no longer called the Executive Director but Chief of Secretariat.

A well rationalised organisational structure is the best starting point for any job. I have looked back at models for running an association such as AfrEA and in my opinion, I did not start in this way. For example, AfrEA should have had key positions managed by competent people in areas that would drive the accomplishments of its strategic objectives. These areas could include conference organisation, membership promotion, finance, communication and information technology. Instead of looking at the human resource requirement for the secretariat before looking for the necessary funding, it appears as if the Association looked at the funding they had before deciding on the personnel they could afford.

I am still baffled by how one person could toy around with the Association for 24 months before his appointment was terminated. Throughout my career I have always worked with teams and have instinctively become a team player. The job at AfrEA left me working with only two other people, which is the smallest team in which I have ever worked. In my opinion, any organisation that wants to open an office should have between five and ten staff to start the operation. Such a team is more likely to succeed through synergy and exchange of ideas than what I had in the AfrEA secretariat.

At this last stop, I look back at my career and recognise the fact that I had learnt a lot in 34 years of facilitating development in several parts of Africa. Most of my learning came from diverse sources, including colleagues and line managers as well as junior staff and the several international organisations for which I have worked. Learning from rural community partners who are sometimes wrongly called beneficiaries, is one of the biggest advantages I have had. From the African Evaluation Association, the biggest lesson I have learnt is the resilience and determination of the board members who were able to bring an organisation that was collapsing back to life and get rid of an individual who had run out of ideas on what to do next. I will forever be grateful to everybody in AfrEA who contributed to this last experience.

PART 3: DIVINE INTERVENTIONS

CHAPTER 42

ACCIDENTS, NEAR ACCIDENTS & SURVIVALS

For any working person, Fridays are the best days of the week, as every worker looks forward to a restful weekend. On this particular Friday at the end of April 1981, I was resting happily with my wife at home in my small bungalow in Bawku Secondary School, where I was teaching Ordinary and Advanced level (O and A-level) Chemistry. I was doing my national service after graduating from university. National service is a programme that was introduced in the early 1970s in Ghana. Students graduating from tertiary institutions were employed in the public and private sectors to get a year's experience of the work environment before proceeding with their careers. At about 7:00 p.m. four leaders of the Scripture Union, a Christian evangelical group in the school, came to visit me because they had heard that I had had a motorbike accident nearly two weeks earlier. My wife and I welcomed them into our home and entertained them as best as we could. I sat there with a bandage on my right foot and narrated the details of the motorbike accident to them.

On the day of the accident one of my friends, David Azari, popularly called Doctor Z (pronounced Zed), who headed the laboratory department of Bawku hospital volunteered to take me from Natinga, a suburb of Bawku to the Secondary School. Dr Z suggested I should ride the Yamaha 100 motorbike he brought while he sat at the back as the passenger. I took the key, kick-started the motorbike and off we were on our way. There was a perception in northern Ghana that young men from Bawku were the best riders in Ghana. With this perception running through my system I sped through town onto the Bolga road. By the time we were approaching the police station, we were cruising at over 100 km per hour. There was a donkey cart in front of me and I imagined that I was going to go past it in a flash. Unfortunately for me, a young man popped out of nowhere just at the time I was at the far end of the cart. I reacted very quickly to avoid hitting him, thus swerving the motorbike to my left. I managed to recover and avoided falling into the gutter on the left-hand side of the road by swerving to the right. At this point, I lost control of the motorbike and fell on the tarred road. The light motorbike dragged for nearly 20 metres before coming to a stop. Doctor Z and I, managed to get on our feet and bring the motorbike to a standing position. We had bruises all over our bodies and I had a deep cut on the top of my right foot. Miraculously when we kick-started the motorbike it was working. We abandoned our mission of getting to the secondary school and Doctor Z took over the bike and we rode back to Bawku hospital.

The nurses in the emergency ward cleaned our wounds and dressed up the deep cut on top of my right foot. As the iodine that was applied to the bruises on my abdomen, feet and legs began to work I felt a massive wave of pain strike through my body. Growing up as young boys in Manga, we were taught that a man must never show visible signs that he is in pain no matter how intense the pain is. I applied "Manga Manly Character 101". I maintained a smile on my face despite the pain.

We returned to my wife who was living in a rented room near the hospital and Doctor Z 'cheerfully' announced to her that we had had an accident. I returned to my bungalow in Secondary School after a few days. Reverend Father Bonnet, one of the staff members of the school, took over the care of my injuries and by the following week all the bruises were gone except for the deep wound on my foot which had also almost gone.

There are several observations to make regarding this accident. None of us on the bike wore a helmet and yet after being dragged on the tarred road for nearly 20 metres we did not sustain any head injuries. We escaped without any broken bones. Despite the amount of time we spent on the road recovering from the fall and putting the motorbike back on the road, no truck was on the road at that time as this could have resulted in another accident. The scraping of the metal parts of the motorbike on the road must have produced sparks that could have ignited the petrol leaking from the fuel tank and yet this did not happen. We both had bathroom slippers on our feet leaving them unprotected. I look back at all these and I know that this was divine intervention by the mighty hand of God.

After narrating my story to the young students, I escorted them to the school campus and my wife and I went back home. But alas! This was to be the beginning of another episode that would call for divine intervention.

Less than 5 minutes after the students left the house, we decided to heat some water and fill our thermos flask so that it would be easy to make a hot drink during the night if my wife needed one. We went into our second bedroom where a two-ring gas cooker was placed on a low table. I then sat down with the gas cylinder by my legs. In the absence of electricity, I also had a lantern standing on the ground near my legs to provide lighting. I turned the gas on without knowing that the regulator that connected the cylinder to the cooker had been taken out earlier in the day and not properly screwed on. Then came the sharp rush of escaping gas. My wife shouted "Run" and ran for the door. The gas in a fraction of a second was lit up by the naked fire from the lantern and before I could decide what to do an invisible force picked me up from the bed and threw me to the doorway where I hit my wife just as she ran out of the door. I got to my feet and there were burns all over my body. I could see skin hanging from both hands and blisters all over my legs. I walked out of the house and then I was hit by this massive pain all over my body. I sat on the ground and tried to apply the Manga manliness rules but in vain.

My wife was screaming at the top of her voice. The young students who had just left our house were the first to arrive on the scene and in less than two minutes a crowd of students and teachers were all over the place. The fire was still burning on the gas cylinder in the room. One of my students had the presence of mind to run to the chemistry laboratory, pick up a fire extinguisher and come back to extinguish the fire and switch off the gas. A car pulled up near the house and I was told to get up and try and walk to the car. I got into the car and it sped away to the hospital. It was then that I noticed that Rev Father Bonnet who became my nurse after the motor accident had transformed to be my ambulance driver to the hospital.

We got to the hospital burns ward and all the action started. In the absence of telephones, nurses ran helter-skelter to ensure that I was taken care of. Then my best friend in the hospital James Yambor, who was also a nursing tutor at Nursing Training School at the hospital, appeared. I have not yet been able to work out who went to inform him about the accident and how he got to my bedside so fast. James took one look at me and told me that I would just need to bear with the pain a few more minutes. He put on gloves and got to work. Dipping his hand in a solution that was provided, he pulled off burnt skin from my body over and over again until swollen blisters burst and skin was removed and the hanging skin was gone. This was more painful than my circumcision at 11 years old without anaesthesia. They put me on intravenous fluids to replace the body fluids I was losing all over my legs, hands and abdomen. James happily told me that the intense pain I was feeling was good news. Good news!? Why on earth would this pain be described as good news? He explained that the intense pain was an indication of superficial burns. If the burns had been deeper I would never have felt any pain. This would have been more dangerous. But that was really no consolation to me at that moment. I was given a very strong painkiller and a sleeping drug and the world came to a standstill. I slept throughout the night. The next morning, I woke up and the pain also woke up because we had now become very close friends.

After 8 a.m. I had an array of medical personnel around my bed. Dr Schneider, Dr Rowland, Dr Agongo, James Yambor, the pharmacist and several nurses were discussing how to deal with my case. In the end, everybody went away and nurses came back with a pack called 'Bio Gauze'. It took nearly 40 minutes to clean my wounds, put on strips of Bio Gauze on both legs and both hands and bandage me up. A mosquito net was erected around me to prevent flies and mosquitoes from getting access to my wounds. The April heat was unbearable and excessive sweating under the net added to the continuous loss of body fluid from my wounds. A table fan was brought to the ward to increase air circulation and reduce my sweating. The events of the last 12 hours were just unbelievable. After more painkillers and sleeping medication, I went back to sleep. I woke up at 11:30 a.m. and sitting right by my bed was my mother. Somehow somebody had sent a message to her, and she must have come running to my bedside. She just asked one question: "Sammy what is it?". I could not give her a detailed narrative of what happened and she seemed to understand that.

At about 3:00 p.m. that day there was some commotion outside as I had a large number of visitors who were not prepared to come in two or three at a time. They were senior A-level chemistry students and they numbered about twenty-two. They all came in and surrounding my bed most of them weeping openly. My mother left the scene to confront her own pain. The final A-level Chemistry practical examination was only one week away and here I was in the hospital with no evidence that I would be well and get back to the school before the examinations. I managed a brave smile and assured them that I had covered every inch of the syllabus and was confident that anything that would come in the examination had been taught. For the next few days, I had an avalanche of visitors, most of whom were not prepared to come during visiting hours. The most interesting visitors where Dr Agongo (a classmate in Navrongo Secondary School) and Mr Duncan who normally came at 9:00 p.m. and sat down to keep me company until about 11:30 p.m. to keep my spirits high. My other visitors included family members, friends, as well as students and teachers from the secondary school.

Two days to the GCE A-Level final chemistry practical examinations, my colleagues back in the school were able to prepare the laboratory for the exam. They brought the preparatory note for setting up the laboratory to me at the hospital. This gave me an indication of the type of questions that would come up in the examination. I called my students to the hospital and gave them my last advice concerning the examination. I just assured them that nothing would come in the examination that they had not done before without divulging any information. Talking to your students from the inside of a mosquito net with a fan blasting hot air around you is not really the best thing in the world. I was in the hospital for 22 days before I was discharged. I am still unable to tell what physical force literally lifted me out of that fire to the doorway of the room. I can only say this was divine intervention by the mighty hand of the Almighty God.

In the last week of August 1982, I decided to drive from Tamale to Ouagadougou in the then Republic of Upper Volta (now Burkina Faso) to take delivery of armchair cushions and a mattress I had ordered two weeks earlier. Being aware that I did not have enough money to pass the night in a hotel, a return trip on the same day was the most logical travel plan. However, I had to wait until after 5:00 a.m. before leaving my house in order to obey the curfew regulations that existed at the time - a remnant of the December 1981 coup d'état. At 5:30 a.m. I zoomed out of Tamale with my wife and 11-month-old baby as well as a friend and headed for the Ghana border in the north. The trip was uneventful. We crossed the border into Upper Volta. At the town of Po, it took over half an hour to go through the laborious documentation of the immigration and customs. Then we had to go through nearly eight barriers where document checks and registration were done by the security agents. We finally got to Ouagadougou after 12 noon by which time all workers, both private and public, had gone on their lunch break.

The culture of siesta in the afternoon to rest after lunch was introduced to Africa by the colonialists. That culture is practised religiously in francophone Africa. The capital cities of francophone countries in West Africa such as Ouagadougou in Burkina Faso, Niamey in Niger and Abidjan in Ivory Coast can look very paralysed during the lunch break. Indeed in Ouagadougou and Niamey, the lunch break can be as long as 3 hours and it is practically impossible to do official or private business during this break. I therefore parked the car under a mahogany tree and my wife and I proceeded to enjoy our packed jollof rice for lunch. We shared one big bottle of a soft drink called Yuki soda to wash down the rice. Life began to come back to normal at 3:30 p.m. This is the most dangerous time to drive in Ouagadougou. It is the time when everybody is trying to get back to work. The roads are heavily occupied by vehicles of every size and shape as well as motorbikes, mobylettes and bicycles. We gingerly manoeuvred our way to the bank to collect money and then to the shop to collect our cushions and mattress. Then we had to get into a shop to buy 'essential' commodities such as sugar, milk, coffee and tea. These were impossible to get back in Ghana at that time. At precisely 4:50 p.m. we cruised out of Ouagadougou. Miraculously we had negotiated our way out of the city without hitting any motorbike or mobylette. The streets of Ouagadougou with all the bikes are a sight to behold. Now we had about an hour and 10 minutes to drive 160 km from Ouagadougou to the border with Ghana. I simply drove at about 160 km an hour, without any regard for speed limits, and managed to stop and go through the checking processes at the security eight barriers. This is the craziest trip I have ever made in my life. Any incident such as a cow crossing the road or a tyre burst could have led to disaster.

We finally arrived at the border at 10 minutes after 6:00 p.m. It had closed and so we proceeded to beg the immigration and customs officers who were sitting around. I implored, pleaded, explained the difficult situation of a woman in my car with an 11-month-old baby and any other explanation I could give. The only thing I did not do was to attempt to persuade them with money. In fact, there was actually no money to do this. Finally, the immigration authorities let us into the country at 6:30 p.m.

I tried to relax and regain my composure as we headed to Tamale. At Wulugu we stopped and our friend called Peter joined us in the car. Then the second stage of panic started. We had to get into Tamale and home before 10:00 p.m. otherwise we would be breaking curfew and could end up in the police cells. Unfortunately, the road to Tamale was not as good as the road from Ouagadougou to the border. It was full of potholes and I had to try and drive as fast as possible while dodging the potholes by swinging the car from one side of the road to the other. This was compounded by the fact that we were driving in the night. We crossed the Nasia River and our passenger said he felt like vomiting. I had heard about motion sickness and I was now carrying somebody who suffered from it. I could not afford to stop so I asked my wife to give him a bowl in which he could vomit. After all, no aircraft stops for a passenger with motion sickness to vomit. In place of the bags given to you in an aircraft, I gave our friend a bowl. The smell of vomit filled the car because all the windows were closed up to allow the air conditioning to be effective and prevent outside wind from introducing drag and slowing down our speed. After about five minutes our passenger said he wanted to go to the toilet. Wow! I did not have a toilet in the car so I had to stop. Our friend went into the bush to deal with his issues. We took advantage of this break to pour away the vomit and open all the doors of the car to get rid of the smell. He finally came back and we resumed our dangerous drive to Tamale.

At about 9:52 p.m. we were at the Tamale airport junction. We had eight minutes to get home before the curfew. There was not a single car on the road and I sped into town like a racing car. I decided that for our safety our friend had to go home with us and spend the night. As we approached the Agricultural Development Bank in Tamale we saw a military truck with soldiers obviously responsible for enforcing the curfew hours. The siren for curfew went off and it blended with the screeching of my tyres as I turned into the Kalpohin Estates Road. For some reason, the soldiers did not attempt to stop us. We arrived home and our house help was sitting in the hall waiting in expectation of our arrival. After packing the contents of the car into the house I took a seat and tried to relax. My brain was still travelling at 160 km per hour. Finally, I managed to get some rest but in my sleep I found myself driving at 160 km per hour.

This was one of the riskiest journeys I have made, and with hindsight, it could have been better planned to avoid the panic and unnecessary risks taken. If we had slept in Navrongo we could easily have gone to Ouagadougou, done our business and left the city at about 2 p.m. and that would have given us ample time to get back to Tamale. Even in our foolishness and lack of wise planning, the Almighty God can still miraculously intervene and keep us from harm's way.

The month of March in northern Ghana is most likely one of the hottest months of the year. I set off one morning in March 1982 to travel from Tamale to Walewale. This is a 100 km journey. I was riding the Yamaha

100 motorbike that had been sent to me in Tamale in response to my transport challenges. I was cruising on the road at about 120 km per hour. The Bawku rider perception was still in my blood. Just before arriving at the Nasia River, a goat from nowhere ran across the road. A quick calculation told me that I was on a collision course with the goat. I quickly reoriented the speeding motorbike to avoid it. It was almost on the other side of the road when it changed its mind and ran back straight into me. I hit the goat and fell but did not slide down the road because of the big potholes. I got up from my fall, lifted the motorbike off the ground to a standing position and manoeuvred it off the road to give way to an oncoming bus. I noticed I had a few bruises on my hands. The bike had bent slightly but I was able to get back on it and ride to Walewale where the Catholic priests in the Walewale Catholic church dressed up the bruises. Looking all over me I noticed that once again I had come close to an untimely demise. In the course of the fall, my head hit the road so hard that there was a big scratch on the helmet I was wearing. A shoe was also badly damaged. But for the way I had dressed up for this journey I could have had very serious head injuries that could have led to death. This was another miracle in my life and the Almighty God had given me another lease on life to work on this Earth.

In the year 1984 Ghana was emerging from the devastating food shortages of 1983 and many World Vision workers were actively involved in assessing and planning for the delivery of relief goods to communities where we worked. I was on one of such missions once again from Tamale to Walewale. Just before arriving at the Nasia river, I was driving at about 120 km per hour in the Peugeot 504 when I felt a slight sway of the car. After a short distance I felt the sway again. I slowed down the car to 40 km per hour and tried to test its stability. I did this by swinging the car from left to right and right to left. As I swung from right to left something broke from under the car and it went off the road and I crashed into the gutter.

At the speed of 40 km per hour, this was a very minor accident. I got out of the car and realised it was not badly damaged. If this had happened at over 100 km per hour it could have been a real disaster. I abandoned the car where it was and tried to get help. By the end of the day, we managed to tow the car all the way back to Tamale for repairs. Incidentally, this was precisely the moment I received a photographer from the International Office to document the response of World Vision International to the food shortages in Ghana. I was compelled to borrow a Peugeot 504 pickup from the Christian Services Committee to continue my fieldwork. The mechanics in Tamale found out that my lower arm suspension was nearly completely broken and hanging by a small piece and my manoeuvre completed the breaking process which sent me into the gutter. In those days spare parts were almost impossible to find in Ghana so I had to travel to Ouagadougou in Burkina Faso to purchase the spare parts and bring the car back onto the road.

It was in 1987 while driving from Accra to Tamale that I got one of the biggest scares of my life. I was driving a new Peugeot 304 that had just been purchased in Accra by Reverend Father James Archer. We were between Techiman and Kintampo. I was driving at 80 km per hour because Father James had warned me that he did not want me to exceed that speed. He sat in the front passenger seat and behind him was Mahama Tampori, the relief coordinator for the Tamale sub-office. All of a sudden I heard Mr Tampori say "hey! hey! hey!". The car was drifting slightly off the road to my right and rubbing against the grass at the side of the road because I had gone to sleep while driving. I woke up from my sleep and brought the car back to the road and in less than 20 seconds we found that two tankers had crashed and left only a small passage in the middle of the road for vehicles to pass. Had I not woken up 20 seconds earlier I would have crashed straight into one of the stationary trucks. The Almighty God has always been on my side and always stretched forth his mighty right hand to intervene on my behalf. When we passed the tankers, I got some water to wash my face and Father James said if I wanted to go 200 kilometres per hour I was free to do so. Sometimes it is not the speed at which one drives that result in accidents. It is the Almighty God's protection that keeps us alive.

In November 1993 I had to make a presentation to some partners in a workshop organised by World Vision International in the city of Takoradi. My wife was on admission in the maternity block of the Korle-Bu Teaching Hospital in Accra. But this presentation was very important. I therefore planned to visit my wife early in the morning at 6:30 a.m., drive to Takoradi and participate in the workshop and drive back to Accra in the night. The workshop finished at about 5:30 pm. After sharing a meal with the participants I jumped into the car and started driving to Accra. I passed Elmina and approached the University of Cape Coast. I remember seeing the west gate of the university and then I must have fallen asleep. I cannot remember seeing the central gate nor the east gate. Something suddenly woke me from my sleep and the first thing I saw was the State Insurance Corporation building to my left. In reality, I had travelled nearly 4 kilometres on a road that was continuously curving. How I managed to manoeuvre the car along this road is still a mystery to me. I pulled up by the side of the road shaking from head to toe. I composed myself and turned into Cape Coast town and to a friend's house where I asked for a cup of coffee. I got some water to wash my face, drank a cup of coffee and got back on the road to Accra, although the precautions were not necessary because I was kept awake by the frightening experience of driving for a distance while asleep. I have never forgotten how I went through this experience. The moving car must have been guided by the angels of the Almighty God.

It is important for me to say here that the Almighty God in his abundant mercy overlooks our mistakes and lack of experience and delivers us from incidents like this and from similar experiences narrated throughout this chapter. This does not mean that Christians should be reckless in adhering to basic safety precautions in expectation of divine interventions. For example, nobody should be riding a motorbike without a helmet and good leather riding shoes as well as knee and elbow pads that can protect them in the case of an accident. It is advisable and indeed legally appropriate for every person riding a motorbike or driving a car to stay within the appropriate speed limits particularly when in a town, not just for the sake of obeying traffic regulations but for their own safety. Anybody in a moving car should be wearing a seat belt. I learnt my lessons the hard way and I don't expect future generations to learn in the same way.

CHAPTER 43

ALIVE TO TELL A STORY

On the morning of 30th June 2017, three young men, Emmanuel, Steven and Nathaniel, together carried me out of my bedroom and down the stairs in my house in Community 15 Tema. They got me into the waiting car in the yard of the house and then drove through the slow-moving Accra traffic jam all the way to the Korle Bu Teaching Hospital. I was admitted into a ward on the 6th floor of the surgical block. My condition looked rather dire. Paralysis was taking over my whole body. My arms were bent at the elbow and I could not straighten them and so were my fingers which were clawed. My legs were bent at the knees and it was absolutely impossible to stand on my feet. The day passed rather slowly as I waited to see what would become of me. In the evening, the neurosurgeon came to see me and he told me that the surgery would be on my neck and would be carried out the following morning which was the 1st of July at 5:00 a.m. I hardly slept that night.

The events from the month of March that year to that moment ran through my mind. It started with the attempt to see a medical doctor who could diagnose my problem of instability in walking and numbness in my feet and hands. I finally saw an orthopaedic surgeon who asked me to have a Magnetic Resonance Imaging (MRI) scan on my lower back and bring the results to him. That reminded me – did not Professor B A Dadson, one of my lecturers in the University of Cape Coast, tell us in his lectures on systematic identification of organic compounds that magnetic resonance imaging would be used in the future for medical diagnosis? This was going to be the fourth time I would be getting into the MRI machine, the first being in Hull in the UK and the two others in Durban, South Africa. I pushed away the thought of claustrophobia when one got into the machine and went for the scan.

When thee surgeon got the results of the scan, he uploaded the soft copy onto his laptop computer and studied the detailed images of my lower spine from all possible angles and various scales of enlargement. He decided that I needed surgery on the lumbar spine but he needed the advice of a neurosurgeon. I saw the neurosurgeon and he told me that in his opinion, there was a possible bigger problem in the neck with the cervical spine and so he sent me back for another MRI scan of that area. That was my fifth experience in the MRI scanner. The final diagnosis of the neurosurgeon was that I had what he called cervical stenosis and I needed surgery that would cost between 6,000 and 10,000 US dollars. I asked how early this could be done and he gave me a series of options including dates in April, May and June. I told him that I did not have the money at that moment but I would look for resources so that the surgery could be done in June.

Upon leaving the hospital, my son Emmanuel, with a quizzical look on his face, asked me whether I had some money hidden anywhere and why I seemed to be sure that I could do that surgery before the end of June. I responded that I was speaking in faith, depending on the almighty God to work a miracle. As it turned out, the surgery was going to cost 8,000 US dollars and upon sharing my predicament of needing that amount of money for surgery, I received massive support from family and friends, particularly former workers of World Vision International, former classmates from Ghana college in Tamale, former members of The Redemption Singers, the Assemblies of God Church and the Christian community as a whole. I will forever be grateful to the numerous friends in these categories who sacrificed so much to help me in my time of need. But for their support I would have died in my difficulties.

The period from the 30th of May to the time I was admitted in the hospital was full of drama. On this date, my pastor, who was concerned about my health, led me to visit a Korean Reverend Minister who took the soft copies of the MRI scans and sent them to a neurosurgeon in Korea. I received communication from Korea through the Reverend Minister that if I could fly to Seoul, they would perform surgery on my neck for free. My neurosurgeon in Accra and medical doctor friends agreed that South Korea would have better facilities for such an operation than any hospital in Ghana. The arrangement seemed to be going very well until there was a U-turn and the doctors in Korea started asking for an NGO that could write to support my request to come to Korea. We abandoned the idea of going abroad for the surgery at the last minute and started getting in contact with my neurosurgeon in Ghana again. This is the background of how I got nearly 80% paralysed before my admission into hospital for the surgery.

At 4:15 a.m. the nurses came to get me ready for the operating theatre. My wife and children were by my bedside at 5:00 a.m.. I imagined that they must have left the house by 4:00 a.m.. At 5:15 a.m. my bed was rolled out of the ward to the theatre where the team which was going to perform the surgery waited for me. Earlier, I had been given a little tablet to swallow with a spoonful of water and I noticed that this was beginning to have an effect on my senses. The lead surgeon introduced the other surgeons made up of two other neurosurgeons, an orthopaedic surgeon and ... I did not hear the names of the rest as I drifted into unconsciousness. My return to consciousness started with the feeling of a gust of air blowing over my nose and mouth. This was from the oxygen mask held over my face by one of the theatre nurses. Then came the clinking and clanking sounds of what I guessed could be surgical instruments in one of those stainless-steel pans that form part of the theatre paraphernalia. Then all of a sudden, I heard voices around my bed. The oxygen mask was taken away from my face. It looked as if I had been unconscious for a few seconds but when I enquired about the time, I was told that I had been under the anaesthesia for well over 5 hours. In the intensive care unit my wife and children came around the bed. I was alive. Yes! I was alive to tell a story.

Many people have asked how I got myself into this condition. The answer to this question is another emotionally draining narrative. In 1997, while working for the Niger office of World Vision International, I went to the house of an Egyptian surgeon in Zinder to seek medical attention. I was made to take my shirt and singlet off to enable him to examine me. It was one of those examinations where the doctors place a stethoscope on your body and listen to all the sounds they can hear to help them make a diagnosis. After the examination, I started to put my shirt back on and the doctor, looking carefully at me, noticed that I took a long time struggling to fasten the last two buttons. He then told me that he wanted to conduct a small experiment. He left the room and came back with a little paper bag, asked me to close my eyes and hold my open palms upward. He then closed my palms and asked me to tell him what was in my hand. I said there was nothing in my hands and then he asked me to open my eyes. When I opened my eyes and palms, I saw that I was holding cotton wool. He repeated the experiment with a toilet roll, different textures of writing paper and stones, and that enabled him to gauge the level of sensitivity of my palms. Then he broke the news to me that he believed I had a problem in my cervical vertebrae - the discs in the neck were pressing on the nerves and reducing the sensitivity in my palms. He said it was not possible to do any surgery to correct the problem in Niger and advised that if I knew anybody in Europe or the USA, I should get in contact with them as early as possible for help. He warned that if I did not take action very quickly the situation could get worse and I could become paralysed. This was heart-breaking for me and that evening, my wife and I, in a state of disbelief and anxiety, decided that we had been confronted with a problem from which we could not escape and so had to tackle it head on. With this information from the doctor and with hindsight, we immediately saw the tell-tale signs that we had ignored. The difficulty and clumsiness in fastening my shirt buttons, the inability to take a full cup of tea to my mouth without spilling the contents, the inability to put a belt through the belt hooks on my trousers without looking at them - these signs had been with me since 1992.

In my search for support, I turned to one of my long-time friends, Neil Cameron, and after several exchanges of messages and a detailed diagnosis report about my condition written by my Egyptian doctor in Zinder, I had to travel to the United Kingdom for surgery on my neck. The news about this travel brought a lot of concern to my family and friends. I travelled to the UK and was later joined by my wife who came to be by my side during these difficult times. I ended up in the Hull Royal Infirmary where I was seen by a neurosurgeon and then went through more detailed diagnostics including Computerised Tomography (CT) and MRI scans. After what looked like a thorough examination of the results from scans, the neurosurgeon said he had identified the problem and that he was going to carry out surgery to correct it. Then I was informed about all the risks involved in surgery on the cervical spine and they were just too scary to repeat anywhere. I accepted that there was a probability of not coming out alive but went in for it all the same. At the end of the surgery which took place in a Bupa Hospital, a bone was taken from my hip and grafted into the neck. I came out alive. Yes! Alive to continue my work. The medical insurance facility that I had as an international member of staff of World Vision paid for my air passage to the UK as well as that of my wife and for all the hospital expenses. The home of the Camerons in Keyingham, which had served as a base for me in 1992 now became home to my wife and me until I was strong enough to travel back to Ghana and proceed to Niger. The Cameron family was such a tremendous help to me during these difficult times away from home with health challenges. There was not much change in the sensitivity of my palms and the numbness of my hands gradually grew worse.

In the year 2004, my family members noticed that when walking, I unconsciously dragged one of my legs. Then the bombshell came in 2005 when I dived into a swimming pool behind my house in Durban, South Africa and got what looked like a shock in the neck which momentarily paralysed me for a few seconds and I could not move any of my limbs to swim. Long hours of swimming as a child taught me several tricks of survival in water and one of these tricks came in handy. I simply held my breath and when I could move my limbs again, I rolled up and sunk right to the bottom of the pool from where I could kick hard and project myself to the surface of the water, and I then swam to the edge of the pool. The following day, I went to the Entabeni Hospital and I was directed to see a neurosurgeon who decided that he wanted an MRI scan of my neck and lower back. I quickly got in touch with the neurosurgeon who did the first surgery in the UK and then got the shock of my life. When he realised that I was going to have a second detailed scan of my neck, he said "By the way, I did not tell you that the problem in your neck is congenital". Wow! I thought that such things happened only in Africa and that everything was perfect in the UK. Now, here I was, talking to a specialist who had withheld personal medical information from me for eight years before giving it to me when he realised that I might be about to discover it. My wife and I went through another night of worrying. We were trying as hard as we could to figure out what it meant to say the problem was congenital. We both understood it to mean that I was born with the problem but my wife thought that nothing could be done about it. When I was given an option for immediate surgery, I opted out because my trust in surgical specialists had just been badly dented. I was even more sceptical because I knew that the neurosurgeon who did the first surgery in the UK was originally from South Africa. This incident delayed the attempt to carry out surgery on my neck for 12 years until it was almost too late in 2017.

I then began to investigate the question of my condition being congenital. I attempted to talk to friends from my childhood and schooldays, and all my colleagues from primary school all the way to the university whom I contacted seemed to remember that I always carried myself with my head tilted to one side of my neck. Back at home, one of my cousins remembers that the family noticed the crookedness of my neck when I was barely a year old and attempted a local traditional healing based more on superstition than science. I supposed that carrying loads repeatedly in my childhood could well have made it worse.

From 2005 onwards a new pattern of symptoms began to develop. Anytime I hit my foot against an object on the road, I fell flat on my face. One of such falls in Bujumbura resulted in a severe cut on my upper lip that required two stitches. The falls became more frequent as the years went by, including falling in very embarrassing situations. In 2012, I fell flat on the street in The Hague while walking from my hotel toward the Oxfam Novib office and was helped to my feet by colleague Oxfam workers. And then in 2013, while getting onto an aircraft in Dakar, I hit my foot against the little bump between the gangway and aircraft body and fell straight into the aircraft, and was assisted to my feet by the cabin crew of the airline. For some reason, I seemed to ignore all these symptoms until I was being dragged, as I thought, into the grave in 2017. Between 1997 and 2015, I always had good medical insurance but did not take advantage of this facility to respond to my deteriorating health condition, which became critical at the time when I did not have any insurance. These memories give me the belief that the Almighty God guided and protected me through these experiences to show me his power of deliverance when I had nothing else to hold onto.

During the surgery, four discs were removed between the 2nd and the 6th cervical vertebrae and 8 titanium rods implanted, actually screwed in between the cervical vertebrae to hold them in place. Immediately after the surgery, I was able to straighten my fingers and my arm and legs but I had lost a lot of muscle strength and nerve coordination. On the 6th day after my surgery, I was discharged from the hospital and a new drama unfolded. The only elevator that carried people up and down the six-floor building had broken down on that day. Although I was discharged at about 9:00 a.m. we waited until 5:00 p.m. and the elevator was still out of use. My children decided to find a way of bringing me from the sixth floor to the ground floor using the stairs and with the assistance of a ward orderly. This was tedious and slow and having just come out of spinal surgery, every little move resulted in pain. At the end of the day, we got out of the hospital, joined the busy evening traffic of Accra and slowly went home.

After six weeks of intensive physiotherapy and rehabilitation, I made the first effort to walk with the help of the physiotherapists who helped me onto my feet and assisted me in taking a few steps, walking and supporting myself with a Zimmer frame.

By October 2019, I had attained a reasonable level of mobility, albeit impaired. Then the symptoms of paralysis started to emerge again. This took me back to the hospital for another MRI scan, and back to the Hospital for yet more surgery on the spine. This time, the disc which had shifted out of place was pushed back and sealed without the need for metal implants. I shudder to think that neurosurgeons have intruded three times into my spinal column with all the risks of a single procedure multiplied by three and I am still alive. I believe I am just alive to tell a story which I have tried to tell as best as I can. I have more functions of the body than I can recount that require accurate communication through nerves coming from the cervical spine. The easiest to describe is that I have lost the ability to hold a pen and write, and all functions that require coordination of my hands. Meanwhile, the problem of a slipped disc on my lower back has had to be ignored because the neurosurgeons think that additional surgery could be very risky. Despite these setbacks, I have battled through life with significantly impaired mobility to write this autobiography.

While the Almighty God has kept me alive to tell a story, the telling of the story was accompanied by several challenges. I started this book as a blog entitled "Memoirs of a Development Worker in Africa". The first article on the blog was published on 30th April 2020. On the 5th of May 2020, with my wife sitting in front of me to help me with my early morning cleaning up, I suddenly felt as if everything in sight was blurred and spinning and then I lost consciousness. The next thing I knew was that I was lying on the right-hand side of my body and somebody was trying to get a pillow under my head. My wife later described what happened. Looking at my face, she realised that saliva was coming out and dripping down the left side of my open mouth. Instinctively, she pushed me down on the bed and raised my legs up and then called for help. My son Emmanuel and his wife Sarah, a medical doctor, lived next door and they rushed in to help. I was given initial medication to calm me down and sent to a nearby hospital in the afternoon after Sarah had assessed the situation. I was given oxygen in the hospital and admitted for 5 days after which I was discharged after several diagnostic scans, laboratory tests and medical interventions. What I had experienced was a mild stroke and it resulted in my losing a significant percentage of the muscle strength and coordination I had gained through several months of physiotherapy. Despite the setback I continued to make weekly publications on my blog by dictating what I wanted to write using voice recognition software and then getting assistance from my children to edit the writing and produce a document that could be published.

In the month of June 2020, I thought I had recovered enough to continue working on my blog on the computer. My children set up a desktop computer for me to work on and then I found out that I could not read anything on the computer screen. Investigations in an eye clinic revealed that I had cataracts in both eyes and I needed surgery. I continued to use the voice recognition software without being able to read the final products of my work on the blog. I stopped posting material on my blog at the end of December 2020 and had surgery on my left eye on the 31st of December 2020 followed by another on the right on the 5th of March 2021. I have regained my sight fully with the assistance of spectacles. Because of the surgeries I suspended my physiotherapy sessions throughout the month of January to April 2021 and this resulted in losses in the recovery of my muscle strength and coordination.

My writing improved as I stopped posting on the blog and was in the process of transforming it into this book. The writing went on successfully with the support of my editors until the 12th of July 2021 when I became ill. On the 17th of July my health deteriorated so badly that I was taken to hospital and after several tests and examinations it became evident that I needed to be admitted into the hospital. With the intervention of my daughter-in-law, I was brought back home and given medication that was administered under hospital conditions recreated at home. On the 28th of July, tests conducted on samples taken from me established that I had Covid-19. It was a very difficult situation but at the time of finishing this autobiography I had recovered from the illness. Unfortunately I had also lost the gains I had made in my muscle coordination and strength since December 2019. Beyond being alive to tell my story, I am alive to complete the narrative and fighting back to recover my muscle strength and coordination.

These narratives are just a sample of the many many times I have had such divine interventions. I owe my being alive today to the Almighty God to whom belongs all praise and glory and thanksgiving. Anyone who has enjoyed reading my memoirs and experiences, narrated to include my

childhood and development facilitation experiences, and learnt any lessons I have tried to share, should remember that this documentation has only been made possible by the divine intervention of God in my life. We have a miracle-working God!

--- THE END ---

BISSA GLOSSARY

Bissa (singular: Bissa; plural: Bissanor; language: Bissa;) is an ethnic group that populates southern Burkina Faso, northern Ghana, northern Togo and northern Benin with cultural practices similar to other ethnic groups in the savannah ecological zone. Below is a list of Bissa (lebre dialect) words used in this book and their English meanings. Work on a Bissa -English dictionary is still incomplete and the spelling here may be different from the spellings that will appear in the final dictionary.

Figure 11: Bissa glossary

Bissa	English
baambuurey	millet food in the form of a paste
beyisga	Bissa food made from bean leaves
biyo	middle of the rainy season
bungkaare	flute, made from sorghum stalk
buyaa	wet foot disease
dabsi, or sassi	loom heald
duubaambureh	Bissa food – steamed millet food
feerr	flute, clay or wood
ferr	tamarind tree, Tamarindus indica)
gaazi	traditional kitchen in the open compound
gancor	vegetable that germinates quickly in the early rainy season
gawurr	steamed black-eyed bean food
gendri	spindle
genla che	kitchen, traditional in a room
gintareh	vegetable that grows throughout the rainy season

gyisiga	warp (weaving)
gyissi	kapok tree, Ceiba pentandra
jengira	guitar, one-stringed
kanni	metal rod used with a stone to press out cotton seeds
kansa	bean food that looks like a pancake
kansannereh	African locust bean pod powder
kanteega	cubit
kariyaama	Bissa food
karr	African locust bean tree, Parkia biglobosa
konni	guitar, two-stringed
koosey	bean food –like donuts deep fried in oil
kourr	shea nut fruit or tree, vitellaria paradoxa
kusor	footwear
kuyeh	dry season
kwereh or gombo	loom reed
laalorr	praise singer
lanni	cotton plant or cotton wool
lanni gya	cotton stone used in combination with a metal rod to extract cotton seeds
lanni sira	house farm / kitchen garden where cotton is grown
lemaar	hot dry season
mosa	harvest season and end of rainy season
naga	sorghum variety
nyaasi	millet ball snack

nyaasipi	millet ball water
nyeim	cold dry season, harmattan
nyimbu	shea butter residue
pipirr	Bissa food
poh	baobab tree, Adansonia digitata
pumpunni	Bissa food
sassi, or dabsi	loom heald
sigiley	planting season
siirey	planting season
torta	festival when sacrifices are made to deities
tunto nyaasi	Bissa food
wu	Tuo Zaafi (TZ)
yawre	communal farm work
yirr	game played with 48 stones and 12 shallow holes dug on the ground or on a piece of wood
zare pumpunni	bean food